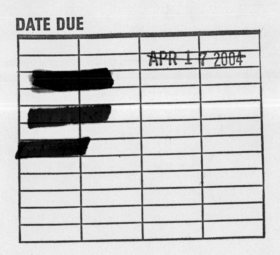

John Donne
and Francisco de Quevedo

UNIVERSITY OF NORTH CAROLINA
STUDIES IN COMPARATIVE LITERATURE

Number 61

WERNER P. FRIEDERICH, *Founder*
EUGENE H. FALK, *Editor*

John Donne
and Francisco de Quevedo

POETS OF LOVE AND DEATH

L. Elaine Hoover

Chapel Hill
THE UNIVERSITY OF NORTH CAROLINA PRESS
1978

Copyright © 1978 by
The University of North Carolina Press
All rights reserved
Manufactured in the United States of America
ISBN 0-8078-7061-7
Library of Congress Catalog Card Number 77-29128

Library of Congress Cataloging in Publication Data

Hoover, L. Elaine, 1942–
  John Donne and Francisco de Quevedo.

  (University of North Carolina studies in comparative
literature; no. 61)
    Bibliography: p.
    Includes index.
    1. Donne, John, 1572–1631—Criticism and
interpretation.   2. Quevedo y Villegas, Francisco
Gómez de, 1580–1645—Criticism and interpretation.
3. Literature, Comparative—English and Spanish.
4. Literature, Comparative—Spanish and English.
I. Title.   II. Series.
PR2248.H6   809'.03'2   77-29128
ISBN 0-8078-7061-7

for my parents

Contents

Acknowledgments

I wish to thank Professors Robert Voitle and J. B. Avalle-Arce for their careful readings and many helpful suggestions during the writing of this book.

Grateful acknowledgment is made to the following for permission to quote from copyright material: Editorial Planeta, for material from *Francisco de Quevedo: Obras completas. Poesía original*, edited by José Manuel Blecua (Vol. 1, 1968); and Oxford University Press, for material from *John Donne. The Elegies and The Songs and Sonnets*, edited by Helen Gardner (1965).

Introduction

The interests and many aspects of the lives of John Donne (1572–1631) and Francisco de Quevedo (1580–1640) were similar, although they never knew each other and most probably did not know of each other. Donne's Protestant England and Quevedo's Catholic Spain were enemies throughout the lifetimes of both poets.

Perhaps the most obvious parallel in the lives of Donne and Quevedo was their inordinate thirst for knowledge and their years of ceaseless study. Their predilection for the contemplative life was equalled, however, by their mutual zest for the activity of the court and the glory of public life. They also shared a disillusionment with the politics of power as they watched their formerly powerful associates fall from the graces of their respective sovereigns. The execution of Essex had a great effect on Donne, and Quevedo was profoundly affected by the imprisonment and death of his former patron and friend, the duque de Osuna, accused of open rebellion against the Spanish crown. Banished from court for long periods, both poets found solace in meditation and the study of philosophy and theology.

Foiled in his political ambitions, Donne was forced to enter the religious field.[1] The courtier's arts which he cultivated throughout his life consistently failed to gain him favor at court, but they did ultimately insure his election in 1621 as Dean of St. Paul's. After years of avid study and constant preaching, Donne became sick in the autumn of 1630. His illness worsened and in February, 1631, he preached at court what was then recognized to be his own funeral sermon, *Deaths Duell*. He had ultimately become reconciled with the divine will he perceived in his life that had led him to spend twenty fruitful years in the ministry.

Quevedo was a critical witness to the corruption of the courts of Felipe III and Felipe IV and to the continuous decline of the Spanish nation and empire, which provoked much of his satirical poetry and prose.[2] Like Donne's, his religious study was unceasing. His prodigious humanistic endeavors consisted of the constant study of classical authors, languages, philosophy, and theology. In 1639 Quevedo was whisked off to prison under mysterious circumstances, and the true cause of his imprisonment to this date remains unknown. He was imprisoned for the following four years and suffered great physical hardship. Only after Olivares' fall from Felipe IV's favor was Quevedo granted his freedom. The strain he underwent those four long years no doubt hastened his death, which occurred in 1645. Like Donne, Quevedo had an uncanny awareness of his impending death. It is said that when his doctor declared that he would live only three more days, Quevedo replied correctly that he had only three hours to live. Like Donne, he knew death well, had become reconciled to its inevitability, and recognized its insistent approach all too clearly.

Donne's and Quevedo's literary production is colossal and comprehends many fields, including politics, theology, philosophy, satire, and secular and sacred poetry. Donne's first *Satires*, as well as most of the elegies and some of his love lyrics, disclose a skeptical and cynical outlook. This attitude acquires a different manifestation in his melancholic apology for suicide, *Biathanatos*, written during his years at Mitcham on the outskirts of London. The years 1607–1610 were ones of great spiritual despondency, which Donne spent in grave doubt of his salvation and consequently in terror of death. He rejected the king's suggestion that he enter the church, clearly preferring to seek political advancement.

During these years, spent between Mitcham and London, following the court and seeking an appointment, Donne continued his constant scholarly study and meditation and wrote his three prose pieces. In addition to *Biathanatos*, he also wrote *Pseudo-Martyr* and *Ignatius His Conclave*. The majority of his *Divine Poems* and most of the prose *Paradoxes and Problems* were also written in these years.

In 1614 Donne became a member of Parliament for the second time, but his hopes for state employment were irrevocably destroyed by King James' advice once more that he enter the church. In 1615 he was finally ordained deacon and priest at St. Paul's Cathedral. His career as one of the outstanding preachers of English history thus began only after all chances for public employment were gone. Although most of his energy was thereafter devoted to preaching, he continued to study avidly and write ceaselessly, producing *Devotions upon Emergent Occasions*, prompted by his illness of 1623.

Quevedo, at a young age, was also a productive scholar. His correspondence with the famed Belgian humanist Justus Lipsius, who like Quevedo was a devoted scholar of Seneca, began when he was only 25. Lipsius declared then that Quevedo was Spain's supreme man of letters. Although he finished his theological study and received the lower orders of the priesthood, Quevedo, like Donne, possessed one overriding obsession, the securement of responsible posts in the government. Just as Donne spent his life in and out of London, devoting his energies to the court, to travels abroad, and to his own meditation and study, so too did Quevedo spend his time in and out of Madrid, dividing his energies between the court, trips abroad in the diplomatic service, and study and contemplation in the little village of Torre de Juan Abad. Just as Donne referred to his home in Mitcham as a prison, so too would Quevedo refer to Torre as his prison. It in fact served as his prison during his exile from the court and Madrid. It was in his Torre that Quevedo would find refuge from the world and a haven for study and writing. There he would spend his last days and prepare himself for death in much the same manner as Donne.

In 1606 Quevedo wrote his *Sueños*, which like Donne's *Ignatius His Conclave* is a biting prose imitation of Dante's *Divina Commedia*. In 1608 he began the *Buscón*, a picaresque novel similar to his *Sueños* in its devastating indictment of the Spain he knew so well. Prior to one of his many trips to Italy in 1613, Quevedo spent several years of fruitful study and writing. During this period he produced *Lágrimas de un penitente,* a book of verse resembling in many ways Donne's *Holy Sonnets.* It reveals perhaps Quevedo's profoundest kinship with Donne, an irrepressible obsession with his own spiritual state. This mutual concern reverberates throughout all of their literary works, including their amorous verse. In 1613 Quevedo also began *La cuna y la sepultura,* which like *Biathanatos* reflects its author's obsession with death. *Las lágrimas de Jeremias,* a poetic reflection of the prophet's lamentations following the fall of Jerusalem, similar to Donne's own *Lamentations of Jeremy,* was published in 1613.

In 1621 Quevedo was exiled to his Torre for his association with the allegedly traitorous duque de Osuna, and there he studied and wrote in solitude. The years spent in exile from the court parallel in many ways Donne's trying years at Mitcham. Sickness, mental depression, and a kind of hopelessness were Quevedo's constant companions. It is during these years that his study of Senecan stoicism provided him with an immeasurable degree of mental peace. It is also during these years that Quevedo wrote *Política de Dios,* his outline of a government based on the scriptures. Only in 1633 did he finally finish and publish *La cuna y la sepultura.* The ascetic and theological emphasis in this latter period of his life resulted in the production of several other important prose works.[3] *La vida de San Pablo, Los remedios de cualquier fortuna* and *La sabiduría del Espíritu Santo* were either produced or published in the important year of 1633. In 1634 Quevedo's translation of Sales' *Introducción a la vida devota* was published, followed in 1635 by his *Virtud militante.* These works present Quevedo's own eclectic philosophy, a combination of Christianity, asceticism, and stoicism.

During his four years of imprisonment, Quevedo underwent spiritual growth and maturation similar to that which Donne experienced in his final years in the ministry. He continued to study feverishly and produced several lengthy prose works of a clearly religious nature, entitled *La constancia y paciencia del santo Job* and *Providencia de Dios.* Living in enforced solitude and silence, surrounded by his beloved books and accompanied only by his ever-increasing meditations on death, Quevedo spent the last years of a hectic life in productive contemplation, in search of spiritual solace.

His *La vida de San Pablo* reflects a serenity and reconciliation with life and death. Through constant study and conscious attempts to find the truth wherever it might be found, Quevedo, like Donne, moved continually toward a deeper comprehension of death's relationship to life. In his final scholarly endeavors, he worked on the *Vida de Marco Bruto* and compiled the vast amount of poetry he had composed throughout his lifetime.

Donne and Quevedo were men of their time and of their shared traditions. They were undeniably human, proud, and often self-serving. They were possessed by an inordinate desire for knowledge, an abiding concern for the moral character of their nations, and a deep need for intimacy with the divine. Their lives were filled with political activity and religious, philosophical, and poetic endeavors. After lifetimes spent in religious study and philosophical and poetic meditations on the nature of death, the final years of John Donne and Francisco de Quevedo were characterized by a continual progression toward God and toward a peaceful and personal reconciliation with the deaths that awaited them.

Among the most valuable studies of the Baroque in recent years are Frank J. Warnke's *European Metaphysical Poetry* and *Versions of Baroque*. In his exploration of the thorny issue of what precisely is meant by the terms "Baroque" and "Metaphysical," Warnke formulates the clarifying theory that the "term 'baroque' . . . can most profitably be used as a generic designation for the style of the whole period which falls between the Renaissance and the neoclassical era. . . . As the designation of a period, 'baroque' refers not to a precisely definable style but a cluster of related styles. One of these is Metaphysical."[4]

According to Warnke's definition, still the most compelling to date, Donne and Quevedo are poets of the all-encompassing period of the Baroque. Their "spare, witty, intellectual, paradoxical"[5] style is characteristic of the Metaphysical manifestations of the Baroque time period. Similarly, as poets of the Baroque period, Donne and Quevedo reflect the themes and traditions that were dominant in their lifetime.

The world view prevalent in the Baroque and particular to the

Metaphysical orientation of poets such as Donne, Quevedo, Herbert, Marvell, Sponde, Huygens, and Fleming involved a rejection of Renaissance equilibrium, optimism, and esthetic proportion. The intention of this study is to explore the intellectual as well as the stylistic particularities that characterize the love poetry of two of the outstanding poets of the Baroque. As major exemplars of what Warnke defines as the Metaphysical style and what I would characterize as the Baroque world view,[6] Donne and Quevedo provide the comparatist the valuable opportunity of investigating the particularities of the Metaphysical style and its relationship to the Baroque vision.

In what ways does the Baroque approach to life, love, and death impose itself on the esthetic productions of Donne and Quevedo? How does their particular Petrarchan or anti-Petrarchan stance correlate to their Baroque vision and Metaphysical style? How do their often-similar thematic obsessions reveal their intellectual and esthetic affinities? How do Donne's and Quevedo's amorous poetry compare and contrast, and in what ways do their differences, as well as their similarities, illuminate their respective positions as major Baroque figures of England and Spain? In short, as Metaphysical poets of the Baroque period and as simultaneous adherents to the particular world view dominant after the disintegration of Renaissance optimism, what can be learned by juxtaposing their love poetry and subjecting it to a rigorous thematic and stylistic examination? How often do apparently contradictory attitudes and themes, upon close analysis, reveal profound similarities in tone, vision, and sentiment? In what respects can we ultimately declare that Donne and Quevedo shared a common *Weltanschauung*? That is, did they share merely a coincidental contemporaneousness, or despite specific differences and conflicts of opinion, as major poets of their era, can an extensive comparison of their stylistic recourses and thematic obsessions elucidate their relationship as poets, indeed as kindred souls, of the Baroque? In Segel's words, in what ways do we find "distinctly recognizable patterns of thought or artistic expression"[7] in the poetry of Donne and Quevedo? This study will analyze the love poetry of Donne and Quevedo in terms of Warnke's concept of the Metaphysical style within the Baroque time period and Segel's assertion that a particular world view distinguishes each literary period, including the Baroque.

In the Baroque, as in the Middle Ages, much emphasis was given to the concepts of death and mutability. Like the *Vita Nuova* before it, Petrarch's *Canzoniere* had reflected man's eternal interest in death's role in his life, in his love. As the joyous Renaissance celebration of life began to wane, this interest was reaffirmed and poets once more expressed a fundamental concern with death. In their anguished view of life, love, and death, Quevedo and Donne reflected the mentality of an age that was beginning to take less and less for granted the grandeur and omnipotence of man. They felt intensely the reality that man is after all simply a mutable and temporal creature who is guaranteed only the certainty of his inevitable non-existence.

A genuine concern with death was accompanied by an obsession with death's accomplices, time and mutability. These themes were not new; what *was* new was the intensity with which men like Donne and Quevedo expressed their intellectual and emotional apprehension of time's passage. Their poetry is characterized by a finely-wrought tension between their keen sensitivity to time's inexorable movement toward death and the poetic objectification of this deeply-felt awareness. Accompanying corollaries to the Baroque interest in death and time were the psychological concepts of pessimism and disillusionment. These themes, again, were not unique to the Baroque period. They simply assumed greater significance and dominance in the literature of the day, and *desengaño*, the dissipation of false illusions, was indeed "el tema barroco fundamental."[8]

Eduardo Camacho Guizado has correctly articulated the relationship between the Baroque's obsession with death and its constant theme of disillusionment, finding that death is one of the prime causes for this sense of disillusionment: "Más que un desengaño más, la muerte, para el poeta del siglo XVII, es uno de los orígenes de ese sentimiento pesimista y desilusionado."[9] The threat of death, of nothingness, was indeed one of the primary causes of the Baroque sense of disillusionment, of *desengaño*. In his study of time and the temporal, Georges Poulet's observation is also to the point. He asserts that all thought in the seventeenth century was "one long meditation on the phrase of Saint Augustine: 'If God should withdraw his creative power from the things he has created, they would fall back into their primal state of nothingness.'"[10]

Death, time, and disillusionment thus became inseparable obsessions of the Baroque mentality. It was not time itself, however, that interested men like Donne and Quevedo, but rather the *passage* of time.[11] Time in itself was innocuous enough. It was what it inexorably led to that captivated the imagination of Donne and Quevedo. Time's movement was symbolic of death and consequently elicited the same profound disillusionment as death itself. Ironically, it was in part the fear of the stasis and the nothingness of death that motivated their visceral fear of the dynamics of time.

These fears and obsessions assume a prominence in the love poetry of Donne and Quevedo, asserting their strength through the traditional love themes inherited from Petrarch and the *amour courtois* tradition. The allied themes of love and death, although certainly not a new alliance, assume greater profundity and central importance in their poetry. As seen in Donne's sermons and prose works and in Quevedo's prose and poetry in general, death and time are of major interest in all of their writings. It is, nevertheless, in their love poetry that this obsession acquires its most paradoxical significance. The theme of death assumes a role which, like the theme of love itself, varies from poem to poem.

This study will analyze the manifold imagistic and thematic interrelationships between death, time, and love in Donne's *Songs and Sonnets* and Quevedo's amorous poetry, primarily his *Poema a Lisi*. Quevedo wrote a great deal of amorous poetry, much of which is similar to many of Donne's love poems in its emphasis on cynicism, misogyny, and argumentativeness. Because this study will deal solely with the relationship between death and love, it will therefore concentrate on his *Poema a Lisi*. Like Donne, Quevedo possessed the contradictory capacities for cynicism and tenderness in love. Both poets wrote within the Petrarchan tradition and could adhere to that tradition in many forms and degrees as well as react heartily against it. Neither approach necessitated the exclusion of the other, however, for Donne and Quevedo shared the intellectual heritage of Western Europe and consequently possessed an all-inclusive conception of love and of life itself.

The union of love and death, although clearly within the Petrarchan tradition and likewise a literary phenomenon typical of their times, was not merely a superficial or infrequent theme in the poetry of Donne and Quevedo. Both poets keenly perceived the inevitability of their own deaths. This haunting awareness permeated their love poetry, more because of an internal necessity than because of any externally imposed poetic commonplace—hence, the passionate intensity of the love poetry of Donne and Quevedo. Because their lifelong obsession with death infused their work, the love poetry that emerged was vigorously original, albeit frankly within or expressly rebelling against well-known poetic conventions and traditions.

The contemplation of death not only pervades their love poetry but is also a dominant theme in their religious poetry. Donne's *Holy Sonnets* and Quevedo's *Lágrimas de un penitente* and *Heráclito cristiano* reflect most intensely their shared anguish. The prose works of both poets also abound with their meditations on death. From Donne's relatively youthful *Biathanatos* to his mature *Devotions upon Emergent Occasions, Essays in Divinity*, and sermons, death is the leitmotif that unites his thoughts. Quevedo's obsession with death also characterizes the majority of his prose satires and philosophical works, such as *La cuna y la sepultura* and *Sentencias*, his translations and paraphrases of Seneca. The single abiding truth that pervades Quevedo's works and philosophy of life is that man is born to die. Death, his grand obsession, determines the tone of his prose and poetry alike.

Quevedo is perhaps the most important poet of death ever produced by Spain, just as Donne is one of England's most significant death poets. Although an investigation of their obsession with death as manifested in some or all of their prose and poetry would be most enlightening, the thematic and imagistic manifestations of death in their love poetry alone will serve as the limiting factor in this study. Quevedo's satirical love poetry will, therefore, not be stressed, for it usually deals only marginally with the theme of death. Quevedo's great sonnets of metaphysical anguish, his religious poetry, and Donne's *Holy Sonnets* must also be excluded, for they do not present the theme of love.

Critics of both Donne and Quevedo have curiously employed the same phrase in their explanation of each poet's obsession with death. John Hayward has declared that Donne "was in love with death, not merely acquainted with it, as Montaigne was in his early years, and the idea of death is the constant companion of his thoughts from the first of the *Songs and Sonnets* to the last, and in its description of death, the greatest of his sermons, 'Death's Duel.'"[12] Rafael Alberti has similarly observed that Quevedo was in love with death, which for him was his friend, his wife, and his lover: "Todo diálogo de Quevedo con el amor es más bien un diálogo con la muerte. Nunca se ha visto a enamorado más prendado de ella. . . . Muerte amiga, esposa y amante."[13] These are significant observations, for it is in the love poetry of Donne and Quevedo that the great irony of their obsession with death is most clearly seen. The paradox of love poetry which is often more expressive of the poets' enamorment of death than with the beloved unites Donne's anti-Petrarchan *Songs and Sonnets* and Quevedo's Petrarchan *Poema a Lisi*. Their poetry, like the *Vita Nuova* and *Canzoniere* that preceded it, deals with ladies who are not really objects of love. They are objects of meditation whose sole purpose, like that of Beatrice and Laura, is not to be served by the lover, but rather to serve him as they elicit and elucidate his metaphysical obsessions with himself, his emotions, his temporality, and his mortality.

Georges Poulet's observations are again pertinent: "An intimate awareness of an ever actual existence, an acute sense of the discontinuity of duration, and a total dependence upon a creation continually reiterated—these are indeed the essential traits of human time in the seventeenth century."[14] Quevedo and Donne belonged to their age in spirit and thought. The temporal anguish of their times and a profound awareness of the discontinuity of duration permeate the *Poema a Lisi* and the *Songs and Sonnets*.

The Baroque is often defined as a period in which the use of antitheses characterizes its search for truth and unity.[15] The dualities of life and death, dreams and reality, eternity and temporality, illusion and disillusionment reflect a world of mutability, constant movement, and disorder. In their love poetry, Quevedo and Donne sought to transcend the negative aspects of each duality by replacing the temporality, illusion, and death of life with permanence in love. Donne sought this transcendence of time and death through the union of requited love. Quevedo expressed his own solitary conquest of the dualities of existence through the purity, invincibility, and immortality of his unrequited love for Lisi. His love thereby overcame temporality, death, mutability, illusion, and darkness. In his most memorable love sonnets, the Spanish poet most famous for his cynicism, satire, and naturalism asserts that his eternal love will transcend death itself. Despite Donne's and Quevedo's aspiration of transcendence, few of the poems in *Poema a Lisi* and *Songs and Sonnets* reveal love's ideal conquest of its enemies, time and death. They disclose instead the anguish with which Donne and Quevedo ponder love's mutability, the destructive power of unrequited adoration and the beloved's disdain, the deathlike qualities of the lovers' parting and absence, or the actual death of the beloved herself. Time and death are strong adversaries, capable of destroying love, the lover, and the beloved. Consequently, in Quevedo's Lisi sonnets, as in Donne's love poetry, the Baroque theme of *desengaño* often defines their love, be it requited or non-requited.

In his description of the poetry of Donne's day, Patrick Cruttwell puts his finger on the Baroque predilection for antitheses, noting that the "taste for incongruities, and a need to express and, if possible, reconcile them—lie at the centre of the new style. The cynical and the idealist, the realistic and the fantastic, the homely and the exotic, the grotesque and the beautiful, the mortality of the graveyard and the sensuality of the living body—these are some of them; and deepest of all is that of love and death."[16]

Nowhere is an attempt to reconcile the deepest of all these incongruities, love and death, so apparent as in the love poetry of John Donne and Francisco de Quevedo. Of the many antitheses that accompany this basic duality of love and death in their amorous poetry, the most pervasive are temporality and eternity, illusion and reality, and the body and the soul.

In addition to their mutual penetration of the basic duality of love and death, these three pairs of dualities are themselves inextricably interrelated. As Arthur Terry has observed, this interaction of antitheses is typical of the Baroque, "the basic opposition . . . [being] between the body and the spirit—the temporal and the eternal seen under the action of death."[17] In the same poem, therefore, Donne may express his love in terms of death and his consequent concern with the relationship between the body and the soul at death. Similarly, Quevedo often expresses the duality of love and death in terms of time and eternity. Both Donne and Quevedo employ all three dualities in their expression of the relationship between love and death. Appearance and reality is the all-pervasive duality which, like the mood of *desengaño*, permeates the Baroque in general. Warnke's observations are again pertinent: "Baroque poetry [reflects] a concern (thematic, but consistently mirrored in technique) with the relations of appearance and reality. The Baroque vision . . . has as its core a systematic doubt in the validity of appearance, a doubt which expresses itself as an obsessive concern for appearance."[18]

In the poetry of both Donne and Quevedo, time is often expressed in spatial terms and vice versa. The complementary dimensions of time and space define the physical reality of the human condition. Man is a creature severely limited by both time and space, and no one has ever perceived this reality more intensely or felt its harshness more acutely than Donne and Quevedo. The moment of death is the most crucial manifestation of the antithesis of the time-space continuum and eternity, and indeed of all the dualities that define existence. Only in that instant are the dualities of time and eternity, immanence and transcendence, the body and the soul, space and infinity in maximum tension.[19]

Donne and Quevedo sought through love and through death to overcome this world of relativity limited by time and space. The achievement of this desire, however, constitutes only one facet of Quevedo's Lisi sonnets and Donne's *Songs and Sonnets*. Each poet's approach to death varies throughout his work. Death is at times courted, sometimes transcended through love, and often feared. Indeed, love's transcendence of death and love's destruction by death constitute the central antithetical relationship between love and death expressed in the *Songs and Sonnets* and *Poema a Lisi*.

Death is thus the crucial factor which must be acknowledged in any serious contemplation of the relationship between the body and the soul, between eternity and the dimensions of time and space, or between appearance and reality—the three inseparable antitheses of *Poema a Lisi* and the *Songs and Sonnets*. Compounded by an obsession with life's evanescence and mutability, the inter-relationship between these antitheses is strengthened by the consequent association of life and death. At the moment of death, the body and the soul are irrevocably sundered. Just as time and space are overcome through death, so too is the soul released from its bodily imprisonment. The material, temporal, and spatial worlds yield to the realms of eternity, immutability, and spirituality, and love itself may either perish or triumphantly endure.

The third significant duality that pervades the love poetry of Donne and Quevedo is the antithesis of illusion and reality, of *ser* and *parecer*. Both poets believed that through death man is released from the material limitations of this world and of his body, and consequently from terrene nescience also. Appearance and illusions yield to death's irrevocable relevation of Reality. While he remains in this world, man inevitably fails to distinguish illusion from reality. What he sees only through a glass darkly in this world, he will one day see face to face in the clear light of eternity. Death is the final and omnipotent instrument of man's *desengaño*. It is the great unveiler of Reality and the omnipotent conquerer of the illusions of this life, of man's inherent ignorance.

Despite life's deceptive appearances that would camouflage ultimate truth, the bitter realities of time and death will always impose themselves on the sensitive observer. Donne and Quevedo shared an acute sensitivity to the realities of death; and, consequently, their love poetry reflects this shared perspective of time, mutability, and love. For Quevedo, death was a terrible experience to undergo, but it was also the greatest avenue for learning and for man's conquest of his hopeless nescience. He often wrote that death is hard and painful, but that it is also the most valuable of life's learning experiences. Donne held a similar view of death as the great unveiler of truth and clarity, as seen in his use of the image of death bringing a taper to life's darkness in *The second Anniversarie*.

The actual instant of death is the moment of the unveiling of absolute reality, when the shadows of this world's appearances are destroyed by death's clarifying light. Just as the spiritual is cleft from the material and the soul abandons the body, so too does the eternal destroy the temporal and spatial, while ultimate Reality vanquishes the appearances that deceive man in his sub-lunar existence. The many dualities, incongruities, and antitheses of life are resolved in this supreme moment of enlightenment.

Donne and Quevedo shared a mental and emotional propensity to view life in its unity, its wholeness. The perception of the equal validity and interdependence of antitheses is consequently central to their poetry. The apprehension of the fusion of life's dualities, antitheses, and incongruities in a single whole resulted in a style that reflected the unavoidable tension arising between these antithetical, yet inseparable, elements of reality. As Arthur Terry has pointed out, the tension that characterizes the metaphysical conceit "lies, not in the structure of the conceit, but in the nature of the problem this embodies." The problems Terry correctly perceives embodied within the metaphysical conceit "are deep philosophical questions of the relation of the One to the Many, the soul to the body, the eternal to the temporal, and so on."[20] These problems puzzled Donne and Quevedo all their lives, dominating their love poetry, which consequently is metaphysical in nature. The subtlety of thought with which Donne and Quevedo present these problems and paradoxes also characterizes their poetry, which occupies a significant position in what Warnke calls the "international European phenomenon [of] metaphysical poetry."[21]

To express their perception that each aspect of reality, by its very existence, implies its opposite, Donne and Quevedo often employed the conceit. Quevedo, the Spanish leader of *conceptismo*, and John Donne, long acknowledged as the English master of the metaphysical conceit, based their themes on the recognition of the inherent contradictions and unity of reality. Hence, an unrelieved tension defines their poetry.

Through their mutual recognition of the underlying profundity of the trivial, they transcended material reality, thereby gaining a deeper awareness of metaphysical truth. Donne and Quevedo viewed all components of reality, irrespective of their humility or grandeur and despite their apparent antagonism, as mutually inter-dependent participants in a higher, all-encompassing unity. All phenomena, including the seemingly insignificant, possess the same potential for transcendence. In the exposure of the dualities inherent in existence and the simultaneous assertion of a funda-mental unity, paradox logically emerges as a significant unifying factor. Like the conceit, paradox coalesces, unifying the most seem-ingly disparate elements of reality, the trivial and the profound, the material and the spiritual.

The view of reality permeating the love poetry of Donne and Quevedo reflects this recognition of the interdependence of the mundane and the mysterious, and the essential oneness of imma-nence and transcendence. Their love poetry, like their religious poetry, is metaphysical because it reveals their predilection for per-ceiving the universal in the specific, the cosmic in the quotidian. It is metaphysical in its paradoxical affirmation of the simultaneous duality and unity of reality and in its vision of mutability and death from the dual perspectives of time and eternity.[22]

Either or both perspectives may be employed in one's medita-tion on love and its relationship to the dualities that define man's existence. Throughout the *Songs and Sonnets* and *Poema a Lisi*, the relationship between love and death consequently varies, and in different poems contradictory attitudes towards death, love, and the beloved prevail. Death is at times feared as the eventual de-stroyer of love, while on other occasions it is utterly vanquished by love's power. While disparateness, duality, contradiction, and par-adox permeate the love poetry of Donne and Quevedo, each poem considered in this study provides its own perspective on the nature of love and love's relationship to death, and thereby contributes in its uniqueness to the unity, richness, and totality of the *Songs and Sonnets* and *Poema a Lisi*.

The complexity of unresolved tensions; the compulsive search for unity through duality; the intensity of the obsessions with death, time, mutability, illusion and reality, the body and the soul; the propensity to view reality in terms of eternity and universality; the predilection for the metaphysical conceit; and a persistent tone of disillusionment are the salient characteristics that pervade the *Songs and Sonnets* and *Poema a Lisi*. In this study, we shall investigate the interdependence of these characteristics, antitheses, and incongruities in relation to the interdependence of the primary antithesis—love and death. The intensity with which Donne and Quevedo rationally perceived the omnipotence and finality of death, as well as the vigor of their purely emotional response, create a unity of tone within thematic variety.

Beneath the varied reactions of both poets abides an awareness of their own inescapable solitude before death. Donne's haunting sense of metaphysical solitude, despite love's requital, and Quevedo's obsession with his own existential isolation in an alien world pervade their love poetry. Quevedo felt all too acutely the unavoidable reality that man is born alone and dies alone, and that his life is a solitary pilgrimage towards death from one point in time and space to the next. In his Lisi sonnets, this solitude is compounded by his unrequited love, which knows only the pain of isolation and solitary wandering. Solitariness before death and in love defines the mood of Quevedo's Lisi sonnets, and even in Donne's greatest celebrations of love's requital, uncertainty and death are ominously present.

The intensity with which Donne and Quevedo felt their inescapable metaphysical solitude was accentuated by their search for escape through love. Despite the attempts at self-consolation, rationalization, and escape, each individual nevertheless remains isolated before the inevitability of his own death, accompanied only by his anguished consciousness. This shared awareness of death, occasionally relieved by an optimistic aspiration toward transcendence, constitutes the most significant similarity between Quevedo's Petrarchan *Poema a Lisi* and Donne's anti-Petrarchan *Songs and Sonnets*.

The similarities and significant disparities between the love poetry of Donne and Quevedo do not indicate, nor will this study suggest in any way, the possibility of influences, mutual or individual, between the works of these two poets. Rather, this study proposes to elucidate the particular Baroque sensibility shared by both poets as manifested in the recurrent themes of their love poetry.

It is true that the iconoclasm of nearly all, if not all, of Donne's *Songs and Sonnets* and the traditionalism of Quevedo's *Poema a Lisi* constitute major differences in approach. Yet, the similarities in both poets' world view and the metaphysical obsessions reflected in theme and style make for a rewarding confrontation between Quevedo's *Poema a Lisi* and Donne's *Songs and Sonnets*. As leading representatives of Baroque sensibility, style, and aesthetics, Donne and Quevedo articulated, perhaps with greater anguish than any of their fellow poets, the Baroque consciousness of temporality and mortality.

Having acknowledged the similarities in style and the particular dominance of the theme of death in the love poetry of both men, we must then proceed to a more detailed inquiry into specific similarities and differences within the framework of this theme. What are the particular manifestations of the theme of death in the amorous poetry of Donne and Quevedo? In what ways do these manifestations reflect the Baroque world view? In what ways do they employ the Metaphysical style and technique?

We shall see that the particular thematic organization which imposes itself on the comparative analysis of the *Songs and Sonnets* and *Poema a Lisi* reflects major trends of the Baroque and often, particularly in Donne's poetry, significant departures from the preceding Renaissance world view. The Baroque obsession with time, death's essential ally, acquires several significant thematic articulations, one of the most prominent of which is old age. Time, in its passage, leaves indelible traces, and for all living beings, these traces indicate continual decline and decay. As major Baroque poets, Donne and Quevedo express their obsession with time's passage and time's ravages, with mutability and the very personal effects of its omnipotence on humanity's frailty.

Death, the major obsession of Baroque literature, dominates the love poetry of Donne and Quevedo in various ways. The concept of death's omnipotence, a significant change in emphasis and tone from Renaissance optimism and the unrestrained joy of life, characterizes a good part of the amorous poetry of Donne and Quevedo. The annoying sense of impermanence and mutability leads ultimately to an overwhelming awareness of impotence when faced with one's own inevitable extinction. The ramifications of this awareness in the amorous poetry of the Baroque acquire an intensity unparalleled in the European love lyric; and we shall see that in the poetry of Donne and Quevedo this awareness provokes some of the Baroque's most powerful articulations of metaphysical anguish.

The occasional assertion of the transcendence of death through love is, again, not unique to the Baroque, but it does acquire the fervor and insistent tone typical of the Baroque in the poetry of Donne and Quevedo. Both poets express this illogical concept through the paradoxical argumentativeness typical of the intellectual, witty Metaphysical style.

In the Baroque the inherited theme of absence in love becomes virtually synonymous with the theme of the absence of death. Absence in love, be it a temporary separation or the eternal absence of death, is a theme which in Baroque literature acquires an unprecedented intensity. The imposition of the theme of death on the poetry of love's absence thus becomes a major Baroque phenomenon. In the poetry of Donne and Quevedo, particularly, this aspect of the Baroque vision acquires a significant manifestation. The spiritual absence of nonrequital, like the physical absence of lovers, is often expressed in terms of death in their amorous poetry.

The theme of death acquires another significant manifestation in the poetry of Donne and Quevedo, which reveals, perhaps with as much importance as the concept of love's omnipotence, the Baroque's debt to the tradition of *amour courtois* and Petrarchism. Donne and Quevedo, as Baroque heirs to this rich and imposing heritage, bestow on the well-worn *topoi* and metaphors of death-by-love and death-for-love a pervasive tone of uneasiness and elemental despair. The beloved-assassin figure is perhaps the dominant representation of this violent relationship between death and love.

The mockery of serious themes, like the imposition of metaphysical considerations on inherited *topoi*, constitutes part of the Baroque reaction against Renaissance tradition. Donne and Quevedo, as major representatives of the Baroque aesthetic, provide a valuable opportunity for understanding this aspect of the Baroque world view. Their humorous and cynical expressions of traditional concepts and attitudes reveal a basic nonconformity with life as well as with their literary heritage. Hence, the humorous Quevedo, although not in evidence in his frankly traditional *Poema a Lisi*, is very much in evidence in his satirical, iconoclastic poetry. Donne and Quevedo often achieved humor through paradox, irony, and verbal ingenuity as well as through the audacity of their stylistic and thematic rebellion against the sober, idealistic, and properly staid poetry of their Renaissance predecessors.

As participants in the Baroque disillusionment with past ideals and beliefs in the realms of science, politics, and theology—of physics and metaphysics—Donne and Quevedo expressed their consciousness of this disparity between past illusion and present reality in humorous as well as in tragic terms. Once again, we perceive the all-encompassing capacity of the Baroque mind and spirit. The disparity between illusion and reality is the fundamental component of comedy and of tragedy. The point of view of the beholder determines whether the thespian mask wears a frown or a smile. Existential incongruities thus supply the sensitive artist with innumerable manifestations of this fundamental paradox of the human condition. The artist may focus either on the comic aspect or the tragic aspect of this basic reality, and although the Baroque artist tended naturally to stress the tragic facts of life, his unique capacity for simultaneously viewing seemingly contradictory truths often led him to don the comic mask, never quite losing sight, however, of its contradictory, yet complementary, counterpart.

In the succeeding chapters, through the comparative analyses of the love poems of Donne and Quevedo in which one of the major Baroque themes, death, enjoys its most significant and varied manifestations, we shall seek a deeper comprehension of the essence of the Baroque, indeed an intimate familiarity with its very heart and soul.

John Donne
and Francisco de Quevedo

1

European Love Poetry:
The Troubadours and Petrarchism

Coming as it does in the first half of the seventeenth century, the love poetry of Donne and Quevedo follows centuries of development in the European love lyric. Their spontaneity and originality do not deny the fact that the themes of Donne and Quevedo also echo traditional concerns and reflect universal preoccupations.

In his *Medieval Latin and the Rise of European Love-Lyric*, Peter Dronke elucidates the status of the European love lyric and asserts that the themes and emotions of *amour courtois* expressed by the troubadours of southern France and later Petrarchists are indeed universal poetic property, irrespective of culture or epoch, and are "reflected in the earliest recorded popular verse of Europe."[1] According to Dronke, the ideals of *amour courtois*, the human aspirations of ennoblement, of spiritual fulfillment, of transcendence through love-longing and love-service, are not unique to one time period or region, as propounded by countless scholars, such as C. S. Lewis, Ernst Robert Curtius and Reto Bezzola (p. 2).

The troubadours of southern France, instead of discovering a new emotion previously unknown to the human heart, simply celebrated and propagated more extensively the cult of love-service in search either of love's requital or transcendence through non-requital. Reflecting universal human aspirations, this *amour courtois* acquired a prominence which, perhaps because of its unprecedented influence ultimately throughout Italy and the rest of Europe, led scholars to assume that its themes were new and previously unknown in the history of mankind. Dronke admirably and exhaustively demonstrates that the *amour courtois* of eleventh-century Provence had as its precedents the learned or popular poetry of such regions as Egypt, Byzantium, Georgia, Mozarabic Spain, Iceland, and Germany.

His most comprehensive example of *amour courtois* outside Provence is what he calls the "greatest monument in a Caucasian literature, . . . Shotha Rusthaveli's *The Man in the Panther's Skin*, written probably between 1196 and 1207" (p. 16). The philosophy of love expounded therein foreshadows with astonishing precision the values of Western Europe's troubadours and Petrarchists:

> *I speak of the supreme Love, species of divine essence,*
> *(it is hard for human language to tell of it):*
> *a celestial activity, lifting the soul on its pinions—*
> *whoever aspires to it must endure many griefs.*
>
> . . . .
>
> *A lover must have beauty, beauty like the sun,*
> *wisdom, humility, generosity, youth—and lots of time;*
> *he must be eloquent, understanding, enduring and heroic—*
> *no one can be a lover who is not all these.*
>
> *Love is beautiful, hard to define:*
> *true love is not lust, it is utterly different,*
>
> . . . .
>
> *The lover must be constant, not wanton, impure, faithless;*
> *parted from his beloved, he must sigh and sigh again.*
> *His heart set on one, he must bear her anger or grief.*
> *I hate insensitive love clinches, sloppy-sloshy kisses.*
>
> *Do not call it love, you lovers, when men long for one today*
> *and tomorrow another, unconcerned with grief at parting.*
> *Such worthless playing at love is childishness.*
> *The true lover bears the sorrow of a whole world.*
>
> *Perfect love does not show its wounds, but hides them;*
> *the lover cherishes them alone, seeks always to be alone.*
> *From far-off fainting, dying, far-off branded, aflame,*
> *he must face his loved one's anger, he must stand in awe of her.*

He must never betray the secret of his love,
nor vulgarly groan, shaming his beloved.
In nothing may he show his love, in no way disclose it.
For her he sees sorrow as joy, for her would be cast into flames.

The poets who wrote at the height of the Petrarchist vogue and those who wrote in its wake during the seventeenth century either embraced or belittled (in the case of poets like Donne who often abjured *amour courtois*) the values embodied within this definition of love: constancy in suffering, faithfulness and long-suffering patience, the grief of parting, the unrequited lover's measureless burdens, the secrecy of emotions, the necessity of solitude, the paradoxically bittersweet nature of love's anguish, and the lover's aspiration toward transcendence. What distinguishes the later European love lyric from this and many other poems expressing the feelings typical of *amour courtois*, however, is its intellectual orientation. According to Dronke, this significant and unique transformation in the expression of universal human emotions is due to the mystical, philosophic, and religious influences in Western thought:

> From the first troubadours whose works survive to the end of the thirteenth century there is an immense development, a deepening and subtilizing of thought in the love-poetry. The new ways of thought and expression came gradually, and while around 1100 there is very little love-poetry the content of which needs special explanation, . . . by 1200 there is considerably more, and by 1300 we must know our philosophers and mystics, cosmologists and theologians at least as well as the poets whom we are studying did (p. 86).

Interestingly, the same assertion is often and quite rightly made regarding the metaphysical poetry of John Donne.

Guido Guinizelli, the author of "perhaps the most influential love-song of the entire thirteenth century" (p. 57), "Al cor gentil ripara sempre amore," as well as his contemporaries and to some extent his twelfth century predecessors, employed an idiom which was greatly influenced by three kinds of language: "mystical, noetic (deriving from Platonic and Aristotelian theories of knowledge) and Sapiential (deriving from 'Solomonic' books of the Old Testament)" (p. ix). The mystical concept of union with the divine, of transcendence of the awesome disproportion between the human and the divine, expressed in terms of human love, in turn lent itself to the expression of aspirations toward the requital of an earthly love. The result of such mystical unions was an obvious unity-in-diversity, which was reinforced by the Aristotelian theory that passive human intelligence of "intellectus possibilis" is activated by the "agens intellectus" (p. 70), the dynamic divine force. The first Western commentators of Aristotle thus theorized that "in the soul, as in the whole of nature, there must be two factors: passive potentiality and an activating principle. Here the first is the mind's potentiality of knowing and of becoming one with what it knows; the second, which actually brings this knowledge about, . . . makes the soul become all the things that it knows potentially" (p. 72). The relationship between earthly and divine love is finally resolved under the same philosophic concept as the mystical union: unity-in-diversity. "There was only one way in which the two lovers could be one and still be themselves—in a unity-in-diversity such as this unity of active and possible intellect. There need be no separation of lover and beloved: they can be united *in* the divine union. Thus Dante's Beatrice, . . . in so far as she is the courtly lady ennobling her lover and raising him to her blessed self, is at the same time the Angel raising him with herself to God" (p. 75).

Another influential philosophic concept in twelfth-century Europe was the Platonic theory of the "Anima Mundi which is the intermediary between unity and diversity, between the indivisible and the divisible, partaking of both and thus overcoming the dualism between them" (p. 76). The problem of unity and multiplicity is firmly entrenched in this theory and was to intrigue poets far into the seventeenth century. "Thus in the notion of the Anima Mundi we again find a possible answer or paradigm for the love-poet's preoccupation. . . . By its irradiation [it] draws the mind into knowledge, and . . . thus forms the link between the human and the divine, in such a way that the human, in being united to it, is not rejected but transfigured. Once again fulfilment suggests a unity-in-diversity" (p. 78).

The third and final significant influence which Dronke perceives as affecting the *courtois* themes is the figure of Sapientia in the Solomonic books of the Old Testament. "With her we come perhaps closest of all to the secret springs of the love-poetry" (p. 87). The identification of the intellect with love as well as that of human love with divine love is achieved through this figure:

> In the Book of Wisdom (VII. 22 ff.) she is given a long series of commendations. . . . She is the brightness of the eternal light, the unstained mirror of God's majesty, the image of his bounty. Following from these metaphors is one in which she figures unity-in-diversity: since she is one, she can become all things, and remaining in herself she makes all things new. Then the notion of love appears for the first time! God cannot love anyone who does not dwell with Sapientia. . . . Because of her [Solomon] says, 'I shall have splendour and honor among men, through her I shall have immortality' (pp. 87–88).

Thus the religious and philosophic orientation of Western Europe influenced immeasurably the evolution of a love poetry which was distinct from that of other cultures and epochs, not because of the emotions it expressed, but rather because of the intellectual tension with which it presented the universal themes and feelings of *amour courtois*.

The troubadours of eleventh-century Provence were followed by the Sicilian school which gradually transformed the poetry of Provence into Italian. It was in Italy that the link between earthly and heavenly love reached its supreme expression. The sonnet emerged, and the sweet new style ultimately achieved greatness in Dante's *Vita Nuova* and *Divina Commedia*. The *stilnovisti* imbued the troubadour's love plaints with philosophy as they speculated on the nature of love. The confessional nature of the troubadours' poetry was transformed into an even more introspective and intellectual form of speculation. The beloved became less and less important as the poets' interests focused more and more on themselves, their own emotions and states of mind. The new style triumphed in Dante's *Divina Commedia*, in which pure love was firmly established as the path to theological truth and spiritual transcendence. After the *stilnovisti* had adapted the patterns of troubadour love poetry to metaphysics, Dante in his *Vita Nuova* added the concept of the "love of the disembodied spirit."[2] Contrary to the *stilnovisti*, Dante portrayed a love that was not earthbound, sad or restless. Through his recognition of his own, as well as Beatrice's, mortality, he transcended the physical desires of the *stilnovisti* that preceded him and the Petrarchists that emerged years later in the wake of the *Canzoniere.*

It was through the perception of correspondences between terrene reality and cosmic truth, between mutable human love and the immutability of the spheres, and between love and death that the intellectual nature of the *dolce stil* manifested itself. Extreme joys and sorrows were fused in their poetry as they portrayed the constant and inevitable disappointment of an all-consuming adoration. There is an inescapable paradox integral to the unrequited lovers' pose. As Maurice Valency has noted, despite the pretensions of pure love, the desire for physical rewards from the lady was never successfully overcome.[3] The tension between the spiritual and the sensual, between heaven and earth, thus characterizes the poetry of the *stilnovisti*. The resultant psychic conflict between desire and denial, between expectation and alienation, provided an appropriate springboard for the metaphysical concerns of Donne and Quevedo, and in fact would constitute the fundamental reality of the poetic vision of both men.

As they sought reconciliation in love, so they pursued release from the intellectual and emotional torments experienced in the contradiction between consciousness and aspiration. The conflict between experiential reality and imaginative ideality, between the rational apprehension of death and the emotional yearning for transcendence, virtually defines their poetry. Like the troubadours, *stilnovisti*, and Petrarchists before them, Donne and Quevedo expressed their compulsive self-concern in the tireless probing of their own emotional, intellectual, and corporal reality.

The joy-sorrow antithesis which defines *amour courtois* is a paradoxical, yet quite valid manifestation of the unrequited lover's emotional endurance. As Dronke observes, "This is the unique quality of love, that it can transform the greatest sorrow into the greatest joy, *dans impossibilibus facilem eventum*. In Ficino's words, 'Love is a voluntary death. As death it is bitter, but as·voluntary it is sweet'" (p. 330). In the poetry of the *dolce stil* the lover, saddened by his unfulfilled desires, often expressed his despair in terms of his death. His metaphorical death was thus his most profound means of expressing poetically his inner torment. It is this self-contemplation, this utter obsession with the lover's bittersweet anguish, that dominates Quevedo's *Poema a Lisi*. Donne's interest in the psychology of the lover also prevails in his *Songs and Sonnets*. Although few of his poems present the plaintive lover as a helpless victim of unrequited love, Donne often contrasts love's requital with the tradition from which he so radically deviates. Similarly, despite the fact that non-requital, a major aspect of the Petrarchan phenomenon, is inimical to Donne, he employs much of the imagery, *topoi*, and points of view of Petrarchism as he carefully examines the myriad psychological possibilities in diverse love relationships. Love's drama is as inward and personal for the anti-Petrarchan Donne as it is for Quevedo in his Petrarchan poems.

It was Petrach, then, more than Dante who dominated the course of European poetry. Like Dante, he concentrated on the beloved's death, but Petrarch's Laura shed the allegorism of Dante's Beatrice and emerged as a woman of flesh and blood, a woman of emotion. It was through death that Petrarch found his solution to the tension of his unrequited and "impure" love, for in death Laura became more approachable than she had ever been in life. The tension between the sensual and the spiritual, characteristic of Petrarch's *Canzoniere*, reflects the influence of the Provençal troubadours, the *stilnovisti*, and through them of the wealth of mystic, theological, and philosophical concepts and language that had infused the European love lyric. Petrarch brought together the traditions, themes, and styles of the "currents of Latin literature, Romance literature and Augustinian meditation. . . . Petrarch's Augustinianism . . . is . . . a major aspect of the *Canzoniere*. It resides in Petrarch's confessional introspection; in his knowledge that the will is radically corrupt; and in his deep dissatisfaction with the mutable, his restless complaints against the inadequacy of the world, and his consequent turning to God."[4] These Augustinian qualities characterize the secular and sacred poetry of Donne and Quevedo alike. In their love poetry, be it through Donne's conversational approach or Quevedo's meditative monologues, the motivation is introspective. Writing within the Augustinian-Petrarchan tradition, Donne and Quevedo infused the familiar restlessness, introspection, self-awareness, and concern for the mutable with an intensity reflecting the profundity of their own turmoil.

Following the intellectual orientation of *amour courtois*, Donne, Quevedo, and their Baroque contemporaries employed metaphysical concepts inherited from the mystical, noetic, and Sapiential literatures. The concept of unity-in-diversity, of the illogical yet conceivable simultaneity of multiplicity and unity, central to the intellectual heritage of Western Europe, was to occupy a prominent position in the philosophical foundation of seventeenth-century metaphysical poetry.

Petrarch, himself deeply influenced by the many centuries of philosophic and poetic evolution, the intellectual and emotional stance of the *stilnovisti*, in turn so influenced the course of European poetry that it is safe to say that Petrarchism and the Renaissance love lyric are one and the same. Most of the sonnet sequences of the Renaissance followed the pattern of the *Canzoniere*, reflecting Petrarchan emotions, images, and themes. Petrarchism is characterized by the union of the universal attitudes of *amour courtois* and the intellectual heritage of Western Europe; by

> amorous devotion, dependence, adoration, dolor and despair. . . .
> Another chief element of Petrarchism is its collection of conceits: its
> fires of passion, tempests of sighs, dying and resurrected lovers. . . .
> A third element of Petrarchism is its collection of commonplaces of
> amorous philosophy: for example, the two-in-oneness of lovers, the
> distinction between base and spiritual love, and the Neoplatonic
> amorous ladder. . . . Finally, there are stock Petrarchan situations,
> such as the initiation of love, the parting of lovers, and the despair-
> ing poet complaining of his lady's hardness.[5]

The first group of internationally important Petrarchists were Chariteo, Tebaldeo, Serafino, and their imitators, the *quattrocentisti*. Throughout Europe, poets of the Renaissance created countless variations on Petrarch's Laura. The sonnet sequences that constituted the poetic production of Renaissance Spain and England were introduced into Spain by Juan Boscán and Garcilaso de la Vega and into England by Wyatt and Surrey. Poets such as Camoens of Portugal, Ronsard and du Bellay of France, and Sidney, Spenser, and Shakespeare of England were profoundly influenced by Petrarchism.

In the sixteenth and seventeenth centuries, extreme variations of Petrarchan style and content developed. On the one hand, Petrarchan style, conceits, and metaphors were deflated into the classical concision of Malherbe, Ben Jonson, and Berni. Reactions to Petrarchism also went the other way, however, through the tendency to out-Petrarchize Petrarch himself. A predilection for antitheses, hyperboles, and exaggerated conceits characterized the poetry of Marino, Góngora, Quevedo, and Donne. The emergence of *culteranismo* in Spain was fostered by Góngora, who, like Marino, emphasized the cult of words and exaggerated style and manifested less interest in ideas and argumentation. Quevedo, on the other hand, represented the trend towards *conceptismo*, which emphasized the intellectual potentialities of poetry through the use of the metaphysical conceit. Donne, like Quevedo, emphasized this facet of poetry which had been introduced by Guinizelli and the *stilnovisti*. Both poets, through their unique perception of the underlying correspondences between antithetical qualities, established valid analogies between disparate phenomena. The *conceptista* of Spain and the metaphysical poet of England transformed inherited Petrarchan themes, attitudes, and poetic conventions through their wit or *agudeza*, their subtlety of thought, and through the shocking exploration and metaphorical expression of intricate and unforeseen relationships.[6]

In the changing attitudes toward the content of Petrarchism the divergence was as varied as the reaction against Petrarchan style. The beatification of Dante's Beatrice was paralleled by the emergence of an earthly worship of the Virgin herself. Crashaw, Luis de León, and San Juan de la Cruz were among the poets who spiritualized Petrarchan devotion. This reaction was paralleled by an antithetical response, however, for there were those who tired of the frozen adoration of an unresponsive lady. Quevedo, Donne, Berni, du Bellay, and Marino were among those who revolted against the Platonism of the past. Their mistresses were very much of this world, at times highly unidealized, and their love was outspokenly carnal.

Quevedo and Donne were thus involved in a reaction in style and content against the Petrarchan tradition. Since the days of the

Provençal troubadours, the Sicilians, the *stilnovisti*, Dante, Petrarch, and the many followers of Petrarch, the European love lyric had been continually transformed. Quevedo and Donne would also contribute to the further development of the ideas and ideals of Petrarchism.

Donne and Quevedo have often been called anti-Petrarchists. In reality, both poets were deeply entrenched in the literary traditions of their times. The satirical poems that constitute a good proportion of Quevedo's poetic work are expressly anti-Petrarchan, anti-idealistic, and anti-Platonic.

In Poem 440,[7] for instance, Quevedo relates to Floris his recent dream of his sexual conquest of her:

> *De beso en beso me vine,*
> *tomándote la medida,*
> *desde la planta al cabello,*
> *por rematar en las Indias.*

(ll. 50–54)

This humorous metaphorical expression of the lover's ultimate sexual triumph resembles Donne's frankly anti-Petrarchan poems in theme and in tone. Total freedom in amorous relationships characterizes many of the poems that are not part of Quevedo's Petrarchan cycle.

Quevedo's anti-Petrarchan verse ranges from this subtle humor to harsh criticism and scatological terminology. In Poem 640, for instance, the traditional Petrarchan lover's complaints and beloved's restraints acquire a flippant, undignified tone quite foreign to the high seriousness of Petrarchism:

> *Ya, mi Belisa, ya rabiando aúllo*
> *tu ingrata sinrazón y mi cuidado,*
> *y del yugo y maromas me escabullo.*
>
> ....
>
> *¡Oh, lo que gritarás mi atrevimiento!,*
> *diciendo: "¿Este mordaz (y aquí te entonas)*
> *se atreve a una mujer de mi talento?"*

> *Pero volviendo en ti, mi lengua abonas,*
> *y viendo que no puedes desmentirme,*
> *por encubrir la caca, me perdonas.*

(ll. 3–36)

This crudely humorous relationship between lovers is completely alien to the sublime adoration and respectful distance that separated previous lovers of the Petrarchan persuasion from their beloveds. Platonic purity of intention is plunged into a scatological mire. The beloved's non-responsiveness here assumes a humorous twist as she herself, rather than the lover, actively demeans his worthiness in contrast to her view of her own superiority. The vocabulary of Petrarchan submission and humility is replaced by typically Quevedesque terminology—satirical, violent, without illusion or dignity, completely devoid of any sense of love's ennoblement.

Quevedo expresses his divergence from the purely spiritual orientation of the past through various forms of materialism. Thus, economic as well as sexual claims are quite common in Quevedo's satirical, disillusioned vision of love. Poem 626, for instance, begins:

> *Si el tiempo que contigo gasté lloro,*
> *¿qué haré, Marica, el oro?*
> ....
> *Juzgué cuando por rara te vendías,*
> *que diez piernas tenías,*
> *seis barrigas, dos frentes,*
> *y eres, al fin, como las otras gentes:*
> *tienes una barriga, un cuerpo, un cuello,*
> *que no hay sastre ni pícaro sin ello.*
> ....
> *Holgarme sólo quiero*
> *cuando gozo, Marica, tus despojos;*
> *no me vuelvas los ojos;*
> *lo que te di me vuelve, y mi dinero.*

This frankly materialistic view of love for pay contrasts with the idealized and distant adoration of the courtly lover. The lady's physical charms have been enjoyed completely by the speaker, who then belatedly loses all illusions. The courtly lover's constant experience of unrequited yearning does not allow for such a disillusionment. When yearning and desire are requited, they often yield to the boredom of requital and to the sad realization of the disparity between illusions and reality. The frankly sexual relationship expressed here constitutes a significant descent from the spiritual heights of Dante's love and of Petrarch's as well.

Most of Donne's *Songs and Sonnets* are undeniably anti-Petrarchan and emphasize the fact that he shares none of the courtly lover's illusions. Physical love is as important for Donne as it is for Quevedo in his anti-Petrarchan verse. The elegy "Loves Progress," for instance, begins with the assertive remonstrance:

> Who ever loves, if hee doe not propose
> The right true end of love, hee's one which goes
> To sea for nothing but to make him sicke. [8]

Clearly, the traditional *amour courtois* pose of disinterest in the lady's ultimate sexual favors is Donne's object of derision.

In "The Extasie," instead of belittling the traditional ideals of spiritual sublimity, he argues for sexual union by frankly basing his logic on the Platonic ideal:

> So must pure lovers soules descend
>   T'affections, and to faculties,
> That sense may reach and apprehend,
>   Else a great Prince in prison lies.
> To'our bodies turne wee then, that so
>   Weake men on love reveal'd may looke;
> Loves mysteries in soules doe grow,
>   But yet the body is his booke.

Clearly aware of the basic opposition between his argument and the preceding centuries of Platonic-Petrarchan idealism, Donne recognizes the value of spiritual love but adamantly denies its exclusivity. The mutuality of corporal and spiritual love, he claims, corresponds to the complementary facets of man's united body and soul. Like Quevedo in his satirical love poetry, Donne challenges the traditional values of unrequited adoration. In this case, he exalts physical love rather than reducing it to the vulgar presentation of sexual love often seen in Quevedo's anti-Petrarchan verse. Unlike Quevedo, Donne rarely, if ever, expresses love in negative or crass terms.

In "Loves Progress," for instance, perhaps Donne's frankest exploration of anti-Petrarchan possibilities, he continues the opening metaphor of "going to sea" in truly outspoken images, which nevertheless do not express the hostility, alienation, or scabrousness that pervade Quevedo's harshest anti-Petrarchan poems. Instead, Donne employs the same tone and writes for the same purpose as Quevedo does in Poem 440. He narrates the progressive exploration and conquest of his lady, and he expresses his ultimate destination with the same metaphor employed by Quevedo:

> And Sailing towards her India, in that way
> Shall at her fair Atlantique Navell stay;
> Though thence the Current by thy Pilot made,
> Yet ere thou be where thou wouldst bee embay'd,
> Thou shalt upon another Forest set,
> Where many Shipwracke, and no farther gett.

Donne's frankness regarding his anti-Petrarchan desires equals Quevedo's boldest departures from tradition. The final explicit example here of Donne's anti-Petrarchan stance (which we will see again and again in the following chapters) is perhaps the most blunt of his challenges to Platonic idealism. Entitled "To his Mistris Going to Bed," Donne's explicitness is shocking from beginning to end:

> Come, Madam, come, all rest my powers defie,
> Until I labour, I in labour lie.
> ....
> Full nakedness, all joyes are due to thee.
> As souls unbodied, bodies uncloth'd must bee
> To taste whole joyes
>
> ....
> As liberally as to a midwife showe
> Thy self; ....
> To teach thee, I am naked first: Why than
> What need'st thou have more covering than a man.

Donne and Quevedo also wrote numerous poems that are Petrarchan in varying degrees. Quevedo's *Poema a Lisi* is strongly Petrarchan in its exploration of the poet's enamorment, complaints, sadness, and intense despair because of his unrequited love for the aloof and highly idealized Lisi. The complete Petrarchan sequence characterizes *Poema a Lisi*, as Lisi eventually dies and the forlorn lover continues to love her in death.

Even Donne's greatest anti-Petrarchan poems are firmly established in the Petrarchan tradition. The Petrarchan assumptions upon which they are based vary, as do their manifestations. Donne's tendency toward introspection, toward an intense concern with his own feelings and a lack of interest in the lady herself, characterizes his poetry. Similarly, *Poema a Lisi* possesses these qualities that so greatly defined the poetry of the *stilnovisti* and Petrarch.

The *Songs and Sonnets* are not, like *Poema a Lisi*, a sonnet sequence in the Petrarchan tradition. They include such famous anti-Petrarchan poems as "Womans Constancy," "The Indifferent," and "The Flea." They nevertheless contain poems which, however they may diverge from pure Petrarchism, are most definitely based on Petrarchan concepts. Many poems, in fact, are simultaneously Petrarchan and anti-Petrarchan. "The Apparition," for example, is based on the traditional metaphor that the beloved's harshness can kill the lover whose adoration is all-consuming. Donne's wit transforms this fundamental Petrarchan notion into something which is most decidedly anti-Petrarchan, the setting being in the beloved's bed, a province Petrarch never dared to enter.

Many of the *Songs and Sonnets* in some way reflect the Petrarchan tradition, either in their utilization of the lover's Petrarchan stance; in the beloved's unyielding harshness; the Petrarchan conceits and images; the mystical and noetic concept of unity-in-diversity as seen in the two-in-oneness of lovers; the resurrection of lovers; or the death of the beloved. Although Quevedo's satirical and misogynistic love poetry is decidedly anti-Petrarchan, his *Poema a Lisi* is purely Petrarchan in its idealization of love and the beloved and in its expression of the unmitigated suffering endured by the unrequited lover.

Donne and Quevedo, then, did not write in a vacuum. In their coupling of death with love, their recognition that they, like the beloved, were mortal, and their ceaseless introspection regarding the relationship between life, love, and death, they echo with haunting intensity the preoccupations of poets since the days of the *stilnovisti*. They were steeped in centuries of poetic themes and philosophical and religious theories. While both poets accentuated particular inherited ideas and forms and slighted others, they also reflected the interests and obsessions of their time. Donne and Quevedo brought to the traditions they inherited their individual poetic genius and insight and in so doing contributed to the further development of the European love lyric.

The Petrarchism of Donne and Quevedo differs primarily in the fact that Donne never devoted himself to a sonnet sequence in the Petrarchan tradition such as Quevedo's *Poema a Lisi*. Indeed, his *Songs and Sonnets* do not contain even one purely Petrarchan poem. Instead, Donne's Petrarchism is always at the service of his anti-Petrarchan arguments. The simultaneous revivification and mockery of Petrarchan convention found, for instance, in "The Canonization," "The Apparition," and elsewhere in the *Songs and Sonnets* is quite rare in Quevedo's verse. Indeed, Donne is much more obviously aware of his departure from Petrarchan tradition in the *Songs and Sonnets* than is Quevedo in his satirical verse.

Thus we find that Quevedo is either purely Petrarchan, following the tradition to the letter in *Poema a Lisi*, or he is obsessed in his satirical poetry by cuckoldry, whores, money, and conniving, ugly, or treacherous women. Although his anti-Petrarchism is extreme, indeed much more than Donne's, Quevedo makes few references, direct or indirect, to the tradition from which he so radically deviates. Donne, on the other hand, deliberately makes countless references to the Platonic-Petrarchan idealism with which he so heartily disagrees. Indeed, much of the irony and subtle humor of Donne's poetry derives from this *conscious* contrast of past lovers and ideals with his iconoclastic expression of love. In contrast, the humor in Quevedo's anti-Petrarchan verse is crude and cruel, based on biting insults, *double entendre*, and vulgar conceits.

As seen in "The Extasie" and in most of Donne's direct expressions of anti-Petrarchan sentiment, he views the sexual experience as either the necessary corollary of, or the culmination of, the lovers' spiritual relationship. The spirit and the flesh are friendly associates, not hostile adversaries.

For Donne, the flesh possesses spiritual value. Quevedo, in his harsh anti-Petrarchan stance, on the other hand, totally denigrates love's physical expression through his emphasis on scatology, cuckoldry, infidelity, and debauchery.

In Poem 641, for instance, we observe Quevedo's typically satirical pose:

> Que pretenda dos años ser cornudo,
> a título de humilde y chocarrero,
> un hombre malicioso y nada rudo,
>
> sin duda que le vale gran dinero;
> que ya son cuernos píldoras doradas
> que las pasa el señor y el escudero;
>
> mas vienen de otra suerte preparadas,
> pues purgan excrementos por la frente,
> que, por ser más cornudos, dan cornadas.
>
> (ll. 1–9).

This poem, in its crudeness, its emphasis on cuckoldry and excrement, is quite different in tone from Donne's *Songs and Sonnets* and related only in some degree to several of his *Elegies*. The Petrarchism and anti-Petrarchism of Donne and Quevedo differ in that Donne's anti-Petrarchan stance involves a simultaneous revivification and mockery of Petrarchan tradition, while Quevedo effects a purely Petrarchan pose in the *Poema a Lisi* and in his satirical poetry makes few overt references to the tradition from which he so radically departs.

In the following chapters, the particular manifestations of the obsession with death shared by Donne and Quevedo also reflect important influences of Petrarchism, either direct or indirect, on their poetry. An awareness of some of the similarities and significant contrasts with specific poems in the *Canzoniere* may deepen our understanding of the Baroque reaction in general toward the inherited Petrarchan tradition.

The particular expressions of the theme of death in the love poetry of Donne and Quevedo that has imposed itself on this study was neither anticipated, nor forcibly evoked, by the author. Instead, the themes of old age and mutability; love's transcendence of death; the omnipotence of death; the relationship between absence, love, and death; and finally, the imagistic and thematic relation of shadows and dreams to the Baroque interest in illusion and reality vigorously asserted themselves as the organizing principle on this investigation of the love-death poetry of Donne and Quevedo. Upon a consequent comparison of the *Canzoniere* with the poetry of Donne and Quevedo, we discover similar unforeseen relationships between the initiator of Western Europe's most important poetic articulation of love and two of the final poets to be significantly affected by the Petrarchan experience.

Many of the particular manifestations of the theme of death in the poetry of Donne and Quevedo are deeply indebted to Petrarch directly or indirectly, and we find that they either react against, or deliberately extend, inherited images, situations, and attitudes of the Petrarchan mode.

We find, for example, Petrarchan precedent for Donne and Quevedo's obsession with time's passage and old age. Although he did not articulate the fervent obsession with time and mutability so prominent in the Baroque orientation of Donne and Quevedo, Petrarch was deeply concerned with time's passage and its effect on his life and on his love for Laura. *Rime* No. 12, for instance, precedes Quevedo's and Donne's declarations that the beloved must yield to time's relentless destruction:

> *Se la mia vita da l'aspro tormento*
> *Si può tanto schermire, e da gli affanni,*
> *Ch'i' veggia per vertú de gli ultimi anni,*
> *Donna, de' be' vostr'occhi il lume spento,*
>
> *E i cape' d'oro fin farsi d'argento,*
> *E lassar le ghirlande e i verdi panni,*
> *E 'l viso scolorir, che ne' miei danni*
> *A lamentar mi fa pauroso e lento,*

Pur mi dará tanta baldanza Amore,
Ch'i' vi discovrirò de' miei martíri
Qua' sono stati gli anni e i giorni e l'ore;

E se 'l tempo è contrario a i be' desiri,
Non fia ch'almen non giunga al mio dolore
Alcun soccorso di tardi sospiri.

In this, one of the early sonnets of his series, Petrarch is already concerned with mutability, imagining that after the passage of time Laura's eyes will someday lose their brightness, her hair turn grey, and her face lose its youthful hue. Time, its years, its days, and its hours and its relation to love's constancy and love's pain, constitute the subject of this sonnet.

We shall see how the concept of the lover's martyrdom through love, not original with Petrarch, but rather an inherited *topos* in his day, is expressed centuries later by Quevedo and radically transformed by Donne. In Petrarch's sonnet, the relationship between the lover's martyrdom and time's passage clearly concerns the poet. In the initial stage of his enamorment, he already imagines an aged Laura and confidently foresees his own immutable constancy. Although the corporal will yield to time's ravages, the spiritual will remain impervious to change.

In "The Autumnall" ("No *Spring*, nor *Summer* Beauty hath such grace, / As I have seen in one *Autumnall* face."), Donne also deals with the concept of an aged beloved, while Quevedo in Poem 487 ("Ya que pasó mi verde primavera, Amor, en tu obediencia l'alma mía.") explores the relationship between mutability and the lover himself. Quevedo treats the exhaustion and old age of the lover, who despite his weakness and physical mutability demonstrates an emotional, spiritual, and volitional constancy similar to Donne's in "The Autumnall" and Petrarch's in *Rime* No. 12.

Petrarch's *Rime* No. 122 is another sonnet that reveals his affinity with, and probably influence on, Donne and Quevedo. Petrarch in this sonnet expresses a love which, like Donne's love in "The Autumnall," is not impetuous or headstrong, bur rather patient, serene, and immutable:

Dicesette anni ha giá rivolto il cielo
Poi che 'mprima arsi, e giá mai non mi spensi;
Ma quando aven ch'al mio stato ripensi,
Sento nel mezzo de le fiamme un gielo.

Verò è 'l proverbio, ch'altri cangia il pelo
Anzi che 'l vezzo; e per lentar i sensi,
Gli umani affetti non son meno intensi:
Ciò ne fa l'ombra ria del grave velo.

Oi me lasso!, e quando fia quel giorno
Che mirando il fuggir de gli anni miei,
Èsca del foco, e di sí lunghe pene?

Vedrò mai il dí che pur quant'io vorrei
Quel'aria dolce del bel viso adorno
Piaccia a quest'occhi, e quanto si convene?

Here we see a concern, like Donne's in "The Autumnall" and Quevedo's in Poem 487, with time's passage, with a love now mature in years whose flame is vulnerable to the frost of old age and eventual death. Although man ages, his emotions nevertheless remain immutable, declares Petrarch, as he, like Donne and Quevedo, awaits his death and his own Platonic form of love's requital. Donne's "The Anniversarie" ("The Sun it selfe, which makes times, as they passe, / Is elder by a yeare, now, then it was / When thou and I first one another saw"), like Quevedo's Poem 471 ("Diez años de mi vida se ha llevado / en veloz fuga y sorda el sol ardiente"), echoes Petrarch's custom, as seen in this sonnet, of periodically pausing to ponder the relationship of his love to time's passage, to mutability, and in essence to eventual finality.

Petrarch's numerous anniversary sonnets reveal his profound concern with the frailty of humanity, its pitiful vulnerability to time's scythe. In *Rime* No. 101, for instance, which celebrates fourteen years of strife between his amorous desire and his reason, he devotes the first three stanzas to man's temporal insecurity:

Lasso!, ben so che dolorose prede
Di noi fa quella ch'a nullo uom perdona,

E che rapidamente n'abandona
Il mondo, e picciol tempo ne tien fede;

Veggio a molto languir poca mercede,
E giá l'ultimo dí nel cor mi tuona:
Per tutto questo Amor non mi spregiona,
Che l'usato tributo a gli occhi chiede.

So come i dí, come i momenti, e l'ore,
Ne portan gli anni; e non ricevo inganno,
Ma forza assai maggior che d'arti maghe.

La voglia e la ragion combattuto hanno
Sette e sette anni; e vincerá il migliore,
S'anime son qua giú del ben presaghe.

This sonnet reveals a profound kinship between Petrarch and his Baroque heirs. The painful consciousness of evanescence and the imminent dissolution of being provoked him to write it, as did his tendency to ponder the relationship between time's passage and his love.

As in *Rime* No. 12, Petrarch demonstrates his keen sensitivity to the components of time and to the often unapprehended, yet fundamental, relationship between the hours and the years of man's life. Petrarch's interest in mutability's role in life and in love is not merely a random phenomenon in the *Canzoniere*. Indeed, his consciousness of time, of the days and the years, determined the number of poems he included in the *Canzoniere* as well as the precision with which he noted the exact date of his first encounter with Laura and the diligence with which he wrote the consequent anniversary poems.

Like his Baroque successors, Petrarch also articulated his own search for, and indeed fervent belief in, the immortality of his love, in his love's conquest of time. Perhaps the most significant Petrarchan antecedent of the sonnets in which Quevedo and Donne assert their love's transcendence of time and death is *Rime* No. 145, in which Petrarch declares that regardless of where, how, or when he is buried, he will nevertheless continue to live as he has lived and to love as he has loved the past fifteen years. As in the other anniversary sonnets, time's passage since his first view of Laura is precisely noted:

> Pommi ove 'l sole occide i fiori e l'erba,
> O dove vince lui il ghiaccio e la neve;
> Pommi ov'è 'l carro suo temprato e leve,
> Et ov'è chi cel rende, o chi cel serba;
>
> Pommi in umil fortuna, od in superba,
> Al dolce aere sereno, al fosco e greve;
> Pommi a la notte, al dí lungo ed al breve,
> A la matura etate od a l'acerba;
>
> Pommi in cielo, od in terra, od in abisso,
> In alto poggio, in valle ima e palustre,
> Libero spirto, od a' suoi membri affisso;
>
> Pommi con fama oscura, o con illustre:
> Sarò qual fui, vivrò com'io son visso,
> Continuando il mio sospir trilustre.

Like Donne's and Quevedo's view of transcendence, Petrarch's notion of love's relation to death reflects universal human aspirations, as manifested throughout *amour courtois* poetry. Dronke quotes, for example, fragments of the seventh-century Islamic poet Jamil al-'Udhri that reflect this universal desire for love's transcendence of death:

> My spirit was bound to her before we were created,
> after our first drop of life, and in the cradle.
> It grew as we grew, gaining strength,
> and will not break its bond when we die,
> but live on in every state of being
> and visit us in the darkness of the tomb.

(p. 19)

Thus we see that the search for love's transcendence in the Baroque echoes a universal poetic theme and reflects mankind's age-old desire to conquer death. This desire, which was articulated in the *Canzoniere* of the fourteenth century, ultimately found its most extensive and compelling articulation in seventeenth-century Europe.

The search for immortality in Petrarch's poetry and in the poetry of Donne and Quevedo also involved a recognition of the transcendent relationship between the poet-lover and future lovers. In effect, the essential kinship of lovers ignores the time barrier, uniting them in spirit across the ages because of their essential likeness. In fact, in the opinion of the poet-lover, lovers may transcend time because of their paradoxically-shared uniqueness. Petrarch affords a host of significant antecedents to the poetry of Donne and Quevedo in which he manifests great interest in lovers of the future and the impression his love, and particularly his poetic expression of his love, will have on them. *Rime* No. 88, for instance, reveals his implicit concern with the lover's transcendence of time, as well as his recognition of an atemporal alliance and mutual responsibility among those who suffer affairs of the heart:

> *Poi che mia speme è lunga a venir troppo,*
> *E de la vita il trappassar sí corto,*
> *Vorreimi a miglior tempo esser accorto,*
> *Per fuggir dietro piú che di galoppo;*
>
> *E fuggo ancor cosí debile e zoppo*
> *Da l'un de' lati, ove 'l desio m'ha storto;*
> *Securo omai, ma pur nel viso porto*
> *Segni ch'io presi a l'amoroso intoppo.*
>
> *Ond'io consiglio voi che siete in via,*
> *Volgete i passi; e voi ch'Amore avampa,*
> *Non v'indugiate su l'estremo ardore;*
>
> *Chè, perch'io viva, de mille un no scampa:*
> *Era ben forte la nemica mia,*
> *E lei vid'io ferita in mezzo 'l core.*

As he belatedly tries to turn away from Love, he warns beginning lovers to take heed and not to delay in fleeing Love's dart. The relationship between lovers separated by time, possibly by centuries, but united by the emotion they share is likewise an important theme in the poetry of Donne and Quevedo. In "The Canonization," for instance, Donne imagines the lovers' transcendence of time through love and poetry:

> We'll build in sonnets pretty roomes;
> As well a well wrought urne becomes
> The greatest ashes, as halfe-acre tombes,
> And by these hymnes, all shall approve
> Us Canoniz'd for Love.

Quevedo's Poem 478 articulates the same sense of responsibility toward lovers who might be influenced by the poet-lover that we just saw in *Rime* No. 88:

> Si por su mal me sigue ciego amante
> (que nunca es sola suerte desdichada),
> ¡ay!, vuelva en sí y atrás: no dé pisada
> donde la dio tan ciego caminante.

Donne and Quevedo shared with Petrarch a fundamental interest in this form of the poet-lover's transcendence of time through time. Petrarch, however, much more than either Donne or Quevedo, expressed a major interest in transcending time and death and achieving immortality through his poetry. In his search for this particular form of transcendence, he indeed outdoes his Baroque successors, for the *Canzoniere* contains numerous examples of his search for immortality through the communication of his love for Laura to future lovers. Thus he ponders in *Rime* No. 60 the effect his poetry may have on future lovers, indicating his confidence in its communicative power:

> Che porá dir chi per Amor sospira,
> S'altra speranza le mie rime nove
> Gli avessir data, e per costei la perde?

Again, as in Quevedo's Poem 478, the poet lover's influence ironically is detrimental to those who would follow his example. This does not negate, however, the transcendental power of the poet's poetry or of the lover's love.

Petrarch also deals seriously with the theme of the omnipotence of time and death in the lives of lovers, as do Donne and Quevedo centuries later with the added vigor of Baroque doubt and despair. In the *Canzoniere* Laura dies, and the poet ultimately perceives the imminence of his own demise and the reality of his defeat by time. Petrarch's dolorous sonnets following Laura's death often express the same intimate relationship between the despondent lover and his physical environment that characterizes many of Quevedo's sonnets and Donne's "A Nocturnall" in particular. Among them is *Rime* No. 338, in which Petrarch bemoans Laura's loss in terms of his own profound grief and nature's obligation to sympathize with him:

> Lasciato hai, Morte, senza sole il mondo
> Oscuro e freddo, Amor cieco et inerme,
> Leggiadria ignuda, le bellezze inferme,
> Me sconsolato, et a me grave pondo,
>
> Cortesia in bando et onestate in fondo:
> Dogliom'io sol, né sol ho da dolerme;
> Ché svelt'hai di vertute il chiaro germe:
> Spento il primo valor, qual fia il secondo?
>
> Pianger l'aer e la terra e 'l mar devrebbe
> L'uman legnaggio, che senz'ella è quasi
> Senza fior prato, o senza gemma anello.
>
> Non la conobbe il mondo mentre l'ebbe;
> Conobbil'io, ch'a pianger qui rimasi,
> E 'l ciel, che del mio pianto or si fa bello.

What immediately strikes us here is the significant contrast between the poet's environment and the environment so often a part of Donne's and Quevedo's love plaints.

In "A Nocturnall," for instance, Donne does not merely cry out that nature should bemoan its great loss at the beloved's death. As in his *Anniversaries*, nature herself is in fact mortally wounded because of her supreme loss in the death of the lady. The same holds true in Quevedo's poetry, not only because of the death of Lisi, but primarily because of the deathly effects of the poet-lover's non-requited love. In Quevedo's poetry, the lover's solitary pilgrimage through desert wastes and desolate shores parallels the death of the world in Donne's poems. In the *Canzoniere*, however, we find that Petrarch does not reach this fatal extreme. He merely imagines that nature's reaction should be thus. In *Rime* No. 338, although he begins by asserting that death has left the world without its sun, gloomy and cold, this preview of the Baroque mood weakens progressively and Petrarch ultimately hints at some form of reconciliation between nature and his grief in the final line: "E 'l ciel, che del mio pianto or si fa bello."

Nature for Petrarch, then, remains a vital factor which does not die when its symbolic sun dies. He merely hints at the despondence, potential chaos, and sterility that will ultimately overwhelm the world of the Baroque poet. In his post-Medieval, pre-Renaissance orientation, Petrarch believes in nature's potential sympathy with man's grief and in its capacity to somehow prevail over loss through its beauty and its essential oneness with humanity. In the Baroque breakdown of confidence in this reassuring theory of man's union with nature, actual grief and non-requital in love become causes for nature's total desertion of the lover. Unlike the nature of Garcilaso or Spenser, nature for the Baroque poet neither sympathizes with nor consoles the bereaved or desolate lover.

Petrarch's grief following Laura's death at times motivated his search for death as a release from his earthly torment and also as a means of joining her. *Rime* No. 332 is an extended plea in the midst of his unbearable pain, and it prefigures both Donne's and Quevedo's search for death as a release from grief or love's non-requital:

> Amor, i' ho molti e molt'anni pianto
> Mio grave danno in doloroso stile,
> Né da te spero mai men fere notti;
> E però mi son mosso a pregar Morte
> Che mi tolla di qui, per farme lìeto,
> Ove è colei ch'i' canto, e piango in rime.

Death thus becomes Petrarch's greatest hope, replacing Love itself. Precisely because of death's omnipotence, he recognizes in an earlier stanza the paradoxical truth that against Death there is no hope but Death ("Né contra Morte spero altro che Morte."). Like Donne in "The Dissolution" ("Shee'is dead; And all which die / To their first Elements resolve; / And wee were mutuall Elements to us, / And made of one another."), and Quevedo in Poem 492 ("¿Cuándo aquel fin a mí vendrá forzoso . . . que por verte muero, / con la vida me estorba el poder verte."), Petrarch before them expressed the intimate relationship between love and death. Because of love and because of the death of the beloved, all three poets expressed a desire for death as an escape from their earthly sorrow and as the only means of reunion with the departed beloved. Petrarch's Baroque successors thus repeated, with greater intensity and desperation, his articulation centuries previous of death's positive value for the lover overwhelmed by loss and unrelieved desolation.

Thus, the dominant themes in the love-death poetry of Donne and Quevedo—old age and mutability; love's transcendence of death; death's omnipotence in nature and in love; and the intimate relationship between death, absence and love—were foreshadowed by centuries of love poets and by Petrarch in particular, who expressed many of the same interests, images, and perceptions of the intricate and varied relationships between love and its adversaries, time and death, that would dominate with unparalleled fervor the amorous poetry of the Baroque.

The final similarity between our two Baroque poets and their most significant predecessor in European love-death poetry is their common presentations of the frequently violent relationships between lover and beloved, or between the lover and love itself. In the courtly love tradition, Petrarch often presents the violent encounter between the lover and his imminent death because of Love. In *Rime* No. 73, for instance, he articulates this reality:

> *Ma le ferite impresse*
> *Volgon per forza il cor piagato altrove;*
> *Ond'io divento smorto,*
> *E 'l sangue si nasconde, i' non so dove,*
> *Né rimango qual era; e sommi accorto*
> *Che questo è 'l colpo di che Amor m'ha morto.*

The pre-Baroque physiological specificity of death's reality is an interesting characteristic of *Rime* No. 198 and prefigures the corporal particularities of Donne's "rack'd carcasse" and Quevedo's *medula* and *polvo*:

> *Non ho medolla in osso, o sangue in fibra,*
> *Ch'i' non senta tremar, pur ch'i' m'apresse*
> *Dove è chi morte e vita inseme, spesse*
> *Volte, in frale bilancia, appende e libra.*

Petrarch provided important precedent for many of the expressions of violence in the amorous lyrics of his Baroque successors. We shall observe, for instance, in Quevedo's Poem 366 ("Soñé que el brazo de rigor armado, / Filis, alzabas contra el alma mía . . ."), the repetition of the powerful visual image of *Rime* No. 202:

> *Morte, giá per ferire alzato 'l braccio,*
> *Come irato ciel tona o leon rugge,*
> *Va perseguendo mia vita che fugge;*
> *Et io, pien di paura, tremo, e taccio.*

The significance of the dream motif in Baroque literature is evident in its prose and its drama as well as in its poetry. The dream-experience of Don Quijote in the cave of Montesinos, like the dream-experience of Segismundo in *La vida es sueño*, reveals the same uncertainties regarding the differentiation between reality and dreams expressed in the poetry of Donne and Quevedo. There is also Petrarchan precedent for this typically Baroque phenomenon. Prior to Laura's death, Petrarch suffered premonitions, which took the form of dreams. He expounded one such dream in *Rime* No. 251, in which, like the lover in Quevedo's Poem 337 ("Mas desperté del dulce desconcierto; / y vi que estuve vivo con la muerte, / y vi que con la vida estaba muerto."), and Donne in "The Dreame" ("Therefore thou wakd'st me wisely; yet / My Dreame thou brok'st not, but continued'st it, / Thou art so truth, that thoughts of thee suffice, / To make dreames truths; and fables histories"), Petrarch expressed the intricate interrelationship between the world of dreams and the world of waking reality:

> *O misera et orribil visione!*
> *È dunque ver che 'nnanzi tempo spenta*

>..
>
> *Or giá Dio e Natura no 'l consenta,*
> *E falsa sia mia trista opinione.*

The beloved-as-murderer motif and the motif of Love-as-murderer, significant in the poetry of Donne and Quevedo, are often presented also in the *Canzoniere*. Two examples shall suffice to reveal the tradition which Donne and Quevedo intensified through their own particular metaphysical sensibility: *Rime* No. 172 presents the beloved's destruction of the lover, a destruction repeated in Donne's "The Dampe" ("When I am dead, and Doctors know not why, / . . . When they shall finde your Picture in my heart") and in Quevedo's Poem 366 ("Y que luego, con golpe acelerado, / me dabas muerte en sombra de alegría"), but without the Petrarchan expression of ultimate confidence in Love's way:

> *Non, perché mille volte il dí m'ancida,*
> *Fia ch'io non l'ami, e ch'i' non speri in lei;*
> *Che s'ella mi spaventa, Amor m'affida.*

In *Rime* No. 184, Petrarch presents Love's murder of the lover, a destruction to be echoed with the haunting Baroque intensity of Donne's "Loves Exchange" ("Kill, and dissect me, Love; for this / Torture against thine owne end is, / Rack't carcasses make ill Anatomies") and Quevedo's Poem 475 ("¡Qué perezosos pies, qué entretenidos / pasos lleva la muerte por mis daños!"):

> *Amor, Natura, e la bella alma umíle,*
> *Ov'ogn'alta vertute alberga e regna,*
> *Contra me son giurati: Amor s'ingegna*
> *Ch'i' mora a fatto, e 'n ciò segue suo stile.*

Hence, Donne's and Quevedo's Baroque articulations of amorous hostility follow a long poetic tradition, expressing Love's often violent alienation and the lover's frequently dangerous position vis à vis his beloved, Love itself, and his own physical and metaphysical actuality. This inherited motif acquires a specificity and dramatic immediacy which was suggested, but rarely exaggerated, in the

Canzoniere. It remained for the Baroque successors of Petrarch and the courtly love tradition to infuse this motif with their characteristic obsession toward death and their unparalleled emotional and intellectual apprehension of its intimate relationship with Love, the lover, and the beloved.

Love's Relationship
to Time, Mutability, and Old Age

Donne and Quevedo, as poets of the Baroque, although they assumed quite different amorous poses, shared a vision of the world which for each poet was his own very real torment, but which nevertheless reflected a common reaction to the scientific, religious, and political upheavals of their age. The harsh reality of disorder, impermanence, and change, on the grand scale of the heavens and traditional human institutions, reverberated throughout the Baroque consciousness, and its repercussions were felt in the lives of sensitive men throughout Europe.

The discontent voiced by Lope de Vega in *La Dorotea* reflected the widespread apprehension of his day:

> No puede durar el mundo,
> porque dicen, y lo creo,
> que suena a vidrio quebrado
> y que ha de romperse presto.
> (Act I, Scene 4, ll. 167–70)

In *The first Anniversary*, Donne voiced the same complaint:

> And new Philosophy calls all in doubt,
> The Element of fire is quite put out;
> The Sun is lost, and the earth, and no
>   mans wit
> Can well direct him where to looke for it.

....

Tis all in peeces, all cohaerence gone;
All just supply, and all Relation.

(ll. 205–14)

In the minds of Baroque writers, the disintegration of man's world, its "discord and rude incongruitie" (*The first Anniversary*, l. 324), simultaneously affected and reflected the decline of man's life itself. Donne's view of man's close relationship to his decaying earth expresses the pervasive Baroque desperation regarding man's own frailty and transitoriness:

Then, as mankinde, so is the worlds
    whole frame
Quite out of joynt, almost created lame:
For, before God had made up all the
    rest,
Corruption entred, and deprav'd the
    best:
....
The noblest part, man, felt it first; and
    than
Both beasts and plants, curst in the curse
    of man.
So did the world from the first houre
    decay.

(ll. 191–201)

This decay and disintegration is felt in life through the relentless aging process, as youth's beauty fades and its powers wane. Man's painful temporality and time's savage destruction of his life, his aspirations, and his love thus become major Baroque themes.

Luis de Góngora in his "Alegoría de la brevedad de las cosas humanas" writes:

Aprended, Flores, de mí,
lo que va de ayer a hoy,
que ayer maravilla fuí,
y hoy sombra mía aun no soy.

(ll. 1–4)

This awareness of self-disintegration, of the inexorable dissolution of life's potency, characterizes Baroque poetry in general, and in the poetry of Donne and Quevedo we find that it is a significant part of their world view.

The passage of time, the emotional and intellectual perception of the imposition of mutability and death on the lovers, and the sentiment of love are intricately interrelated themes of the Baroque love lyric.[1] In Donne's and Quevedo's love poetry, the preoccupation with time's effect on the lover, the beloved, or love itself bestows a poignant tone, at times nostalgic, at times sinister. They often employ similar metaphors and images in their varied emotional reactions to these seemingly disparate themes.

The themes of mutability, time, and death, for instance, are fused with the theme of love in "The Blossome" by Donne and in Quevedo's Poem 446, both of which are initially motivated by each poet's meditation on the life of a flower. The contemplation of the ephemeral beauty of flowers, although quite unusual in Donne's case, is a common poetic experience often resulting in an emotional apprehension of time's passage and death, as well as a consequent *desengaño*, or loss of illusions. *Desengaño* indeed pervades "The Blossome," a frankly anti-Petrarchan poem whose title and first stanza reflect a traditional Petrarchan interest in nature. Donne's imagery rarely deals with nature and is clearly more innovative and revolutionary than that of Quevedo or other Petrarchists. In this unusual appearance, the blossom serves nevertheless as the basis for Donne's severe anti-Petrarchan rebuke of the beloved who refuses to accept the corporal as well as the spiritual manifestations of love's unity. Entitled "Ofrece a Lisi la primera flor que se abrió en el año," Quevedo's sonnet does not deal with *desengaño*, one of his most recurrent obsessions. It is rather a song of praise for an idealized beloved in the Renaissance spirit. The beloved metaphorically bestows eternity on the normally evanescent first spring flower. Although their motivations differ, both poets, inspired by their love for a woman, employ the forces of mutability and death in the expression of their individual reactions toward the beloved. Quevedo joyously exclaims:[2]

> *Ésta, por ser, ¡oh Lisi!, la primera*
> *flor que ha osado fiar de los calores*
> *recién nacidas hojas y colores,*
> *aventurando el precio a la ribera;*
>
> *ésta, que estudio fue a la primavera,*
> *y en quien se anticiparon esplendores*
> *del sol, será primicia de las flores*
> *y culto con que la alma te venera.*

He calls Lisi's attention to the first spring flower whose beauty has anticipated the sun's splendor and the spring's loveliness, asserting that through its veneration of Lisi it will have precedence over all other flowers.

The splendor of the quatrains is muted, however, by the following tercet, which introduces the threatening notion of evanescence:

> *A corta vida nace destinada:*
> *sus edades son horas; en un día*
> *su parto y muerte el cielo ríe y llora.*

In his treatment of the brevity of the flower's life, Quevedo expresses his metaphysical apprehension of time's compression, a central concern throughout his and Donne's work. The contrast of eternity and infinity with earthly time and space logically results in a heightened sense of the illusory and temporal nature of man's terrene existence.[3]

In Quevedo's expression of the fleeting quality of the flower's existence, there is that same compelling intensity with which he ponders his own mutability and imminent death in the *Poemas metafísicos*. Like man's life, the flower's ages are mere hours, and in one short day the heavens simultaneously celebrate its birth and grieve its death. In many of his sonnets dealing specifically with the nature of human existence, Quevedo telescopes the past and the future into one single instant. Man is virtually equal to the evanescent flower, being as ephemeral and fragile. When viewed from the vantage point of eternity, the time span of both rapidly accelerates, thereby accentuating their common insignificance.

Interestingly, there is precedent for this in the *Canzoniere*. Petrarch himself expressed with alarm his own existential encounter with time and eternity. He begins *Rime* No. 32, for instance, with the articulation of his intellectual and emotional recognition of time's ever-increasing velocity as he draws nearer his final hour:

> *Quanto più m'avicino al giorno estremo*
> *Che l'umana miseria suol far breve,*
> *Più veggio il tempo andar veloce e leve,*
> *E 'l mio di lui sperar fallace e scemo.*

Quevedo's final tercet reflects a mood markedly different from the spirit in which Donne wrote "The Blossome." Following centuries of philosophic, religious, and amorous works, Quevedo's Lisi, like Dante's Beatrice, possesses the qualities of a goddess, for the flower gains eternal life through its association with her:

> *Lógrese en tu cabello, respetada*
> *del año; no mal logre lo que cría:*
> *adquiera en larga vida eterna aurora.*

She is a metaphysical variant of the *flos florum* tradition which "carries the intimation that the beloved is at the same time earthly and heavenly," who not only unites "in herself all the diverse beauty to be found in the world,"[4] but like Solomon's Sapientia can bestow immortality on the evanescent.

"The Blossome" begins with a concern for mutability, the effects of time's passage, and death's inevitability as Donne addresses a blossom whose birth and growth he has witnessed. (In contrast to Quevedo's meditative monologues addressed to a mute, unresponsive Lisi, Donne's dramatic monologue serves as the vehicle through which action-in-progress is transmitted. Quevedo's sonnets usually present analyses of situations and states of mind, whereas Donne's poems imply the dramatic experience of human intercourse in their presentation of the ratiocinative process.)

Although the blossom presently enjoys the zenith of happiness and maturity, Donne is well aware that henceforth all change will be towards decline and decay:

> *Little think'st thou, poore flower,*
> *Whom I have watch'd sixe or seaven dayes,*

> *And seene thy birth, and seene what every houre*
> *Gave to thy growth, thee to this height to raise,*
> *And now dost laugh and triumph on this bough,*
> > *Little think'st thou*
> *That it will freeze anon, and that I shall*
> *To morrow finde thee falne, or not at all.*

Donne refers to the flower in this first stanza only and then abandons this Renaissance and Petrarchan interest in nature for another aspect of Petrachism, the investigation of the poet's own being, emotional and psychological. In the following four stanzas, he addresses his own heart, echoing these initial warnings to the blossom. After six or seven days of growth, the blossom must rapidly decay and die. In contrast to Quevedo's sonnet, no redeeming spirit, no idealized beloved bestows eternity on the unfortunate blossom. The woman in Donne's poem, in fact, will be the *cause* of mutability, ironically through her own immutability, her own "stiffenesse." Quevedo ultimately counters his first tercet, in which the flower's life is compressed into a few paltry hours, with the final tercet's assertion of the beloved's miraculous powers to transcend time. In Donne's poem, however, the blossom's life span is mercilessly "sixe or seaven dayes," and the precipitous nature of its mutability presages the argument he makes to his own heart:

> > *Little think'st thou poore heart*
> > *That labour'st yet to nestle thee,*
> *And think'st by hovering here to get a part*
> *In a forbidden or forbidding tree,*
> *And hop'st her stiffnesse by long siege to bow:*
> > *Little think'st thou,*
> *That thou to morrow, ere that Sunne doth wake,*
> *Must with this Sunne, and mee a journey take.*

Like the blossom, his heart is subject to mutability and unanticipated change. Because of Donne's anti-Petrarchan stance, the constant adoration of a cold and stiff beloved is unthinkable. Just as the blossom must fall and die, so too must his heart leave its "siege" and seek another less "forbidden and forbidding" beloved.

In this dialogue between the lover and his heart, Donne dramatically demonstrates his predilection for Augustinian-Petrarchan self-analysis. The metaphor of the journey emphasizes the lover's dynamic spatial separation from his heart. The spatial and temporal dimensions involved in making a journey are central in the poetry of Donne and Quevedo, as in the poetry of Petrarch before them. In their love poetry, the journey implies separation from the beloved, either the actual moment of parting or literal spatial-temporal separation; and in most of Quevedo's sonnets the metaphor of the journey indicates spiritual estrangement, as well as physical separation, from the beloved.

Donne and Quevedo were certainly not alone in their tendency to stress spatial movement. Morris W. Croll has observed regarding Baroque art in general that "the motions of souls, not their states of rest, had become the themes of art."[5] Throughout *Poema a Lisi*, this spiritual tension indeed underlies the metaphor of physical movement, of aimless solitary wandering.

In "The Blossome," the journey more than symbolizes the dynamic motion of the lover's soul, for it is also a concrete spatial conceptualization of mutability. Just as the blossom's inevitable demise demonstrates mutability's temporal manifestations, so the journey symbolizes change while elucidating the spatial aspect of the time-space continuum. Inevitability, compounded with the metaphor of the journey, intensifies the sensation of inescapable mutability in life and in love.

Donne also emphasizes mutability by subtly contrasting the inevitability of the heart's journey with the immutable beloved's unrelenting "stiffenesse." The beloved's immutable coldness prompts the mutability of the lover's warmth and his heart's journey, for, like the blossom and all temporal commodities, love itself is subject to change. Despite the contrast between Donne's non-responsive beloved and the idealized bestower of immutability in Quevedo's sonnet, both poets express their differing conceptions of the beloved in terms of death. In "The Blossome" the beloved is death's accomplice, whereas in Quevedo's sonnet she conquers death.

In the following stanzas, Donne strengthens the oblique relationship established earlier between the blossom, the beloved, and the lover's heart:

> *But thou which lov'st to bee*
>   *Subtile to plague thy selfe, wilt say,*
> *Alas, if you must goe, what's that to mee?*
> *Here lyes my businesse, and here I will stay:*
> *You goe to friends, whose love and meanes present*
>   *Various content*
> *To your eyes, eares, and tongue, and every part.*
> *If then your body goe, what need you a heart?*
>
>   *Well then, stay here; but know,*
>   *When thou hast stayd and done thy most;*
> *A naked thinking heart, that makes no show,*
> *Is to a woman, but a kinde of Ghost;*
> *How shall shee know my heart; or having none,*
>   *Know thee for one?*
> *Practise may make her know some other part,*
> *But take my word, shee doth not know a Heart.*

This relationship between the beloved, the lover, and his heart, this dialogue, and this separation of the heart from the body are all clearly within the *amour courtois* and Petrarchan tradition. Petrarch's *Rime* Nos. 242, 243, and 249, for instance, present, almost consecutively, variations on this theme of the separation of the lover's heart from his being. In *Rime* No. 243, Petrarch recalls:

> *Il mio cor che per lei lasciar mi volle,*
> *E fe' gran senno, e piú se mai non riede,*
> *Va or cantando ove da quel bel piede*
> *Segnata è l'erba, e da quest'occhi è molle.*
>
> *Seco si stringe, e dice a ciascun passo:*
> *—Deh fusse or qui, quel miser, pur un poco,*
> *Ch'è giá di pianger, e di viver, lasso!—*
>
> *Ella sel ride; e non è pari il gioco:*
> *Tu paradiso, i' senza cor un sasso,*
> *O sacro, aventuroso, e dolce loco!*

The contrast between Donne's situation and Petrarch's is crucial, for whereas Petrarch is the poor wretch, abandoned by his heart which follows Laura and suffering her derision of his supplications and tears, Donne rebelliously leaves his heart behind in search of greener pastures. Donne's inconstancy and imperiousness contrast with Petrarch's humility, constancy, and long-suffering patience. Thus, Donne radically diverges from this inherited Petrarchan motif.

Just as Donne will inevitably find the blossom "falne, or not at all," so too will the beloved inevitably believe his unaccomodated lover's heart to be "a kinde of Ghost." Donne's declaration that to a woman "a naked thinking heart" is "but a kinde of Ghost" is a witty variation on Petrarch's assertion in *Rime* No. 129 that without his heart, he himself is a ghost:

> Ivi è 'l mio cor, e quella che 'l m'invola;
> Qui veder pòi l'imagine mia sola.

Upon the separation of the heart (a symbol of the spiritual) from the body, Petrach assigned non-existence to the material, to the corporal, whereas Donne attributes deathly non-existence to the spiritual.

Utterly incapable of perceiving the deeper truths and spirituality that appearances and materiality may conceal, the woman who denies corporal love ironically can only recognize the lover's corporality. In his scathing attack of the woman who has rebuked him, Donne asserts that she, like all women, can apprehend man's heart, unsheltered corporally, only in terms of death's insubstantial essence. She then suffers his ultimate insult through his implication that whereas the "show" of the merely corporal represents life to her, the purely spiritual signifies death.

The final couplet hints that, through her associations with others, she may have developed her knowledge of other parts of the human anatomy, external parts to be sure. So the irony is finely tuned as Donne subtly upbraids the lady from whom he futilely demands corporal as well as spiritual love for having physical, but certainly not spiritual, knowledge of love.

"The Blossome" concludes not with Donne's original concern of mutability, but with a plea for unity, as he insists on a love both corporal and spiritual. He affirms the interdependence of the material and the spiritual worlds, asserting the equal validity, yet inherently contradictory nature, of the disparate manifestations of the One:

> Meet mee at London, then,
> Twenty dayes hence, and thou shalt see
> Mee fresher, and more fat, by being with men,
> Then if I had staid still with her and thee.
> For Gods sake, if you can, be you so too:
> I would give you
> There to another friend, whom wee shall finde
> As glad to have my body, as my minde.

Unrequited adoration will most decidedly not satisfy Donne, cursed with a beloved like Lisi, like Laura. In the Petrarchan tradition, the lover portrays his reaction to his beloved but shows little interest in the woman herself. While Quevedo idealizes his beloved in the highest terms, transforming her into a goddess, Donne angrily insults and belittles his lady because, in her relationship with him at least, she is as distant as Quevedo's beloved. The ideals of disinterested adoration are not enough for him, as they *seem* to be for Quevedo. Demanding both poles of experience, Donne emphasizes the value of the corporal, as well as the spiritual, for the lover's body is as worthy in love as is his mind. His stress on the equal validity of love's multiple facets, of love's unity in diversity, characterizes the *Songs and Sonnets* as a whole. He expresses a complexity of emotions and attitudes towards love, countering his poems of cynical promiscuity with poems proclaiming love's exaltation and transcendence of temporality and mutability.

Quevedo similarly expresses every conceivable approach to love throughout the vast range of his amorous poetry. His love poetry at times expresses an unadulterated savage love, while at other times it reflects a passionate search for a more refined and elevated experience. Platonic love has a slight echo in Quevedo's love poems, but it is inherently contradictory to the notes of passion and suffering that so well define his vision of life and love.

In the courtly love tradition, *Poema a Lisi* contains Quevedo's noblest love poetry.[6] Courtly love subjects the pining lover to a bittersweet life of passionate suffering, a life of constant metaphorical dying, continual "passion" in the original sense of suffering as well as the more common understanding of amorous desire. For when unrequited, amorous desire becomes an ecstatic suffering. It is unbearable pain which the lover-sufferer nevertheless bears and often expresses in terms of his impending death. Quevedo's Lisi sonnets, clearly in the *amour courtois* tradition, are always and inevitably expressed in terms of sorrow and death.

According to Shotha Rusthaveli, the perfect lover "sees sorrow as joy" because of his beloved and "for her would be cast into flames." What Otis Green describes as a sombre tone of death in Quevedo's expression of love in the Lisi sonnets results from this dual nature of love.[7] Such a duality is caused by what Green has aptly termed the courtly love conflict between possession and self-sacrifice. Such a conflict of motivation within Quevedo's Lisi sonnets arises because Quevedo, like Donne, indeed like the troubadours and Petrarch himself (who ultimately admitted that his love for Laura was corporal as well as spiritual), articulated an emotion which, despite its strong spirituality, was not purely Platonic.

Like Donne in "The Blossome," Quevedo could espouse corporal as well as spiritual love, although he never blatantly expressed his desires in *Poema a Lisi*. In contrast to Donne's outspoken declaration of the value of physical love, Quevedo, like Petrarch, only hinted at his underlying motivations. Like Petrarch's, his was an impossible love, and the consequent conflict between desire and denial resulted in a poetry characterized by grief and tears. Otis Green was correct in his observation that the intensity of Quevedo's sorrow emphasizes the impossibility of his love for Lisi ever being seriously considered as Platonic. On the contrary, *Poema a Lisi* reveals the agony of a love spiritually and physically unreciprocated.

In the majority of the Lisi sonnets, we observe the sorrowing lover, who metaphorically wanders in an alien world, overwhelmed by his inner torment. Quevedo portrays his obstinacy in loving while asserting his love's transcendence over death. The pendulum swings to the antithetical notion of death, however, as, like Petrarch before him, he eventually pleads for death as the only conceivable release from his misery. As in the *Vita Nuova* and the *Canzoniere*, the beloved herself ultimately dies. Quevedo's love, however, like Petrarch's, is never the purely spiritualized love of Dante. It is, rather, a love like that of the troubadours and the many poets of the *amour courtois* tradition in other epochs and cultures whose spirituality does not deny its corporality, indeed whose spirituality springs from its sublimated corporality.

This conclusion brings us back to "The Blossome," in which Donne insists that he seeks a beloved who will be as glad to have his body as his mind. This desire for the unified duality of love also subtly underlies Quevedo's amorous poetry and assumes varied manifestations.[8]

In Poem 469, entitled "Persevera en las quejas de su dolor y advierte a Lisi del inútil arrepentimiento que viene de la hermosura pasada," Quevedo subtly resorts to the traditional argument of *carpe diem*; although he does not explicitly demand physical love, he does plead for some form of love's requital, basing his argument on the logic of mutability:

> En una vida de tan larga pena,
> y en una muerte, Lísida, tan grave,
> bien sé lo que es amar, Amor lo sabe;
> no sé lo que es amor, y Amor lo ordena.

Like the troubadours and Petrarchists before him, he bemoans his paradoxical fate of knowing what it is to be in love but not knowing what it is to be loved. His life of endless distress in love is a virtual living death. Lísida's coldness and the pains of unrequited love unite life and death. As Pedro Laín Entralgo has observed, Quevedo, in his unifying vision of reality, loved life because it was death, as he loved death becuase it was life. Laín Entralgo then concludes that the key to Quevedo's poetry lies in his dramatic attempt to unite these two concepts in a living reality.[9] Indeed, the initial alliance between life and death in this sonnet is central to Quevedo's total poetic and philosophic vision.

He continues:

> Esa serena frente, esa sirena,
> para mayor peligro, más süave,
> ¿siempre escarmientos cantará a mi nave?
> ¿Nunca propicia aplaudirá a su entena?

Employing the familiar Petrarchan metaphor of the lover in peril on the high seas, he pleads for the lady's favors and the end of her abuse. The following tercets present the crucial thematic turn of thought as he introduces the concept of mutability, forcing the beloved to recognize that while he may be experiencing his own particular kind of living death, she *also* is most assuredly dying:

> ¿No ves que si halagueñas tiranías
> me consumen, que, mustio, cada instante
> roba tu primavera en horas frías.
>
> y al ya rugado y cárdeno semblante,
> que mancillan los pasos de los días,
> no volverá a su flor ni amor ni amante?

The opening quatrain has provided precedent for these final tercets, which convey the similar message that life, inescapably related to death, is ultimately and inexorably overwhelmed by it. In the tercets, this interrelationship of life and death is due to unrequited love and simply to the nature of life itself. Quevedo pleads his cause through life's haunting logic, which is founded on mutability, the aging process, and death's inevitability. While the attractive tyrannies of unrequited love visibly consume him, he is quietly revenged by the mustiness of each instant and the coldness of the passing hours that unobtrusively rob the lady of her springtime youth. In the final threatening tercet, he warns the beloved that neither love nor the lover will ever return to a face withered and stained by time's passage. Time is love's enemy just as clearly as it is life's enemy and death's accomplice.

Mustiness evokes the spell of autumn while coldness symbolizes winter. Autumn, an archetypal image for the withering and decline of aging, characterizes the years preceding the winter of old age and death. This image assumes central importance in Donne's own poem devoted to aging, "The Autumnall." Whereas Quevedo descries time's power on the individual, in "The Autumnall" Donne expresses an appreciation for the maturity time brings.

In his important observations regarding many of Donne's love poems, Louis L. Martz, for instance, has pointed out the significance of the constant pressure of Donne's awareness of the shadow of time and death. It is indeed the point from which his poetical 'lectures' all arise. . . . The Autumnall is a poem of quite a different nature from that of the youthful poems that may have composed Donne's 'Book of Elegies.' . . . But this poised and balanced style is appropriate to the poem's theme, which celebrates the beauty of a Lady in her autumnall season. . . . This quiet, 'tolerable' style helps to create the sense of a beauty delicately poised between passion and death, as Donne indicates by the act of denying the presence of the grave in her brow.[10]

Donne earnestly declares age's superiority to youth, asserting that youth's headstrong recklessness and beauty are less worthy than age's serenity. The vivacious springtime youthfulness that permeates "The Blossome," in fact, finds its antithesis in this poetic assertion of the value of age:

> No Spring, nor Summer Beauty hath such grace,
> As I have seen in one Autumnall face.
> Yong Beauties force our love, and that's a Rape,
> This doth but counsaile, yet you cannot scape.

The contrast with Quevedo's previous sonnet is obvious, for youth's beauty, which Quevedo judges essential to attract love and lover, here assumes a distinctly negative quality. Donne prefers the wisdom of age to the compulsiveness of youth.

> Call not these wrinkles, graves; If graves they were,
> They were Loves graves; for else he is no where.
> Yet lies not Love dead here, but here doth sit
> Vow'd to this trench, like an Anachorit.
> And here, till hers, which must be his death, come,
> He doth not digge a Grave, but build a Tombe.

Donne establishes the interrelationship between love and death, uniting the themes and images of old age (wrinkles), death (graves, Tombe), and love (Loves graves). Although her age does not imply that her death is imminent, the beloved's death would entail the death of love itself. Donne asserts the value of middle age, of the lady's "Autumnall face," while indicating his abhorrence of extreme old age in his remonstrance against the horrors of senility, of

"Winter-faces." He thereby rejects three of life's seasons—youth's naive spring and ardent summer as well as old age's frozen winter —clearly preferring the middle autumnall years of consummate ripeness, of mature love's freedom from youth's passion and life's freedom still from death. He continues:

> But name not Winter-faces, whose skin's slacke;
> Lanke, as an unthrifts purse; but a soules sacke;
> Whose Eyes seeke light within, for all here's shade;
> Whose mouthes are holes, rather worne out, then made;
> Whose every tooth to a'severall place is gone,
> To vexe their soules at Resurrection;
> Name not these living Deaths-heads unto mee,
> For these, not Ancient, but Antiques be.

He contrasts life's mellow middle years with its hollow latter years, asserting that the body functions as nothing more than an animated corpse during this final period. When Donne wrote this elegy (1607–08), he himself had not yet reached those mellow years, but he could envision them clearly and declare a preference for their tranquility. The contrast with Quevedo's Poem 469 is again significant, for whereas Quevedo threatens the beloved's youth with time's mutability, inevitable old age, and the consequent loss of his affections, Donne accepts such a reality as a natural occurrence in humanity's movement from birth through life towards death. He includes himself in this process as well, whereas Quevedo's argument for requital is conveniently one-sided, emphasizing the mutability of the lady alone.

Donne concludes:

> I hate extreames; yet I had rather stay
> With Tombs, then Cradles, to weare out a day.
> Since such loves naturall lation is, may still
> My love descend, and journey downe the hill,
> Not panting after growing beauties, so,
> I shall ebbe out with them, who home-ward goe.

This contrast of "Tombs" with "Cradles" brings to mind one of Quevedo's philosophical prose works, La cuna y la sepultura, 'The

Cradle and the Tomb,' in which he asserts over and again that the short span of time between birth and death is comparable to the time required to, as Donne says, "weare out a day." Quevedo, like Donne, recognized that from the viewpoint of eternity, these extremes of life are actually simultaneous events with reciprocal functions. The reciprocity of their functions underlies his view of the interrelatedness of life and death in his declaration that "la cuna empieça a ser sepultura, y la sepultura cuna a la postrera vida." The cradle is man's tomb as he is born into this living death, just as his tomb will be his cradle when he enters eternal life. "Empieça el ombre a nacer y a morir; por esto, quando muere, acaba a vn tiempo de vivir y de morir."[11] Birth is the beginning of life and of death as well. Death consequently terminates the life-long process of dying as well as the process of living.

Donne, also deeply aware of this paradoxical relationship between life and death, eloquently expressed his perception of the union of life and death in his final sermon, entitled "Deaths Duell or, a Consolation to the Soule, against the Dying Life, and Living Death of the Body." His words parallel Quevedo's in *La cuna y la sepultura* and in much of his serious poetry, such as Sonnet 2, in which he cries out that he simultaneously wears *pañales y mortaja,* 'diapers and a shroud.' Donne declares:

> But then this exitus a morte, is but introitus in mortem, this issue, this deliverance from that death, the death of the wombe, is an entrance, a delivering over to another death, the manifold deathes of this world. Wee have a winding sheete in our Mothers wombe, which growes with us from our conception, and wee come into the world, wound up in that winding sheet, for wee come to seeke a grave. . . . We celebrate our owne funeralls with cryes, even at our birth. . . . And we come into a world that lasts many ages, but wee last not.[12]

The macabre tone of this, one of Donne's final gestures towards death, contrasts tellingly with the youthful ease of "The Autumnall," in which he has the temporal luxury to view death serenely, albeit ironically, from the point of view of age. In "The Autumnall," Donne presents an attitude toward death which he does not view as the end of life, but rather as a peaceful descent toward home.

The phrase, "I shall ebbe out with them, who home-ward goe," reflects no sense of regret, nor does it indicate the fear of death and metaphysical anguish Donne expresses elsewhere. He instead effortlessly and gracefully accepts death for the lady and for himself.

In a similar vein, Quevedo's Poem 487, entitled "Pide al amor que, siquiera ya por inútil, le despida," reflects his obsession with his own mutability as he pleads with love to release him now that time's passage and old age have rendered him useless:

> Ya que pasó mi verde primavera,
> Amor, en tu obediencia l'alma mía;
> ya que sintió mudada en nieve fría
> los robos de la edad mi cabellera;
>
> pues la vejez no puede, aunque yo quiera,
> tarda, seguir tu leve fantasía,
> permite que me cuerpo, en algún día,
> cuando lástima no, desprecio adquiera.

Quevedo, like Donne, employs the archetypal images of the seasons' correspondence to the ages of man, the spring's greenery symbolizing his youth, the cold snows of winter his old age. Typically Quevedesque is his juxtaposition of the extremes of such a great expanse of time—his youth and his old age. The word *mudada*, 'changed,' links these extremes while also presenting the central theme of this sonnet—mutability. In "The Autumnall," Donne is repelled by "winter faces" and utterly rejects them as "Deathsheads." For Quevedo, time's passage brings an old age which is also subject to ridicule, if not to pity.

> Si te he servido bien, cuando cansado
> ya no puedo, ¡oh Amor!, por lo servido,
> dame descanso, y quedaré premiado.

Age's effect on the body eventually affects the lover's capacity for love itself. He seeks a rest from loving, a surcease which would be a reward for his years of devotion. Rather than requital, he seeks in his weariness only a release from Love's bonds.

Concédeme algún ocio, persuadido
a que, estando de Lisi enamorado,
no le querré acetar, aunque le pido.

He finally recognizes, however, that the strength of his love for Lisi will not allow him to accept the release from Love he has sought so fervently. The results of old age, the loss of youth and the inevitable movement towards death, ultimately lack the power to overcome his love's strength. Love will endure until the end and only then would Quevedo, like Donne, prefer to ebb homeward, accompanied by his unfailing adoration of Lisi.

Through three sonnets by Quevedo and "The Blossome" and "The Autumnall" by Donne, we have seen that each poet was very much concerned with love's relationship to time and mutability and assumed antithetical poses regarding both themes. Thus we see that the distant heritage of Western Europe's mystical, philosophical, and religious literature, which proposed in one way or another the theory of unity-in-diversity, ultimately influenced the Metaphysical poets of the seventeenth century as well as the Medieval troubadours and *stilnovisti* and the Renaissance Petrarchists before them.

Just as in "The Blossome" Donne poses as a scathing lover interested in physical rewards from his lady, so too is Quevedo's stance harsh and demanding in Poem 469. Each employs mutability to his own advantage in an attempt at logical persuasion. Both poets could also be tenderly provocative and gentle, however. The forces of old age and mutability in "The Autumnall" and Poem 487 affect each speaker as well as his beloved; and their respective loves reflect a mellow maturity. This aspect of their all-inclusive vision complements its antithesis, the youthful springtime vibrance of "The Blossome" and Poem 446, and the derided youth of the unreceptive lady in Poem 469.

The themes of time, mutability, and old age in the love poetry of Donne and Quevedo thus assume varied antithetical manifestations, which in their Petrarchan and anti-Petrarchan stances reflect their shared propensity to perceive the unity of existence through diversity. Life's springtime and autumn are significant temporal reflections of the extreme variations possible in love as well. The impetuosity of passionate anti-Petrarchan love and the comparative serenity of Petrarchan love in turn reflect these temporal antitheses of human existence.

As poets of the Baroque, Donne and Quevedo reflect their age in their obsessive concern with time and the transitory. Their interest, intellectual to be sure, was also emotional. In the Baroque period, temporality acquired an acuteness, a crucial significance never before expressed with such widespread fervor, emotional commitment, and analytical intensity.

Donne and Quevedo articulated this Baroque obsession with mutability, revealing a metaphysical attitude toward the transitoriness of their own lives. They are distinguished, for instance, from their Medieval predecessors not so much by theme as by the profound emotion with which they express themes dominant in Medieval literature. Time's passage and the inevitability of old age and ultimately of death are painful topics in the Baroque. Medieval equanimity, objectivity, and passive acceptance of the rules of life and death do not return to the seventeenth century, as does the Medieval preoccupation with death. Instead, there is a profound imbalance, a painful inability to cope with the dilemmas and unanswered riddles of temporal existence. The comparatively serene objectivity of the Medieval period is replaced in the Baroque by an intellectual acuteness, a constant questioning, an analytical intensity that reveals a basic inconformity with things as they are. The Medieval passive acceptance of temporality yields ultimately to the Baroque active disagreement with life's rules, no doubt because of the influence of the intervening Renaissance period of enchantment with life, love of its beauty, and joyous recognition of its inestimable value.

Baroque poets such as Donne and Quevedo are distinguished from their Renaissance predecessors by their themes, as well as by the loss of stylistic proportion, of optimism, and of emotional-intellectual equilibrium. They stress the themes of mutability, time, and death, themes which did not enjoy such wide currency or profound articulation in the Renaissance, dominated as it was by the themes of the glorification of life, nature, and art itself, themes expressed through an esthetic harmony, balance, and restraint.

The explicit theme of old age is, to be sure, a rare phenomenon in the Renaissance. In contrast, together with the obsession of time's passage, it is a major characteristic of the Baroque. The simultaneous analytical and emotional exposition of such themes which have at once personal and universal dimensions defines the metaphysical poetry of Donne and Quevedo. The prevailing Baroque preoccupation with the decay of the world thus reverberated in their lives and in their poetry and characterized their shared vision of life's helpless surrender to the constant encroachment of time and death.

3

Love's Transcendence of Death

Transcendence, an optimistic concept to be sure, acquired great significance in the Baroque, paradoxically because of the prevailing sense of doom and foreboding that distinguished the Baroque vision from the preceding Renaissance spirit of optimism, hopefulness, and certainty of the supreme worth of earthly existence.

Transcendence, as understood in the Baroque, was an unusual concept in the Renaissance, during which there was little motivation for escape from this world. Death itself was a subject rarely explored to any great extent or profundity during the Renaissance. Transcendence usually involved the exaltation of life's vital reality, be it humanity's or nature's actuality. Transcendence in the Renaissance rarely reflected the Baroque obsession to overcome temporality and mortality. Nature itself constituted one of the greatest expressions of earthly transcendence. As God's supreme manifestation on earth, it occupied the position of major significance, a position it would lose in the Baroque. Thus Spain's greatest Renaissance poet, Garcilaso de la Vega, described the ineffable beauty of nature in his "Égloga III," in which he presented the death of his beloved, thereby seeking consolation through this, the most positive expression possible of his profound grief:

> Cerca del Tajo en soledad amena,
> de verdes sauces hay una espesura,
> toda de hiedra revestida y llena,
> que por el tronco va hasta el altura,

y así la teje arriba y encadena,
que el sol no halla paso a la verdura;
el agua baña el prado con sonido,
alegrando la hierba y el oído.

(ll. 57–64)

The greatest transcendence of the limitations of this life in the Renaissance was articulated by the mystic poets. San Juan de la Cruz presented his transcendence of corporality, paradoxically through the supreme expression of man's corporality. As a direct heir to Garcilaso, he portrayed nature, together with human sexuality, as significant manifestations of man's freedom from finiteness in his "Cántico espiritual":

Gocémonos, amado,
y vámonos a ver en tu hermosura
al monte o al collado
do mana el agua pura;
entremos más adentro en la espesura.

The articulation of transcendence in the Renaissance, instead of disclosing a profound concern with death, thus reflected life's vital reality. Life's transcendence of death became a significant theme only in the Baroque, replacing the Renaissance form of transcendence, which was primarily an ascension toward a more elevated form of life in terms of this world. A heightening of life's experiences, rather than a concern for the continuation of life after death, thus constitutes one of the major differences in perspective between the Renaissance and the Baroque.

The theme of the transcendence of death, so dear to the Baroque, assumed multiple manifestations. One of the major manifestations of the search for transcendence beyond this world was the emergence of devotional and meditative prose and poetry. The literary expression of concern for life beyond the grave and for the spiritual realities of this life augmented in astounding proportion as Renaissance worldliness yielded to the spiritual preoccupations of the Baroque. In part, because of the many violent and swift political and religious changes throughout Europe in the waning sixteenth century, Renaissance confidence in this world yielded to Baroque uncertainty, disillusionment, and the consequent search for meaning in spiritual certainties and release from what Donne once referred to as "this holy discontent."

Less existential and much more metaphysical was the Baroque disillusionment regarding the cosmos and the earth's precipitously humbled position in a universe no longer occupied by heavenly bodies but by planets similar in kind to the mutable earth. A consequent psychological discord and metaphysical uncertainty replaced Renaissance optimism regarding the earth's favored position in the universe and its belief in man's harmonic relationship with the cosmos and with nature. The consequent search for salvation therefore acquired an unprecedented urgency, primarily because of the overwhelming power of the fundamental changes in man's position in his cosmic, political, religious, and physical environment.

Donne's sermons and *Holy Sonnets*, like Quevedo's *Heráclito cristiano*, *La vida de San Pablo* and *La constancia y paciencia del santo Job*, constituted only a fraction of the spiritually-oriented works in the Baroque. Baroque poetry as well as prose was distinguished by a substantial proportion of poems that replaced the Renaissance mystics' expression of supreme transcendence with either despair, uncertainty, rebelliousness, or a nagging sense of alienation from the divine. Thus we observe the flaunted attempts at religious transcendence in such Baroque poets as:

Donne, in his Holy Sonnet XIX:

> *Oh, to vex me, contraryes meet in one:*
> *Inconstancy unnaturally hath begott*
> *A constant habit; that when I would not*
> *I change in vowes, and in devotione.*
>
> (ll. 1–4)

Quevedo, in his Salmo V of *Heráclito cristiano*:

> *Como sé cuán distante*
> *de Ti, Señor, me tienen mis delitos,*
> *porque puedan llegar al claro techo*
> *donde estás radïante,*

esfuerzo los sollozos y los gritos,
y en lágrimas deschecho,
suspiro de lo hondo de mi pecho.

(ll. 1–7)

George Herbert in "Deniall":

When my devotions could not pierce
Thy silent ears;
Then was my heart broken, as was my verse:
My breast was full of fears
And disorder.

(ll. 1–5)

Michelangelo in Poema 150:

Le favole del mondo m' hanno tolto
Il tempo dato a contemplare Iddio;
Né sol le grazie sue poste in oblio,
Ma con lor, più che senza, a peccar volto.

(ll. 1–4)

Lope de Vega in his *Rimas Sacras* I:

Cuando me paro a contemplar mi estado
y a ver los pasos por donde he venido
me espanto de que un hombre tan perdido
a conocer su error haya llegado.

(ll. 1–4)

Another significant manifestation of the Baroque search for transcendence is to be found in its amorous poetry. Like the religious poetry of the period, the amorous poetry reflects intense needs, doubts, anguish, and aspirations. In their search for transcendence, both Donne and Quevedo had more success in their amorous poetry than in their religious poetry. The above citations from their religious poetry are typical of the *unrelieved* search in their work for spiritual harmony, mental peace, and reconciliation with the divine.

In their amorous poetry, however, unlike in their religious poetry, both poets expressed the reality of supreme commitment, exaltation, and the transcendence of death. Curiously, both also expressed their most glorious affirmations of love's omnipotence in terms of death. Although Donne's requited love and Quevedo's unrequited yearning reflect the antithetical poles of human love relationships, they nevertheless share fundamental characteristics central to each poet's vigorous self-interest. Donne and Quevedo expressed a deeply-felt transcendent emotion which, were Quevedo given the option, he probably would not have exchanged for a relationship in which he was loved but himself felt nothing. According to the convention of *amour courtois* and Petrarchism, love's grandeur emanates from its ennobling power, from the ineffable spiritual elevation which it bestows upon its steadfast and long-suffering servant. Although requital is a central difference in their poetry, it is thus overshadowed by the fact that both Donne and Quevedo expressed with conviction love's fulfillment, exaltation, and, ultimately, its transcendence of death. For the requited Donne, as for the unrequited Quevedo, "supreme Love" is, as Shotha Rusthaveli described it, "a celestial activity, lifting the soul on its pinions."

Donne and Quevedo shared a zestful self-concern with which this emotion is strangely compatible; for it is ultimately through love that both poets expressed their own transcendence of death. They delighted in loving for the effect it had on them in this world *and* for the ultimate metaphysical transcendence which they perceived in its power. Because they were inextricably bound to this world, they expressed their love's transcendence through the spatial-temporal terms of materiality and mutability.

Quevedo, for instance, gloriously affirmed love's transcendence of death through his own mortal remains in Poem 460, entitled "Amor impreso en el alma que dura después de las cenizas":

> Si hija de mi amor mi muerte fuese,
> ¡qué parto tan dichoso que sería
> el de mi amor contra la vida mía!
> ¡Qué gloria, que el morir de amar naciese!

In her valuable exploration of the stylistic recourses which create the unique tone of Quevedo's sonnets and truly render "inconfundible la voz que vibra en los sonetos quevedianos," Emilia Kelley observes that Quevedo's initial verses resemble a frontal attack on his poetic theme.[1] Whether they be affirmations, negations, hypotheses, rhetorical questions, or violent apostrophes, Quevedo's opening lines convey a sensation of urgency in their establishment of the specific metaphysical problem which the sonnet as a whole progressively explores. The final line, then, either sums up this initial theme or radically alters its conceptual perspective.[2]

In Sonnet 460, for instance, the initial line establishes the theme which, after the sonnet's exploration, culminates in the final line's articulation of the ultimate result of the original hypothesis. Paradoxes abound in the first quatrain and the thought is complex. Paralleling Donne's frequent use of conjunctions, Quevedo begins by envisioning the hypothetical situation *if* his death were the daughter of his love. This conceit of death as the daughter of love logically follows his paradoxical union of *nacer* and *morir*, of 'birth' and 'death.' The reciprocal nature of birth and death, although not original with Quevedo, acquires major significance and an insistent intensity in his works.

Such a conceit is also logical, given the well-worn idea of *amour courtois* and Petrarchan verse that love can cause death. It is then a short, yet unique, step from the concept "to cause" to the concept "to beget," and thus to Quevedo's unusual notion of death as the begotten child of love. This subtle association of birth, death, and love maintains a powerful metaphysical paradox throughout Quevedo's poetry. No two events seem more contradictory than birth and death; yet, Quevedo meditates on their interrelatedness because of his recognition that even the most disparate phenomena share a common essence and are united in the profoundest sense.

This quatrain exemplifies Quevedo's Metaphysical style in its sparse quality, its strictly cerebral orientation, and the absence of decorative imagery. Similarly, Quevedo's syllogistic approach, his penchant for paradox, and the logical imposition of illogical concepts contribute to the Metaphysical style of this sonnet.

Quevedo continues, asserting that man's capacity for love is more powerful than death and may accompany him even to the grave:

> Llevara yo en el alma adonde fuese
> el fuego en que me abraso, y guardaría
> su llama fiel con la ceniza fría
> en el mismo sepulcro en que durmiese.

Quevedo affirms love's omnipotence over death, as he expresses with great intensity the glory of dying for love. He juxtaposes a well-known Petrarchan image, love's living flame, to death's cold ashes, thereby asserting the close union between life and death, even after death. Living fire would continue to inflame his soul, he declares, although his body would only be *ceniza fría*, 'cold ashes.' The soul and the warmth of love's flame would conquer the tomb's coldness and death's destruction of the body.

This active quality of love, which would animate the dead lover's ashes within the tomb, contrasts with Donne's love-in-death poems. Donne expresses love after death either in terms of inanimate passive objects, such as a bone and a bracelet of hair which will communicate his story to others, or in highly grandiose and public terms, such as a new religion that will arise to worship the lovers' relics. In Quevedo's sonnet, however, despite the stark reality of his death, his still-vibrant remains will themselves alone actively proclaim his love's immortality and immutability. Quevedo's love thus strictly adheres to the *amour courtois* tradition of love's secrecy.[3] His omnipotent love will remain self-contained within his corporal being and will have no need for the recognition or approval of others in death as in life. Such privacy and independence contrasts with Donne's assertion of love after death, which is socially oriented and dependent on the world beyond the lover's heart.

Quevedo's vacillation between the realms of this world and the next continues as he denies death its victory:

> De esotra parte de la muerte dura,
> vivirán en mi sombra mis cuidados,
> y más allá del Lethe mi memoria.

In the tercets he grows more adamant and confident in his assertions, replacing the contingency of the subjunctive mood and conditional tense in the quatrains with the certainty of the future tense.

He overcomes the physical realities of death, conquering its more subtle results as well. He will continue to care and to love, albeit in shadows, and, most importantly, his memory will remain intact despite Lethe's powers. He envisions his triumph over time, as the memory of his love transports the realities of the past into the future, thereby transcending death's finality. Lisi's beauty, which Quevedo scornfully predicted would be destroyed by passing time in Poem 469, destroys the forces of mutability and oblivion in this sonnet, but only through the ardent love and memory of her lover:

> Triunfará del olvido tu hermosura;
> mi pura fe y ardiente, de los hados:
> y el no ser, por amar, será mi gloria.

Echoing the first quatrain's paradox of the glorious birth of death through love, "Qué gloria, que el morir de amar naciese!" the final line reaffirms that, through love, non-existence will be transformed into the lover's glory. This glorification of death for love, of physical non-existence in the name of spiritual fulfillment, is also central to the resolution of Petrarch's *Rime* No. 217: "Ma canto la divina sua beltate; / Ché, quand'i' sia di questa carne scosso, / Sappia 'l mondo che dolce è la mia morte."

In Quevedo's sonnet, the beloved's beauty will conquer oblivion, as his pure and ardent faith will overcome the forces of destiny. The lover thus achieves his own apotheosis through death. In his religion of love, the beloved's beauty and the lover's faith will survive the nothingness of the grave's cold ashes.

The religious transcendence in this life, expressed by the Renaissance mystics and often in terms of human love and sexuality, becomes in Quevedo's and Donne's poetry human love's transcendence of death expressed in religious terminology. We see the quite subtle change in perspective between the Renaissance and the Baroque search for transcendence. The dominance of the death theme in the Baroque accentuates the lingering Renaissance love of life and renders it more acute, more insistently painful. The anguish of Baroque consciousness thus results from this head-on encounter between the joyous Renaissance world-view and the ever-growing obsession with life's finality.

Thus the subtle shift in perspective from the Renaissance to the Baroque involved a significant change in priorities. In the Renaissance, we find that writers express spiritual values in terms of this world, which for them has supreme value. In the Baroque, in contrast, the insistent consciousness of death's inevitability leads writers to discredit this life, paradoxically because of the lingering Renaissance zest for living. Through the extreme devaluation of life, Baroque writers sought a psychological escape from the painful reality of its loss.

The Baroque concern with life beyond death in its amorous poetry, as in its growing abundance of meditative works, reflected a widespread search for spiritual consolation. Thus Donne's and Quevedo's search for the transcendence of this world's values, particularly human love, is often articulated in terms of death. Conviction of this life's uncertainty paradoxically impelled sensitive men to seek certainty in the unknown beyond death.

Donne's "The Canonization" resembles Quevedo's sonnet, its central concern being the same alliance between faith, love, and death which emerges in Quevedo's final tercet. Both poems also affirm that love can conquer perhaps the most humiliating result of death, oblivion. Donne begins "The Canonization" by abruptly asserting that his physical state, rather than his love, should be chided. His sickness, encroaching old age, and bad fortune, all reflections of mutability, may make him an object of reproach, but not his love. By contrasting his love with the obvious vital manifestations of change in human life, Donne indirectly affirms the virtual immutability of his love.

> For Godsake hold your tongue, and let me love,
>   Or chide my palsie, or my gout,
> My five gray haires, or ruin'd fortune flout,
> With wealth your state, your minde with Arts improve,
>   Take you a course, get you a place,
>   Observe his honour, or his grace,
> And the Kings reall, or his stamped face
>   Contemplate, what you will, approve,
>   So you will let me love.

Donne's dramatic monologue, here nevertheless directed toward an obvious outsider, contrasts tellingly with the *amour courtois* tradition of solitary introspection. It reflects the social orientation of his poetry, of his non-secretive love. As in so many of his poems, Donne's pose is that of a lover who has no qualms about loving and telling. He does not subscribe to Shotha Rusthaveli's theory that the perfect lover "must never betray the secret of his love. . . . In nothing may he show his love, in no way disclose it."

In the second stanza, he reflects on the many activities with which those who would reproach his love could better occupy themselves, insisting that his love is harmless and hurts no one:

> *Alas, alas, who's injur'd by my love?*
> *What merchants ships have my sighs drown'd?*
> *Who saies my teares have overflow'd his ground?*
> *When did my colds a forward spring remove?*
> *When did the heats which my veines fill*
> *Adde one more to the plaguie Bill?*
> *Soldiers finde warres, the Lawyers finde out still*
> *Litigious men, which quarrels move,*
> *Though she and I do love.*

As Warnke has pointed out, the wit of "The Canonization" and of this stanza in particular depends on Donne's simultaneous burlesque and rehabilitation of Petrarchan hyperbole:

There is nothing inevitably comic or playful in extreme hyperbole of the sort that marks the Petrarchan tradition. . . . The desperate exaggeration and tormented ingenuity of his metaphors operate as fully accurate correlatives for the lover's psychological condition. . . . Typical Baroque hyperbole, even among the heirs of Petrarch, operates rather differently. . . . In Donne's "The Canonization," for example, the burlesque of conventional Petrarchan hyperbole functions simultaneously as a humorous parody, a modest affirmation of the truth of the speaker's emotion, and a highly sophisticated placing of that emotion in a context of recognition of the world outside his amorous sufferings. By virtue of conceding that his sorrows do not affect the external world, the speaker at once admits the existence of that world and asserts the substantial, if limited, validity of his amorous protestations.[4]

As we noted earlier, the simultaneous revivification and mockery of Petrarchan tradition in Quevedo's amorous poetry is a rarity. Quevedo does not often share Donne's tendency to refer to traditional values through the subtlety of indirect allusions or irony.

The third stanza contains a number of paradoxes based on the meaning of the verb "to die":

> Call us what you will, wee are made such by love;
>> Call her one, mee another flye,
> We'are Tapers too, and at our owne cost die,
> And wee in us finde the'Eagle and the Dove;
>> The Phoenix ridle hath more wit
>> By us, we two being one, are it,
> So, to one neutrall thing both sexes fit.
>> Wee dye and rise the same, and prove
>> Mysterious by this love.

"The Canonization" reflects a faith in love's powers and an assurance of the Neoplatonic theory of the two-in-oneness of lovers, of the concept of unity-in-diversity implicit in the intellectual heritage of Western Europe. Donne's debt to the tradition in which he wrote, and against which he often rebelled, is clear. The conceit of the phoenix, of love's metaphorical power to kill and then revive the moribund lover, is also inherited poetic material. However, rather than repeating the commonplace conceit of the lover dying and being reborn in his beloved's mere presence, Donne bestows a blatantly sexual meaning on the phoenix conceit. Just as Quevedo extends a conventional metaphor and creates the striking image of death as the begotten daughter of love, so too does Donne here revivify a well-worn image through ingenuity and a profound understanding of correspondences. The final lines, "Wee dye and rise the same, and prove / Mysterious by this love," refer to the physical realities of the sex act and to the spiritual doctrine of the Christian resurrection, as Donne unites sexual and religious experience through the word "dye." Whatever interpretation we choose, the other possibility imposes itself on our consciousness, forcing us to recognize the equal validity of both realms of experience. Through the humble pun, Donne weaves seemingly disparate threads of reality into a single unified texture, and we must logically accept both interpretations. Warnke notes, "Sexual love and religious devotion are the two great areas in which the experience of contradiction forces its claim upon the imagination most insistently. . . . The fabric of contradiction is tightly woven in Donne's poetry, the absolute of spirituality and the absolute of sensuality repeatedly becoming identified with each other."[5]

Quevedo and Donne exhaustively explore the unrealized meanings of words through puns in their attempt to unify the diverse reality they signify. Characteristic of many of Donne's poems is the power of the single, solitary word, such as his bony name scratched in a window. The potential of the pun to force the apprehension of unusual, indeed paradoxical, similarities in words reverberates in the world of materiality, shocking the beholder into a recognition of the essential unity underlying superficial differences and apparent conflicts. In their predilection for puns and paradoxes, Donne and Quevedo reveal a shared awareness, prevalent in the Baroque, of the interdependence of all manifestations of reality, be they seemingly trivial or profound, similar or antithetical, secular or sacred. For all aspects of reality inhabit the same plane of existence, interacting in unapprehended ways that often seem to conflict until the coincidence of verbal similarities provokes a sudden recognition of their essential union and mutual interdependence.

This interdependence is central to "The Canonization," for sex and religion, like love and death, the Eagle and the Dove, and the lovers themselves, may appear to have separate identities, but in truth are inextricably united. In this interdependence, we perceive the Baroque echo of the Renaissance mystic's expression of his own particular union of opposites. In "The Canonization," as in the mystic experience, this oneness constitutes the mystery of mutual love, as well as the mystery of all existence, of death and rebirth. Donne here echoes Quevedo's assertions that birth and death, the cradle and the grave, and infancy and senility are in essence simultaneous manifestations of life's single, abiding unity.

Donne's riddle of the lovers, who like "Tapers" at their "owne cost die," yet "rise the same and prove / Mysterious by this love," recalls the mystery in Quevedo's sonnet of love's flame that accompanies and virtually conquers death's cold ashes. This shared imagistic correlation between fire and love's power over death suggests a possible similar approach to death itself, which Donne presents in the following stanza:

> Wee can dye by it, if not live by love,
>   And if unfit for tombes or hearse
> Our legend bee, it will be fit for verse;
> And if no peece of Chronicle wee prove,
>   We'll build in sonnets pretty roomes;
>   As well a well wrought urne becomes
> The greatest ashes, as halfe-acre tombes,
>   And by these hymnes, all shall approve
>   Us Canoniz'd for Love.

The first line of this stanza recalls the first line of Quevedo's sonnet, "Si hija de mi amor mi muerte fuese." Central to both poems is the paradox of love's power to destroy life and to then bestow a form of eternal life after death. Love's power over life also constitutes power over the death towards which life inexorably moves. The personal *gloria* that Quevedo envisions after he has died for love is comparable in essence to the public canonization that Donne foresees after the death of the lovers. Love's power to cause death is equalled by its ability to obviate the oblivion of death. Just as Quevedo's own recollection of love would conquer oblivion, so too in "The Canonization" does love assert its spiritual immortality through memory. Quevedo's self-contained "pura fe y ardiente" reflects the faith of others who will later "approve" Donne's dead lovers "Canoniz'd for Love."

In Quevedo's sonnet, the memory, care, and faith of the lover himself will survive death's destructiveness. Donne is not as idealistic about death's effects on love. True, the love he shares with his beloved will continue to exist, he declares, but not in the tomb. Rather, their immmortality will be achieved through the power of the word, for the sonnet, like "the well wrought urne," can eternalize "the greatest ashes" as well as "Chronicles" or "halfe-acre tombes." Their love will be remembered and revered by others in the world of the living, whereas Quevedo's love will continue its hermetic existence in the tomb because of the virtues of the lovers themselves: "tu hermosura," "mi pura fe y ardiente," "mis cuidados," and "mi memoria." Typical of the Petrarchan tradition, the lover's qualities far outnumber the lady's, reflecting greater interest in his emotions than in her charms which first elicited them.

In Donne's final stanza, the lovers' dependence on others contrasts with the independence of the solitary lover in Quevedo's sonnet. He declares that everyone shall approve the canonization of their love:

> And thus invoke us; You whom reverend love
> Made one anothers hermitage;
> You, to whom love was peace, that now is rage;
> Who did the whole worlds soule extract, and drove
> Into the glasses of your eyes,
> So made such mirrors, and such spies,
> That they did all to you epitomize,
> Countries, Townes, Courts: Beg from above
> A patterne of your love!

Because of the sacredness of their "reverend love," the lovers have become saints, who will be invoked by future generations seeking the mystery of their love. Since all aspects of life are simply interlocking fragments of the whole, there is no contradiction between the earlier implications of sexual love and its final transmutation into a love most sacred.

The social dimension of his love is again emphasized through this concern for the reactions and words of unborn generations. Donne's transcendence of time through time, his contrast of the present with the future, acquires an added dimension as, bound in his own time prison of the present, he envisions the future, which is in turn looking back to the past of his present. He expresses his shared love and death through the multiple perspectives of the time-prism as he imagines the words of the future: "You, to whom love was peace, that now is rage."

Donne deftly pivots his dramatic monologue as he imagines the word future generations will address to the dead, non-responsive lovers. His dialogue with the future is in truth a monologue, for the non-existent does not respond. The future's dialogue with the past, Donne's actual present, will also be a monologue, unanswered by the muteness of non-existence.

Non-existence is nevertheless glorious for Donne, as it is for Quevedo in Poem 460. Through their respective religions of love, both poets achieve transcendence of time and the tomb. It is indeed through death, as it is through temporality and corporality, that love achieves its final conquest. The greatest adversaries of love, when defeated by love, thereby accentuate love's utter omnipotence. Donne recognizes that non-existence may be transcended and essentially concludes with Quevedo that "el no ser por amar será mi gloria."

Quevedo's Poem 471, entitled "Amor de sola una vista nace, vive, crece y se perpetúa," also presents love's triumph over death and time's passage. As in Petrarch's numerous sonnets in which he expresses the number of years that have passed since he first saw Laura, Quevedo begins with a reference to his first brief glimpse of Lísida ten years before:

> Diez años de mi vida se ha llevado
> en veloz fuga y sorda el sol ardiente,
> después que en tus dos ojos vi el Oriente,
> Lísida, en hermosura duplicado.

The *fuga*, 'flight,' of time is *veloz*, 'swift,' and *sorda*, 'silent.' The adjective *sorda* modifies the flight of ten swift years which the sun's movement has swept away. As in other sonnets, Quevedo emphasizes the fact that time's flight is as indiscernible as it is rapid. Like solitude, silence is a corollary motif in many of his sonnets. The absolute silence of utter solitude and of time's rapid flight conveys perhaps better than any other image the cosmic loneliness of humanity, utterly helpless before the stealth of time's passage and death's finality.[6]

The notion of human solitude is as integral to Donne's *Songs and Sonnets* and *Holy Sonnets* as it is to Quevedo's *Lágrimas de un penitente*, *Heráclito cristiano* and *Poema a Lisi*. Both poets recognized man's loneliness, manifested in the inescapable solitude of his birth and death and in his attempts to break out of his isolation through the contact of human or divine love. Although Donne and Quevedo sought escape from their own solitariness through earthly and heavenly love, their secular and sacred poetry nevertheless reflects their haunted awareness of man's inescapable solitude in love as well as in life and death.

With the exception of marital love, Quevedo expressed every aspect of love found in the *Songs and Sonnets*. Like Donne's, his amorous poetry also reflects cynicism, bitterness, and virtual misogyny. In the Lisi sonnets, however, his emotional range is limited to the constant veneration of an unresponsive, distant beloved. Donne's *Songs and Sonnets*, "a compendium of Baroque amorous attitudes,"[7] at times cynical, at times idealistic, almost always deals meaningfully with another human being who reacts in some way, be it with disdain or affection. Hence we note the crucial distinction between Quevedo's espousal of the Petrarchan tradition in *Poema a Lisi* and Donne's often dramatic reaction against it. In contrast to many of the *Songs and Sonnets*, Quevedo portrays much more profoundly the inescapable cosmic isolation of the individual in the Lisi sonnets as he emphasizes the futility of his search for love. The Lisi sonnets in fact present variations on the theme of the unrelieved solitude of passionate suffering. Loneliness in love not only mirrors, but also intensifies, the lover's solitude in life and before death.

Here we recognize the crucial difference between Quevedo's poetry and that of the *amour courtois* tradition. Shotha Rusthaveli asserts that "perfect love does not show its wounds, but hides them; / the lover cherishes them alone, seeks always to be alone." This quasi-masochistic attitude is strictly of a uni-dimensional orientation. The lover seeks his solitude the better to enjoy his pain. He isolates himself voluntarily for purely amorous motives. In Quevedo's poetry (and in Donne's as well), by contrast, the lover is thrust at birth into a metaphysical solitude which his love *reflects*, but does not *cause*. His isolation is existential, not amorous, and therefore of far greater magnitude and complexity.

Returning to Quevedo's Poem 471, we see that through the word *ausente*, 'absent,' the loneliness motif appears as unobtrusively and subtly in the second quatrain as did the motif of silence in the first quatrain:

> *Diez años en mis venas he guardado*
> *el dulce fuego que alimento, ausente,*
> *de mi sangre. Diez años en mi mente*
> *con imperio tus luces han reinado.*

Quevedo dedicated a number of sonnets to this notion of painful absence in love. According to his Lisi sonnets, love is perhaps the most painful of all life's manifestations of man's inescapable isolation. He lent a metaphysical profundity to the *amour courtois* and Petrarchan theme of love as an endless torment of solitary wandering, unfulfilled desire, and separation from the beloved.

This sonnet, like most of Quevedo's sonnets, follows the general norm of employing the quatrains for the exposition of the theme and the tercets as the conclusion. In the tercets, Quevedo counters the insistent repetition of the temporal phrase "Diez años" seen in the quatrains with the repetition of the temporal phrase "una vez." He also contrasts the temporality of the quatrains with the atemporal phrase "eternamente" and the lexically ironic affirmation of immortality, of freedom from temporality, through the insistent repetition of the negative conjunction "ni."

This sonnet presents love's paradoxical reality, its many facets reflecting the antitheses that comprise the unity of existence. While underlining, and indeed intensifying, the lover's solitude before life and death, love paradoxically empowers him to overcome the vicissitudes and impermanence of life through the immutability of his idolization of the beloved:

> *Basta ver una vez grande hermosura;*
> *que, una vez vista, eternamente enciende,*
> *y en l'alma impresa eternamente dura.*

Because just one glimpse of the beloved can eternally inflame the lover's soul, it is through love that he envisions his triumph over time and death:

> *Llama que a la inmortal vida trasciende,*
> *ni teme con el cuerpo sepultura,*
> *ni el tiempo la marchita ni la ofende.*

Rather than merely achieving immortality, the lover's flame transcends it. Love is superior to the physical mortality of the body, for it does not fear the grave, nor does swift time's advance wither or offend it. It is hyperbolically and inconceivably more immortal than the soul itself.

Carlos Blanco Aguinaga has perceived that this sonnet was motivated by the same faith in love as Dante's *Vita Nuova* and Petrarch's sonnets to Laura 'in Morte,' a faith in love that overcomes his almost constant and dogmatic Baroque concept of disillusionment.[8] Its title reflects this unusual reprieve from Quevedo's usual *desengaño*. It implicitly contrasts love's superior properties with the capacities of mortal man in its declaration that "Love, because of one single view of the beloved, is born, lives, grows, and perpetuates itself." The implication is that love experiences the same vital processes as man, who is also born, lives, and grows. But man must eventually die; love is thus paradoxically superior to man and the forces of life and death, for, like the phoenix, it can "perpetuate itself."

Donne's "The Good-morrow" also asserts love's immutability and immortality, and in its expression of love's mutuality, it contrasts with the solitary nature of the absent, distant, and unrequited adoration of Quevedo's sonnet. He begins in his characteristic conversational idiom:

> I wonder by my troth, what thou, and I
>   Did, till we lov'd? were we not wean'd till then?
> But suck'd on countrey pleasures, childishly?
>   Or snorted we i'the seaven sleepers den?
> 'Twas so; But this, all pleasures fancies bee.
> If ever any beauty I did see,
> Which I desir'd, and got, 'twas but a dreame of thee.

Recognizing the unseen alliance between the world of reality and the world of appearances, between waking and dreaming, between truth and fancy, Donne affirms the unreality of previous beauty perceived and desired (two of the central characteristics of *amour courtois*) and "got" (Donne's crucial anti-Petrarchan ingredient).

Past amorous experiences pale into the insignificance of insubstantial dreams compared to the quintessential reality of his love for the beloved. Donne here echoes a concern constant throughout the Baroque which Warnke describes as "the radical Baroque conviction that the phenomenal world is illusion."[9] We see this particularly in the Spanish baroque—in *Don Quijote*, in *La vida es sueño*; in poems such as Góngora's sonnet which asserts that the beloved's beauty, like the beloved herself, will be transformed "en tierra, en humo, en polvo, en sombra, en nada;" and in Argensola's sonnet which sums up this central Baroque *desengaño*: "Porque ese cielo azul que todos vemos / ni es cielo ni es azul: ¡Lástima grande / que no sea verdad tanta belleza!"

In "The Good-morrow," Donne presents his own temporal variation of this point of view with his assertion of his love's present fullness and reality as compared to previous phenomena. He presents time in its logical progression from past to present to future. In the first stanza, he reflects on his past life and then contrasts it with the present. In the second stanza, he deals with the present alone, while in the third stanza, he relates the present to the future, asserting love's omnipotence over mutability and death. The three realms of time are united in the present, for the past and the future have their being only in Donne's mental powers of recall and imagination. Quevedo's previous sonnet similarly begins with his recollection of his first view of Lisi ten years before and maintains itself firmly in the present, as Quevedo envisions his love's virtual annihilation of the death and decay implicit in the future.

In "The Good-morrow," this division of time subtly reinforces the duality of illusion and reality. Juxtaposed to the present, the past loses reality and assumes the illusory quality of dreams. Entirely dependent on present recall, it necessarily fades when compared to the tactual and visual reality of the present.[10]

Donne's elaboration on the metaphor of the dream imagistically effects the shift from the illusory past to present actuality. The second stanza begins as he awakens from his past dreams to the reality of his present love:

> And now good morrow to our waking soules,
>   Which watch not one another out of feare;
> For love, all love of other sights controules,
>   And makes one little roome, an every where.
> Let sea-discoverers to new worlds have gone,
> Let Maps to others, worlds on worlds have showne,
> Let us possess our world, each hath one, and is one.

In this final line, Donne develops his own logical argument as he wittily elaborates on a traditional amorous conceit, which Dronke calls the "kindred paradox of lovers—the beloved is one-in-all and all-in-one."[11] In Donne's requited love, however, the lover himself resembles the beloved; hence the reciprocity of being and having, so crucial to the fullness of Donne's mutual love.

We saw Donne's conception of the relativity of space in "The Canonization," in his assertion that "As well a well wrought urne becomes / The greatest ashes, as half-acre tombes," and in his later description of the lovers as those "who did the whole worlds soule contract." Now this same flexibility of space characterizes "The Good-morrow," as Donne expands the space he contracted in "The Canonization." In both poems, he implicitly asserts that the essential oneness of space remains inviolable, its expansions and contractions being mere appearance.

Donne often expresses his metaphysical wonder regarding life and death in terms of space, the space of the universe, of the world's geography, of "a little room," of the spatial attributes of the human body, and of movement through space in particular. Dynamic movement through space is a central theme in the Lisi sonnets as well. The conceit of the journey, as seen in the discussion of "The Blossome," unites many of the shared themes and obsessions throughout the *Songs and Sonnets* and *Poema a Lisi*.

In the second stanza of "The Good-morrow," Donne shifts not only towards the realm of space but also away from the realm of time. Although firmly in the present and with no thought for the past, he now expands his imagination spatially towards an else-where.[12] In the final three lines we see the flexibility of his conceptualization of space, as he asserts that the worlds of the "sea-discoverers" and "Maps" are no larger and no more interesting than the worlds encompassed by both lovers. Like time, space is relative and its essential unity may be viewed from different perspectives.

In the final stanza, Donne broadens love's relationship to the illusion-reality antithesis and the time-space duality to encompass the fundamental antithesis of life and death:

> My face in thine eye, thine in mine appeares,
>   And true plaine hearts doe in the faces rest,
> Where can we finde two better hemispheares
>   Without sharpe North, without declining West?
> What ever dyes, was not mixt equally;
>   If our two loves be one, or, thou and I
> Love so alike, that none doe slacken, none can die.

Continuing to express mutual love in spatial terms, he shifts time from the present to the future. Global geography is Donne's metaphorical ally in his description of the grandeur and permanence of requited love, as the lovers' eyes become virtual hemispheres. Donne's imagery does not adhere with any serious intent to Petrarchan tradition, but instead branches out into all areas of human endeavor. It is far-ranging and draws from astronomy, geography, alchemy, medicine, physiology, law, logic, theology, and philosophy. In this realm, Donne is far more concrete and innovative than Quevedo, for although Quevedo's imagery also draws from areas such as astronomy (see his Poem 458, for instance), it remains firmly within the Petrarchan tradition, revitalizing and lending metaphysical profundity to inherited images and conceits.

In "The Good-morrow," Donne presents love's truth and love's constancy in geographical terms. Seeking to preclude the North's coldness and the West's darkness from their emotional realms, Donne implies that the light and warmth of the never-setting sun characterize the hemispheres of their love. The temporal implication of this idyllic spatiality is that mutual love can stop time's movement. The simultaneity of the reciprocal reflections through space of the lover's eyes has indeed foreshadowed this implicit unity of time and space.

The juxtaposition of the spatial terms North and West with the concepts of darkness and coldness, two of the qualities most often associated with death, similarly foreshadows the introduction of death in the final three lines of this stanza. Because of his fervent desire to establish the notion of Love's immortality, Donne logically denies the existence of death's most telling attributes in love. He does so in spatial, rather than temporal, terms, thereby ironically affirming the integral relationship between time, space, love, and death. Although he enjoys physical love with his beloved, Donne describes a love as idealized as Quevedo's distant adoration, whose lover's flame fears neither time nor the tomb. It is indeed *through* physical love that Donne envisions a transcendence of the physical, just as he transcends the present through the present. Throughout the poem Donne has revealed a confidence in love's mutuality similar to Quevedo's confidence in his solitary, unrequited love, but Donne's final two lines betray this impression of certainty. After asserting that "What ever dyes was not mixt equally," he qualifies the penultimate line with the word "if." The argument of the entire poem now rests not on a certainty, but on a possibility. The purity and quality of their lovers' adoration must never "slacken," "decline" like the Western sun, or turn as cold as the North wind. This is the only condition to their love's conquest of mutability and death.

Whereas Quevedo is certain of the immortality of his solitary passion, the uncertainty that plagues Donne ironically arises from love's mutuality. This is indeed one of the essential differences between unrequited adoration and mutual love. Donne realizes that the lovers' essential oneness and the perfectly balanced mixture of their affections must be maintained, or they will both slacken and die. Quevedo, however, by virtue of the unreciprocated singleness of his passion, need not base his arguments for immortality and immutability on the beloved's unforeseen actions or caprices. Love's mutuality, while decidedly happier than love's non-requital, is inevitably twice as vulnerable to life's vicissitudes. Because of his impossible love, Quevedo wanders in a dark, alien world, ruled by mutability, impermanence, and uncertainty. Although overwhelmed by this oppressive atmosphere, he never once indicates that he is uncertain of his own all-consuming love for Lisi. The Lisi sonnets thus emphatically express one undeniable certainty. In the *Songs and Sonnets*, on the other hand, there is almost always some hint of uncertainty, some indication that even in the warmth of love's mutuality, permanence and certainty are as elusive as ever. Quevedo thus transcends sublunar impermanence more successfully than Donne.

Perhaps this is due to Quevedo's more rigid adherence in *Poema a Lisi* to the conventions, and, to a great extent, to the vision of Renaissance Petrarchism. Donne, in contrast, in the *Songs and Sonnets*, reflects the Baroque awareness of inconstancy and impermanence. Thus, the hold-over of Renaissance values in Quevedo's more traditional approach aids him in his search for some form of certainty in this world, while Donne's iconoclasm and vehement departure from Renaissance and Petrarchan balance and optimism contribute to his fundamental inability to retain the increasingly elusive certainties of the past.

Despite its hints of uncertainty, "The Good-morrow" is nevertheless one of Donne's most positive assertions of love's transcendence of death. Donne's "The Anniversarie" and Quevedo's Poem 472, entitled "Amor constante más allá de la muerte," likewise affirm love's victory over time and death. Yet, although the imagery of Quevedo's sonnet is more spectral, "The Anniversarie" subtly implies that mutual love is indeed as vulnerable to mutability and death as are all other aspects of life.

Quevedo, in contrast, affirms the immortality of the lover's flame after death. As in his previous sonnet, and in contrast to "The Good-morrow," "The Canonization," and "The Anniversarie," the beloved is of very little importance. In Donne's poems of mutual love she is admittedly more significant than the beloved in Quevedo's sonnets of unrequited veneration. Quevedo asserts love's conquest of death solely through the power of his own consuming adoration:[13]

> *Cerrar podrá mis ojos la postrera*
> *sombra que me llevare el blanco día,*
> *y podrá desatar esta alma mía*
> *hora a su afán ansioso lisonjera;*

mas no, de esotra parte, en la ribera,
dejará la memoria, en donde ardía:
nadar sabe mi llama la agua fría,
y perder el respeto a ley severa.

Alma a quien todo un dios prisión ha sido,
venas que humor a tanto fuego han dado,
medulas que han gloriosamente ardido,

su cuerpo dejará, no su cuidado;
serán ceniza, mas tendrá sentido;
polvo serán, mas polvo enamorado.

Arthur Terry has noted that this sonnet is based on the contrast between the spirit and the senses, and that this duality is related to the antithesis of the eternal and the temporal.[14] Significantly, Quevedo expresses both antitheses in terms of the underlying antithesis of love and death.

In the first quatrain, he concedes that death has the power to seal his eyes and to disassociate his soul from his body. The contrast of lightness and darkness reflects the tension inherent in death's final unraveling of the knot uniting the soul with the body. Like Donne, who refers to the declining West in "The good-morrow," Quevedo apprehends death in terms of darkness as he recognizes his own inability to prevent its omnipotent conquest of his body and his eyes and foresees its inevitable destruction of the light of life.

The second quatrain introduces the one aspect of Quevedo's being over which death will have no dominion. It establishes irrevocably the superiority of his "lover's flame" over the "severe law of death," for death must halt its advance upon reaching love's domain. Quevedo employs the familiar image of love's flame, contrasting it with death's cold waters and calling to mind Donne's image of the death-dealing cold of the "sharpe North." Fire's illogical conquest of water intensifies the assertion of his love's omnipotence, for its inexplicability parallels his love's mysterious conquest of death's rigors. The illogical nature of both conquests unites the metaphor with its message.

In this sonnet, like many of Donne's poems, the lover hypothetically leaps into the future as he imagines his own death. The entire sonnet thus occurs in the future and is filtered through Quevedo's dramatic and inventive mind. As in Poem 460, memory's survival is significant, for it insures love's conquest of time and death and the past's survival into the future. Each line in the first tercet functions in conjunction with its corresponding line in the second tercet. In the first line of each tercet Quevedo asserts that the soul, which has been imprisoned in the body, will abandon the body, but the body itself will not abandon the cares and torments of its love. Providing an ironic twist to the second quatrain, the second line of each tercet refers to the veins whose life-giving blood kept love's flame alive. The bone's marrow which once burned with passion will, like the veins, turn to dust and ashes, but the love it once felt will remain throughout eternity.

In this juxtaposition of idealized passion with death's physical reality, Quevedo adroitly maintains contradictory attitudes in perfect balance. Although love cannot prevent death's destruction of the body, it can survive its severity, ironically through that same body's physical remains. Just as Donne seeks spiritual transcendence through physical love, so too is Quevedo, even in his most Petrarchan of stances, avowedly bound to his corporality. He affirms the value of the material world by attributing spiritual transcendence to his veins and marrow.

Quevedo relates love's glorious victory over death to the body-soul dichotomy. Although he must admit that the soul will leave the body in death, he refuses to follow this admission through to its logical conclusion, for this would mean death's victory over the body. He employs instead the fallacy of *secundum quid*,[15] a fallacy often found in Donne's poetry as well. His soul is immortal and therefore his love, which is spiritual as well as corporal, illogically transfers the soul's immortality to the body. His body will therefore simultaneously manifest qualities of death in its ashes and dust and qualities of life in its sentience and passion. The Petrarchan antitheses of fire and water acquire metaphysical profundity, as Quevedo equates love's flame with life and the river's water with death. Carlos Blanco Aguinaga's reflection on the metaphysical nature of Quevedo's poetic concern with time and death is particularly illuminating, for he notes that his poetry is "metafísica . . . cuando el poeta amatorio . . . tropieza inevitablemente con los dos absolutos que se oponen a la razón de existir de su llama: el Tiempo y la Muerte."[16]

Whatever physical vestiges death leaves ironically constitute the basis of Quevedo's transcendent faith in love. Equally ironic is Donne's use of temporality in his assertion of love's eternity in "The Anniversarie." Although "The Anniversarie" presents an argument for love's conquest of death which is ostensibly similar to Quevedo's sonnet, Donne seriously undercuts it with the notion of "Treason," and his final reference to love's endurance is in severely limiting temporal terms. Central to this final hint of treason is the notion of mutuality, a significant contrast with Quevedo's solitary veneration. Like "The Good-morrow," "The Canonization," and Quevedo's previous sonnet, "The Anniversarie" deals with the relationship between life, love, death, and time and presents the possibility of love's endurance despite life's vicissitudes and death's destruction.

In the first stanza of "The Anniversarie," Donne's obsession with time and mutability is of primary importance:

> All Kings, and all their favorites,
> All glory'of honors, beauties, wits,
> The Sun it selfe, which makes times, as they passe,
> Is elder by a yeare, now, then it was
> When thou and I first one another saw;
> All other things, to their destruction draw,
>   Only our love hath no decay;
> This, no to morrow hath, nor yesterday,
> Running it never runs from us away,
> But truly keepes his first, last, everlasting day.

In his observation that it has been a year since he and his beloved "one another saw," Donne establishes a crucial contrast with Petrarchan tradition, in which the distant lover recalls his solitary, unreciprocated first view of the beloved.

The relationship between love and time's decay suggests Quevedo's "Amor constante más allá de la muerte." While Quevedo affirms his solitary love's victory over death's powers, Donne asserts his shared love's invincibility when confronted with time's passage. Quevedo admits that death and decay will convert his body to dust and ashes, yet asserts that his body will remain triumphantly animated by his love's flame. Donne similarly recognizes time's destructive power on "Kings," "honors, beauties, wits," and "The Sun it selfe," but still boasts, "Only our love hath no decay." It is a sad irony that this great assertion of a timelessness which has no tomorrows or yesterdays should occur in a poem celebrating a love which has endured scarcely a year. Donne's reciprocated love is nevertheless the only immutable element in a world of constant change. It is eternal and changeless, free from time's movement, limitations, and destruction.[17]

Donne affirms that his mutual love has been impervious to decay for the past year. Following Petrarch's example, such references to specific periods of time also occur in Quevedo's poetry, seen, for instance, in his affirmation that for the past ten years his love for Lisi has increasingly grown. This assertion, as contrasted with Donne's declaration of his love's immutability in "The Anniversarie," does not deny his love's mutability, but rather employs the logic of change to love's own advantage. For mutability does not necessarily imply decay and death, as suggested in "The Anniversarie." It may also signify birth, growth, and self-perpetuation, as seen in Quevedo's sonnet.

Donne counters his assertion that their love is impervious to earthly decay and mutability with his recognition in the second stanza that their lives are not, like their love, free from time's rigors. Once again the movement is from the recent past to a distant and hypothetical future, presented in terms of a frank concern for the lovers' bodies after death. Like "The Canonization," "The Anniversarie" illustrates Lowry Nelson's observation that "movement toward the future, either full or incomplete, is perhaps the commonest movement to be found in the Baroque lyric."[18]

> *Two graves must hide thine and my coarse,*
> *If one might, death were no divorce.*
> *Alas, as well as other Princes, wee,*

> (Who Prince enough in one another bee,)
> Must leave at last in death, these eyes, and eares,
> Oft fed with true oathes, and with sweet salt teares;
> But soules where nothing dwells but love
> (All other thoughts being inmates) then shall prove
> This, or a love increased there above,
> When bodies to their graves, soules from their graves
> remove.

Donne understands that their bodies and their "eyes and eares," which allowed them to love, must unavoidably decay after death. Quevedo's reaction against death's decay of his body in "Amor constante más allá de la muerte" results in an apotheosis of the body through love. Because Donne shares with Quevedo this abiding concern for the corporal, the thought of death's hideous destruction of the beloved's body, the cause of his grand adoration, or of his own body, the instrument of his grand passion, is unbearable. When Donne asserts that death would not separate the lovers were their bodies buried in the same grave, he articulates a concept akin to Quevedo's "polvo enamorado." Just as Quevedo's solitary adoration will continue after death in the grave itself, so too can Donne conceive of a continued mutual adoration in the grave. Through their decided dependence on corporality to express love's spiritual transcendence, both poets articulate the most significant manifestation of love's unity-in-diversity.

In Donne's musings on death and immortality throughout his sermons and other prose works, there is a firm insistence on the body's integrity and an unshakable belief in its reintegration with the soul on Judgment Day. For Donne the truth of experience is indivisible, equally material and spiritual. Typical of his approach to reality is his unifying view of love affirmed in "The Extasie":

> Loves mysteries in soules doe grow,
> But yet the body is his booke.

Like countless love poets before them, Donne and Quevedo were keenly aware of the importance of the body, despite its many limitations. Although both often employed the familiar metaphor of the world as a prison, they also expressed a profound, almost desperate, affection for it. Even in his most dramatic espousal of death, Donne affirmed his love of life. During his last illness, he made the effort of posing for a statue, a replica of himself, that would remain in this world after his death. As Louis L. Martz noted, this ironic gesture of reunciation was in truth an affirmation of the values of this world and revealed Donne's deep longing to remain in it.[19] We have already seen Quevedo's ultimate poetic expression of his own tenacious grasp on life, albeit as enamored dust.

Both poets expressed poignantly an attraction-rejection attitude toward temporality as they juxtaposed it to eternity. Their attitude toward eternity, juxtaposed to the material world, was similarly varied and contradictory. As we survey their love lyrics, we see that, from poem to poem, faith and hope yield to disillusionment and despair and these are then in turn replaced by faith and hope. Both poets repeat in other poems the familiar assertions observed in "The Anniversarie" and "Amor constante más allá de la muerte." Quevedo, for instance, echoes Donne's concern at death for "these eyes, and eares" in Poem 479. The second quatrain of this sonnet resembles the first stanza of "The Anniversarie."

> Siento haber de dejar deshabitado
> cuerpo que amante espíritu ha ceñido;
> desierto un corazón siempre encendido,
> donde todo el Amor reinó hospedado.[20]

The material assumes importance because the spiritual manifests itself through it. As in "Amor más allá de la muerte," Quevedo deals with his own body, his own passion, and the separation of the body from the soul, while Donne typically treats the bodies of two lovers, the separation of two material entities. "Death were no divorce," he declares, if one grave might "hide thine and my coarse." He views the mutuality of love after death only through the lovers' bodies. In contrast to Quevedo's "Amor constante más allá de la muerte," Donne finds in "The Anniversarie" that the body when separated from the beloved's body will not conquer such a powerful force as death. Quevedo attributes transcendence of his spiritual love to the body, while Donne must attribute the transcendence of requited corporal love to the soul "where nothing dwells but love."

The resolution of Donne's stanza ultimately lies in a concept of the body which is antithetical to the positive view that it is love's instrument. In an attempt at self-consolation, Donne expresses the traditional idea that the body is a hindrance to the spirit, a "Grave" or a prison of the soul. Although the body is love's agent, spiritual as well as corporal, it is subject to nescience, ignorance, disease, and death. Disease interested Donne and Quevedo, for, like death and old age, it poignantly reflects the human existential realities of mutability. Donne pondered his own sickness and disease in general in *Devotions upon Emergent Occasions*, and Quevedo firmly believed and articulated the philosophy that life itself is a sickness, that man is diseased with his own inevitable mortality.

Unlike the soul, the body is heir to the sickness of life, to mutability, and to death. Donne's final line in stanza two, "When bodies to their graves, soules from their graves remove," resembles Quevedo's philosophy that the body is the prison or grave for the soul, just as this life is a form of incarceration or death. The body serves as the grave of the soul for a lifetime until death ultimately severs the body from the soul, condemning it to its own earthly grave. The idea that death is born with life, central to Quevedo's poetry and prose works such as *La cuna y la sepultura*, is clearly the basis for the final line of stanza two in "The Anniversarie." The body's death to this life is simultaneously the soul's birth to a new, unencumbered freedom.

In the first stanza of "The Anniversarie," the central dichotomy was time and eternity. In the second stanza, it is the body and the soul, accompanied by the duality of life and death. In the third and final stanza, the prevailing antithesis is this world and the next, the physical and the metaphysical. Throughout the poem as a whole, there is thus a clear dichotomy between the material and the spiritual which assumes varied, yet mutually reinforcing, manifestations.

The eternal nature of mutual love ultimately envisioned in the second stanza is subtly weakened in the final stanza, however, as

Donne returns from his mental sojourn in the timelessness of the future to the temporal mutability and physical limitations of the present:

> And then wee shall be throughly blest,
> But wee no more, then all the rest.
> Here upon earth, we'are Kings, and none but wee
> Can be such Kings, nor of such subjects bee;
> Who is so safe as wee? where none can doe
> Treason to us, except one of us two.
> True and false feares let us refraine,
> Let us love nobly,'and live, and adde againe
> Yeares and yeares unto yeares, till we attaine
> To write threescore: this is the second of our raigne.

Having praised their love as timeless, eternal, immutable, and immortal in the first stanza, Donne ironically calls for the continuation of their love in finite terms of "yeares." He reduces their love to time's measurement, seeing it as dangerously vulnerable to mutability. On the surface, it is a pleasant realization that each lover is king. The other lover is the sole subject and, therefore, the only person capable of treason. Yet the beloved's treason would be the cruelest and most powerful of all. Donne does not deny the possibility of such an occurrence when he declares, "True and false feares let us refraine." False fears are fears of the outside world, true fears are of the beloved. He recognizes that he cannot completely avoid mutability, not even through love's mutuality, for in this sublunar world love itself may die. This subtle hint of uncertainty undermines what is otherwise one of Donne's most positive expressions of mutual love.[21] It echoes his last-minute introduction of doubt in "The Good-morrow." As in "The Good-morrow," the lovers themselves are responsible for love's victory over time, mutability, and death, and, therefore, for any possibility of love's defeat.

Just as mutability and inevitable death will always threaten the lovers' lives, so too will time and mutability define their love. The title itself reflects the author's awareness of time, its relationship to their love in the past "yeare" and in future "yeares." Love's mutuality thereby ironically creates an uncertainty that subtly undercuts both "The Anniversarie" and "The Good-morrow."

The subtlety with which Donne slips in these hints of mutability parallels, in essence, the subtlety of time's silent, swift flight that characterizes so many of Quevedo's sonnets. Imperceptibility and its result, increased danger, unite these parallel hints of mutability in the poetry of Donne and Quevedo.

In "The Relique," Donne also asserts in his own way requited love's transcendence of death:

> When my grave is broke up againe
> Some second ghest to entertaine,
> (For graves have learn'd that woman-head)
> To be to more than one a Bed)
> And he that digs it, spies
> A bracelet of bright haire about the bone,
> Will he not let'us alone,
> And thinke that there a loving couple lies,
> Who thought that this device might be some way
> To make their soules, at the last busie day,
> Meet at this grave, and make a little stay?

This poem, like many of Donne's sermons and essays, reflects his fascination with Judgment Day when all souls will return to their bodies as well as his obsession with the state of his own body after death. He envisions his future state in terms as stark as those employed by Quevedo in "Amor constante más allá de la muerte"; and, like Quevedo, he insists on his body's continued integrity after death. He envisions that "Last busie day" when souls return to their bodies, thereby reversing death's separation of the soul from the body, which preoccupied Quevedo in "Amor constante." Through the highly visual device of the bracelet of bright hair, he ingeniously attempts to provoke the soul of the beloved to return to that small portion of her body and, therefore, to his newly reunited body and soul.

The contrast of the darkness of the grave with the brightness of the bracelet precisely parallels Quevedo's bright flame in the midst of death's ashes, as both poets assert love's eternity, its conquest of the grave. The brightness of Donne's bracelet of hair and Quevedo's enamored ashes fills their graves with hope and light, thereby providing a paradoxical imagistic juxtaposition to the dark bones of death and the lifeless dust of the tomb.

In "The Relique," Donne expresses hope for the renewal of love at the Resurrection, when souls and bodies will be reunited. As the lovers' souls and bodies are reanimated, their love's fullness will banish the sterility of the grave. There is no indication, as in Quevedo's sonnets, that love's flame will continue to burn in the interim or that, because of love's immortality, the lover's inanimate remains will partake of the soul's immortality. Donne, who dwells so on the importance of corporal love in life, is curiously incapable of making Quevedo's ultimate assertion of corporal sentience in death.

Like Quevedo, however, he expresses his earthly devotion in terms of love's eventual conquest of death:

> If this fall in a time, or land,
> Where mis-devotion doth command,
> Then, he that digges us up, will bring
> Us, to the Bishop, and the King,
> To make us Reliques; then
> Thou shalt be'a Mary Magdalen, and I
> A something else thereby;
> All women shall adore us, and some men;
> And since at such times, miracles are sought,
> I would that age were by this paper taught
> What miracles wee harmlesse lovers wrought.

As in "The Canonization," Donne seeks to inform posterity of his love through poetry and again applies a religious interpretation to this requited love. Whereas in "The Canonization" he emphasized the mystery of their love, in "The Relique" he stresses the miracle of their love. This alliance between love, death, and religion recalls Quevedo's Poem 460, in which the lover's own "pura fe y ardiente" symbolized the nature of his love after death. In "The Relique," as in "The Canonization," Donne imagines that posterity will immortalize the lover's adoration, albeit through "mis-devotion." In Quevedo's corresponding poems, love's immortality depends neither on what future generations might do, nor on the beloved's faithfulness, nor on any attempts by the lover to maintain his love through external devices such as poetry or a bracelet of hair. Quevedo's love is impervious to mundane limitations, and its immortality does not depend on any equally-limited devices of this world. His love's ardor will be as isolated and self-contained in death as it was in life.

Because of their mutual love, the lovers in "The Canonization" and "The Relique" will be immortalized by others. The lovers in both poems will become saints, whereas in Quevedo's poems his solitary love for Lisi will alone thwart death's power. The final stanza of "The Relique" reinforces this basic difference between many of Donne's poems and Quevedo's sonnets:

> First, we lov'd well and faithfully,
> Yet knew not what wee lov'd, nor why,
> Difference of sex no more wee knew,
> Then our Guardian Angells doe;
>   Coming and going, wee
> Perchance might kisse, but not between those meales;
>   Our hands ne'r toucht the seales,
> Which nature, injur'd by late law, sets free:
> These miracles wee did; but now alas,
> All measure, and all language, I should passe,
> Should I tell what a miracle shee was.

The idealization of the beloved reaches the heights already seen in some of Quevedo's sonnets, but as Donne indicates, his relationship with his lady is much more than Quevedo's single glance of Lisi ten years before. It is nevertheless a faithful and chaste relationship, and therein lies their love's miracle, according to Donne. He subtly juxtaposes this unorthodox interpretation of "miracle" to its orthodox meaning from the *amour courtois* and Petrarchan tradition in his hyperbolic praise of the beloved. As Joan Bennett has observed, this miraculous beloved of the final lines contrasts with "the common run of women" of the first stanza who may "some second ghest entertaine."[22]

"The Relique," like "The Canonization," celebrates the joys of mutual love as Donne looks beyond death. As in "The Canonization," "The Anniversarie," and Quevedo's "Amor constante más allá de la muerte," Donne envisions the future which is the setting for the first two stanzas. In the third stanza, the present becomes the past as it is viewed through the lenses of the future. Donne intensifies and compresses time through this complex, but logical, interassociation of the present, the future, and the past. We see the present through the uncertainty of the future and the dim haze of the past. Through the lover's perspective in the final stanza, Donne asserts the essential oneness of time, the inextricable unity of the future, the past, and the present. Through the expansion of *space* in "The Good-morrow," Donne finds that "one little roome" could be "an every where." In "The Relique" he expresses *time's* flexibility through its compression. Although he may articulate the oneness of the dimensions of time and space through expansion or compression, the final result is the same, for ultimately man remains a prisoner of the time-space continuum.

Mutability and death characterize all aspects of life, including love, be it Quevedo's solitary adoration or Donne's shared passion. The disparateness of love experiences only emphasizes death's universality and inevitability. The varied love poems discussed reflect their authors' shared concern with the relationship between love and its adversaries—time, mutability, and death. Each poet asserts in his own way love's transcendence of these limitations. Time's passage and its inevitable results, mutability and death, can never be avoided. Donne and Quevedo nevertheless affirmed that, although love cannot prevent death or ignore the limitations of the material world, of time and space, and of man's corporality itself, it can, and indeed does, transcend all limitations, be they material, temporal, or spatial.

Love, be it human or divine, rarely finds its articulation in the Baroque lyric or in the amorous poetry of Donne and Quevedo as the supreme manifestation of transcendence in terms of this world.

As major representatives of the Baroque, Donne and Quevedo express, rather, love's essential role as the omnipotent adversary of time, death, and oblivion. In contrast to the poetry of such Renaissance figures as Spenser, Garcilaso and San Juan de la Cruz, dominated by sensorial imagery and finely-polished style, the metaphysical poetry of Donne and Quevedo is primarily cerebral, dominated by argumentation that is often illogical, yet paradoxically convincing.

Their metaphysical orientation, like their Baroque obsession with death, bestows on the amorous relationships expressed in their poetry a unique significance far beyond that of ordinary love. Mutability, transience, and death thus yield to the expressed transcendence of the sublunar emotion of love, primarily because of the poets' irrepressible human yearning for immortality. The finite thus becomes infinite and eternal because of the fervent desire, the intellectual acrobatics, and the metaphysical understanding of correspondences revealed by Donne and Quevedo—in short, because of the expressive power of their poetry.

Sexuality no longer reflects life's joyous vibrance, but rather the fundamental human urge toward the transcendence of death. In the Baroque, love's emotion is directed toward the unknown, toward mortality, whereas in the Renaissance it was directed toward the celebration of life, toward the known. Hence, the clarity of Renaissance confidence yields in the Baroque to the dark musings of poets who wander in an alien land, beset by doubts and despair, having lost contact with the center of their being, of nature, and of the cosmos. In their search for transcendence, they nevertheless courageously direct themselves toward the ultimate question which, although it remains unanswered, paradoxically defines the human condition. The essentially tragic orientation of the Baroque is due to this fundamental problem regarding the significance of existence and of non-existence and of the ironic relationship between the two.

A profound awareness of human limitations and of relentless and unending loss dominates the Baroque world-view. The Baroque as a literary period, in contrast with the preceding Renaissance or the following Neo-Classical, is infinitely more courageous in its daring confrontation with the unresolved problems and paradoxes of life. Discontent with the superficial beauty of nature and the classic symmetry of Renaissance art, it strives, rather, to probe the substantive marrow of reality, rejecting facile or shallow solutions to the profound metaphysical questions of existence.

The truly optimistic assertion of the transcendence of the most mysterious phenomenon that besets man—death itself—is quite rare in the Baroque lyric. Hence, when it does occur, we are obliged to take special note, for one such occurrence is worth far more than the countless expressions of transcendence in the Renaissance manner. The monumental effort of Baroque poets to achieve transcendence and to *believe* in the possibility of death's subjugation, despite their obsessive doubts regarding the imponderable and tragic fate of humanity, doomed to the consciousness of its temporality—such an effort and such an expression of transcendence merits our profound admiration and our unequivocal wonder. Thus, Donne and Quevedo, while expressing fundamental Baroque themes, simultaneously achieve one of the major esthetic goals of the Baroque—the provocation of the reader's awe. Through the persuasive fervor typical of their times and through a vigorous expense of mind and spirit in their rare, but consequently ever so more valuable, affirmations of love's transcendence of death, Donne and Quevedo created some of the Baroque's most moving expressions of man's conquest of death.

4

Absence, Love, and Death

Absence in love is perhaps the most common theme in the love poetry of Western Europe. It is a fact that characterizes at one time or another most love relationships in reality and in fiction. In the poetry of the seventeenth century, love's absence in itself acquires various manifestations, depending on the relationship between lovers and primarily on whether love is shared or solitary. If love is mutual, its absence has only one possible dimension, the absence of physical separation, of spatial distance. This physical separation of lovers encompasses the initial moment of parting, followed then by the duration of absence, which may be either short or prolonged.

If love is unrequited, however, if one individual loves alone, his solitary passion suffers an absence which has two dimensions, spiritual as well as spatial. In this relationship, continual physical separation from the beloved is a foregone conclusion, primarily because of the fundamental spiritual isolation particular to non-requital.

Donne often associates death with the parting or absence of lovers, while Quevedo expresses the relationship between death and the solitude of unrequited love in terms of a painful absence.[1] The contrasts between many of the poems of Donne and Quevedo that deal with absence in love exist, therefore, because Quevedo's sonnets are purely Petrarchan, while Donne's, although they clearly succeed the *amour courtois*–Petrarchan tradition, are not bound by that tradition and forge out in new directions, often antithetical to orthodox Petrarchism. Quevedo's association of love with absence and solitary pilgrimage is distinctly indebted to the *amour courtois*–Petrarchan tradition. The theme of absent wandering and nostalgic longing appears in Dante's *Commedia* and his *Vita Nuova*, but in Petrarch's *Canzoniere* the image of the wandering lover, tortured by his beloved's disdain, acquires the intensity of love's pilgrim exiled to unknown seas and lands.[2]

In the Baroque, we find that the inherited theme of absence acquires a profoundly sombre tone as the traditional associations of absence with death become more and more exaggerated and imbalanced. Traditional metaphors acquire an identity all their own and become increasingly independent. The Baroque poets' insistence, and extreme emphasis, on the relationship between absence-in-love and death-in-life reflects the age's preoccupation with finality. As major representatives of their time, Donne and Quevedo articulate the basic Baroque obsession with death's invasion of all aspects of life.

In the Baroque, we also find that the metaphorical association of death with parting, physical separation, and nonrequital in love reflects an acute sense of loss, an awareness and consequent fear of its unavoidable absoluteness. Thus, loss in one realm of human activity mirrors, or presages, the ultimate and total loss that awaits all temporal creatures. Because of this consciousness of correspondences and the prevailing awareness of the profound kinship shared by all factors of life, Baroque poetry of absence in love often emphasizes the logical corollary of absence in life. For the true lover, love is the most meaningful human experience, and hence most closely parallels life's value. Following the parallel logically, the absence of love or the absence of the beloved correspondingly leads to the absence of life itself. As intimate corollaries, love and life thus parallel the antithetical corollaries of the absence of love and death.

The theme of absence, which in varied ways characterizes Quevedo's *Poema a Lisi* and Donne's *Songs and Sonnets*, strengthens the fundamental union between love and death. In "The Legacie," for instance, Donne asserts metaphorically that separation from the beloved constitutes the lover's death:

When I dyed last, and Deare, I dye
  As often as from thee I goe,
  Though it be an houre agoe,
And lovers houres be full eternity,
I can remember yet, that I
  Something did say, and something did bestow;
Though I be dead, which sent mee, I should be
Mine owne executor and Legacie.

After dramatically envisioning a hypothetical situation, which is as usual his own death, Donne equates this death with parting from his beloved and imagines that he has returned from this death to be his own executor and legacy as well. This self-dramatization, which characterizes other poems by Donne and many of Quevedo's sonnets, enables both poets to express the essence of reality more forcefully and, paradoxically, with greater involvement. Through the recreation of the self as character and the consequent enactment of the dramatic role required within the contexts of the poem, they express the subjective and objective perspectives of existence simultaneously. As Warnke has noted, drama is of the essence for the Metaphysical poet: "Donne's poetry like that of Marvell, of Théophile, or Quevedo, is theatrical in that the creation of the self as character and the purposeful playing out of the role on the stage of the poem are felt not as an avoidance of reality but as a unique experience of reality."[3]

This dramatic expression of one's own inner feelings and experiences is simply one further step in the development of traditional Augustinian-Petrarchan self-consciousness. It is paradoxically the externalization of confessional introspection, and thereby always remains firmly rooted in the poet's interior world. As they dramatically externalize their inner lives, Donne and Quevedo thereby disclose their deepest obsessions and emotions. Death is foremost among the concerns revealed.

The dramatic situation in "The Legacie" is thus based on a unique re-creation of reality in which Donne presents himself as a dead man and as that dead man's executor and legacy. In contrast to "The Paradox," in which he affirms, "Wee dye but once, and who lov'd last did die," he declares that he has died *many times* because of love. Petrarch before him employed hyperbolic references to his own repeated metaphorical deaths in his constant endurance of love's nonrequital, of love's spiritual distance and absence. Two such examples are the final tercets of *Rime* No. 164 and *Rime* No. 172:

> E perché 'l mio martír non giunga a riva
> Mille volte il dí moro e mille nasco;
> Tanto de la salute mia son lunge.

> Non, perché mille volte il dí m'ancida,
> Fia ch'io non l'ami, e ch'i' non speri in lei;
> Che s'ella mi spaventa, Amor m'affida.

In "The Legacie," specific sexual *union* does not cause death, as in "The Paradox;" nor does the cruelty of non-requital, as in Petrarch's sonnets, cause the speaker's death. Rather, his death is synonymous with the painful act of physical *separation* from the beloved. This departure, a metaphorical form of death, is nevertheless a corporal and emotional rehearsal for that inevitable and irreversible corporal separation which characterizes death.

In Quevedo's sonnets, separation from the beloved does not assume the form of repeated physical partings. He often describes instead the anguish and torment of his passion's non-requital as an endless spiritual separation from the beloved, unrelieved isolation, and living death. In Poem 473, for instance, Quevedo is a forlorn stranger who suffers on foreign shores, ultimately finding death a merciful release from his solitary pilgrimage and unrequited love's torments. While the theme of absence in the Lisi sonnets arises from a general pervasive mood brought on by love's non-requital, the theme of absence in the *Songs and Sonnets* springs from specific situations between lover and beloved.

In "The Legacie," Donne declares that a single hour for the lover is as expansive as eternity itself and that parting from the beloved means virtual death. Donne here expresses the validity, as well as the antithesis, of the *amour courtois* notion of *pleroma*: "intensity as against mere length, quality as against mere quantity—which seems to reflect the Boethian notion of eternity—holding endless life in one moment, *tota simul et perfecta possessio*."[4] Love's presence transcends mortality, mutability, and all the restrictions of time and space. Conversely, love's absence constitutes a submission to human limitations and renders the lover vulnerable to life's absolute and final restriction, death. Through love, therefore, man himself may transcend all his mortal limitations, or conversely become extremely vulnerable, as love's power accentuates his fragility and temporality. The key to such extremes lies in the assertion that "Lovers houres be full eternity." Like time, all of love's emotions, sorrow as well as joy, are accordingly magnified by love's passion.

Curiously, neither the timelessness, transcendence, nor completeness of mutual love are the themes of "The Legacie." Through the conceit of death, Donne, in a cynical pose, dramatizes instead the beloved's fickleness. In the second stanza, he presents paradoxes, typical of his complexity and subtlety of thought:

> I heard mee say, Tell her anon,
>   That my selfe, that's you, not I,
>   Did kill me,' and when I felt mee dye,
> I bid mee send my heart, when I was gone;
> But I alas could there finde none,
>   When I had ripp'd me,' and search'd where hearts
>   should lye;
> It kill'd mee'againe that I who still was true,
> In life, in my last Will should cozen you.

Donne's capacity for witty argument is at its best in this self-dramatization. As in "The Relique," he dramatizes an encounter between the future and the dead lover. The irony is double-edged here, however, for not only is Donne the projected dead lover; he is also the projected live executor. The self-reference is doubly reciprocal and depends on the juxtaposition of death and life, united paradoxically in the person of the lover. The "I" is a multi-faceted individual who, as lover, wills his heart; and as executor and legacy, rips himself open in search of this heart; and then metaphorically dies once more of shame. Donne often employs the metaphorical paradox of dying twice to further the wit of his poems, and in this poem, of course, the wit lies in the contrast between the lover's sincerity, which provokes his second death, and the beloved's fickleness in love.

In the final stanza, he continues this burlesque hyperbole of lovers' customary metaphorical exchange of hearts. While seeking his own heart after death as a legacy for his beloved, he finds instead her mercurial heart:

> Yet I found something like a heart,
>   But colours it, and corners had,
>   It was not good, it was not bad,
> It was intire to none, and few had part.
> As good as could be made by art
>   It seem'd, and therefore for our losses sad,
> I thought to send that heart in stead of mine,
> But oh, no man could hold it, for twas thine.

Love, which in the first stanza was potentially transcendent and immutable, is ultimately as inconstant as all other aspects of temporal and spatial reality. Donne's ironic humor regarding the lady's faithlessness and ultimately regarding love's mutability and terrene uncertainty is central to the unity of the poem. The seriousness of the problem is countered by this humorous perspective. Yet the humor, for all its incisiveness, does not, and indeed could never, deny the fundamental uncertainties of human existence on which it is paradoxically based. Donne has typically chosen to come to terms with mutability through wit and humor instead of through the more obvious route of despair inherent in *Poema a Lisi*.

"The Computation," like "The Legacie," begins with the notion of lovers' parting. The theme of absence is again united with the themes of love, death, and time. In the final stanza Donne will assert ultimately that absence from his beloved means his death, but in the first stanza he only emphasizes the exaggerated expansion of time caused by his absence from the beloved. Following the logic of the *pleroma* hyperbole in "The Legacie" that "Lovers houres be full eternity," Donne expresses the sorrow of lovers' separation in terms of seemingly endless temporality:

> For the first twenty yeares, since yesterday,
> I scarce beleev'd, thou could'st be gone away,
> For forty more, I fed on favours past,

> And forty'on hopes, that thou would'st, they
>   might last.

Hyperboles abound in his expression of the effect the beloved's absence has had on him. His lover's emotions have highly elasticized an absence that is actually short in real elapsed time. Petrarchan antecedents are again pertinent. Like Donne and Quevedo after him, Petrarch was aware of the subtle distinction between real time and psychological time, between time perceived from the perspective of human temporality and time perceived from the perspective of eternity. He asserted this relativity in *Rime* No. 362, for instance, in which he imagined his presence in heaven before Laura:

> *Menami al suo Signor: allor m'inchino,*
> *Pregando umilemente che consenta*
> *Ch'i' stia a veder e l'uno e l'altro vólto.*
>
> *Responde:—Egli è ben fermo il tuo destíno;*
> *E per tardar ancor vent'anni o trenta,*
> *Parrá a te troppo, e non fia però molto.—*

Quevedo's constant hyperbolic expressions of his lonely sorrow parallel Donne's exaggerations of their intensity and echo Petrarch's sensitivity to time's power over the mind. His Poem 474, entitled "Solicitud de su pensamiento enamorado y ausente," presents the themes of absence and death through images more haunting, desolate, and mournful than Donne's hyperbolic computation of years:

> *¿Qué buscas, porfiado pensamiento,*
> *ministro sin piedad de mi locura,*
> *invisible martirio, sombra obscura,*
> *fatal persecución del sufrimiento?*

Like Donne in "The Computation," Quevedo dramatizes the sorrow he endures because of his absence from the beloved, as his thought characterizes and intensifies his agony. He refers to his *porfiado pensamiento*, his 'contentious thought,' which is many things at once: a dark shadow, the invisible cause of his martyrdom, a merciless minister of madness, and the fatal instrument of his anguish.

Quevedo never reveals his specific thought, allowing instead its singular intensity to dramatize his agonized absence from the beloved. Significantly, one of Petrarch's central concerns was his thought, which, with his memory, constituted the primary force behind the creation of his poetry and his love for Laura. Thought, imagination, memory—primarily intellectual qualities—are ironically the sustaining forces in the emotion of love. Throughout the *Canzoniere* as throughout *Poema a Lisi*, the speaker's thought persecutes him, alienates him from the world, and encompasses him with his inescapable solitude. We see this, for example, in the first quatrain of *Rime* No. 169:

> Pien d'un vago penser, che me desvia
> Da tutti gli altri, e fammi al mondo ir solo,
> Ad or ad ora a me stesso m'involo
> Pur lei cercando che fuggir devria.

In "The Computation," Donne presents his specific thoughts as he dramatizes their intensity through the hyperboles of time. One day has passed, but in his mind it has been one hundred years. For "Twenty yeares," he tried to comprehend the reality of the beloved's absence. He spent "Forty more" years recalling the past and yet another "forty" pondering mutability and hoping that his beloved's past favors would not change in the future. The dangers of requital are once again obvious. The requital and joys of the past create anxiety in the mind of the lover in terms of the future, for his dependence on the beloved's will is absolute. The obvious expansion of time in this quatrain parallels a much more subtle compression of time already seen to be a dominant characteristic of Quevedo's thought. Whereas Quevedo often views human time from the perspective of eternity, Donne here views time from his own vantage point in the present as he recalls the past and looks forward to the future in terms of that past.

Donne thus counters his hyperbolic expansion of time through his own mental compression of time. While Donne expresses his thought through the simultaneous expansion and compression of time, Quevedo here expresses his ideas by merging religious concepts with those of suffering and pain. The terms *ministro, martirio,* and *persecución* evoke the impression of amorous martyrdom. Whereas Donne employed religious symbolism in "The Canonization" and "The Relique" to celebrate the transcendence of mutual love, Quevedo employs it here to reveal the horrors of unrequited love.

Whatever initial divergence in metaphor one may note in this sonnet and "The Computation," metaphoric death, despite its antithetical causes, ultimately defines the absence both lovers endure. Donne concludes:

> *Teares drown'd one hundred, and sighes blew out two,*
> *A thousand, I did neither thinke, nor doe,*
> *Or not divide, all being one thought of you;*
> *Or in a thousand more, forgot that too.*
> *Yet call not this long life; But thinke that I*
> *Am, by being dead, Immortall; Can ghosts die?*

His exaggerations grow bolder as he describes his anguish in terms of his perception of the time elapsed since "yesterday." The final two lines succinctly and effortlessly combine a number of themes, exactly paralleling the final tercet of Quevedo's sonnet. The life-death duality appears in the metaphor of living death. Foreshadowing "The Paradox" and Quevedo's ingenious attempt to thwart death in Poem 489, "The Computation" announces the lover's metaphorical death, as he asserts that the endless torture of the beloved's absence has killed him. Paradoxically, the thousands of "yeares" since she has "gone away" do not constitute a lengthy life; for because of his absence from the beloved, and the consequent exaggeration of his mental years, he is no longer even alive. Here Donne simultaneously employs the notion of *pleroma*, of love's power to intensify time, with the traditional concept of love's power to kill the lover. Through love his time emotionally expands, while paradoxically, because of this same love, he is metaphorically transformed into a living dead man who consequently could not have experienced this long life.

The morbidity of this argument suggests many of Quevedo's sonnets dealing with the power time exercises over mortal man. This poem nevertheless ends with the ingenious assertion that the lover, by being "dead" metaphorically, is also "Immortall" because ghosts cannot die. The logic is as clever as Quevedo's in Poem 474, in which he also argues against the possibilities of dying twice. Both poets, in fact, effect their arguments against death by taking seriously the illogical Petrarchan metaphor of a living death caused by pain in love, thereby expanding the possibilities for witty and shocking subtlety. They then explore the practical implications and relationships that result from this vivid actualization of traditional metaphors. Through this process, Donne and Quevedo are able to express many unusual possibilities within the traditional notions of the relationship between love and death. They thereby employ traditional metaphors and common expressions in untraditional ways by first taking them seriously and then exploring the consequent paradoxical ramifications.

"The Computation" provides a striking parallel with Quevedo's Poem 474 through Donne's metaphoric transformation of the lover into a ghost. In the second stanza, Quevedo dramatically continues to address his own mind in the same tone of self-reference Donne employed in "The Legacie":

> Si del largo camino estás sediento,
> mi vista bebe, su corriente apura;
> si te promete albricias la hermosura
> de Lisi, por mi fin, vuelve contento.

Offering his sight and his life to his murderous thought, he declares that if, because of Lisi's beauty, his thought seeks its reward through his death, then it may return (to Lisi) satisfied. In "The Computation" thought and emotion are so powerful that they can expand time and transform the lover into a ghost; so too can the strength of Quevedo's thought and emotion exhaust his strength and will.

He then addresses Lisi herself, revealing that his thought triumphs in his death:

> Yo muero, Lisi, preso y desterrado;
> pero si fue mi muerte la partida,
> de puro muerto estoy de mí olvidado.

> *Aquí para morir me falta vida,*
> *allá para vivir sobró cuidado:*
> *fantasma soy en penas detenida.*

As he juxtaposes life and death in his evocation of the solitary wanderings of love's lost pilgrim, Quevedo views life as a shadowy exile that ends all too soon in the metaphorical death of absence.

Quevedo expresses the isolation he suffers in terms of imprisonment and banishment. In the first tercet, he juxtaposes the metaphor of death caused by his persecuting thoughts with his assertion that "fue mi muerte la partida." His metaphorical death occurred when he left Lisi, but now, finding himself an exile and utterly alone, his further destruction and ultimate desertion by his cruel thoughts have deprived him even of his memory.

Throughout Quevedo's sonnets, memory plays a significant role in his insistence on love's immortality. Memory, perhaps the strongest weapon against time's destructiveness, assures the continuity of past, present, and future. In this sonnet, however, Quevedo's thought and memory have abandoned him to a mental wilderness of oblivion. In his moribund condition, even he has forgotten himself. Since, unlike many of Donne's poems, there is no consideration that the memory of others may immortalize his solitary adoration, Quevedo's subjugation to death's omnipotence is total.

The final tercet provides a striking correlation with the last lines of "The Computation." The concepts of life-in-death and death-in-life are central to the resolution of both poems, as both Donne and Quevedo are caught between the world of the living and the realm of the dead. The sorrows of unrequited love and his absence from Lisi have made Quevedo a *fantasma*, just as the intensity with which Donne suffers the separation from his lady transforms him into a ghost.

Quevedo spatially and temporally juxtaposes his present situation in an alien land to his plight prior to his separation from Lisi. The sorrows of unrequited love had previously prevented him from living *allá*, and now he finds that the sorrow of separation has stripped him of life *aquí*, thereby paradoxically denying him the release of death. Like Donne, he is an intangible shadow, neither alive nor dead, suspended in a twilight ambiguity. As a ghost, Donne is an immortal being to whom earthly time and corporality mean nothing. Quevedo also becomes a disembodied spirit, not too different from the *sombra obscura* that plagued him in the first quartet. Love has ultimately obliterated time and space.

In "A Valediction: forbidding Mourning," Donne expresses the sorrows of parting lovers in terms of death. Like death, space and the body-soul duality characterize the relationship between absence and love. Donne invokes his beloved to help him insure that their parting be as calm as possible. In so doing, he dramatically employs the metaphor of death:

> As virtuous men passe mildly'away,
>   And whisper to their soules, to goe,
> Whilst some of their sad friends doe say,
>   The breath goes now, and some say, no:

> So let us melt, and make no noise,
>   No teare-floods, nor sigh-tempests move,
> 'Twere prophanation of our joyes
>   To tell the layetie our love.

In his evocation of the lovers' separation, Donne finds the analogy of death's final moment most compelling. In this valediction, as in "The Autumnall," he portrays death as peaceful, inevitable, and mild. The death of "virtuous men" is as indiscernible and silent as Quevedo's secret hours and mute years that silently slide away from the living. The conceit of the disassociation of the body from the soul is integral to Donne's argument, for each parting lover is the soul of the other. Each remaining lover must, like virtuous men who pass mildly away, whisper to his or her soul, the loved one, to go. Parting, which overwhelmed Quevedo in his previous sonnet and which Donne found so formidable in "The Computation," acquires a different complexion here. Paradoxically, Donne employs the conceit of death expressly to avoid the mortal results of separation seen in the previous poems.

The serenity pervading this valediction reflects the spiritual essence of its mutual love. In contrast to the uncertainty and frenzy of the separation in "The Computation," in which the uneasy Donne magnified inherited Petrarchan tears and sighs ("Teares drown'd one hundred, and sighes blew out two,"), he here remonstrates against such shows of distress, counselling the beloved that they should quietly and indiscernibly "melt" apart and "No teare-floods, nor sigh-tempests move." Like Quevedo, who expressed the lonely anguish of his suffering in religious terms (*ministro, martirio, persecución*), Donne expresses the sacred quality of the lovers' mutual devotion through words such as "prophanation" and "layetie." As in the *amour courtois* tradition, the complete joy of their mutual love depends on secrecy. This is an interesting note in Donne's valedictions which contrasts with the social orientation of his poems discussed in the previous chapter. His philosophy of love-in-life thus often follows the *amour courtois* belief in love's secrecy, while in his philosophy of love-in-death the awareness of the outside world is necessary.

The resigned, tranquil tone of Donne's poem recalls the serenity of "Amor constante más allá de la muerte," in which Quevedo recognized his own inherent vulnerability to the forces that would disassociate his soul from his body. Like Donne in this valediction, Quevedo rose above the rigors of death and separation through his love's invincibility. Donne here also loses "el respeto a ley severa" and affirms the superiority of spiritual love over the lovers' physical separation in life or through death.

In his analysis of absence's effect on their love, Donne pursues his concern with the interrelationship between the soul and the body. After comparing movement in the earth with the movement of the spheres, he then associates such a contrast with the differences between the absence of lovers' bodies and the absence of souls:

> *Moving of th'earth brings harmes and feares,*
> *Men reckon what it did and meant,*
> *But trepidation of the spheares,*
> *Though greater farre, is innocent.*

> Dull sublunary lovers love
> (Whose soule is sense) cannot admit
> Absence, because it doth remove
> Those things which elemented it.

> But we by'a love, so much refin'd,
> That our selves know not what it is,
> Inter-assured of the mind,
> Carelesse, eyes, lips, and hands to misse.

Just as the earth's movement causes "harmes and feares," so too does the body's absence destroy the love of those "dull sublunary lovers, whose soule is sense." The trepidation of the spiritual spheres, however, is much more innocent than that of the material earth. Similarly, those whose love is "so much refin'd" and "Inter-assured of the mind," may part without fear or loss. The proximity of their bodies is not essential for their continued devotion, for their love is ethereal, free from the bonds of the tangible world. It is not of the earth's materiality, but of the spheres' spirituality.

Donne expresses the serenity of love's mutuality through the concept of the lover's own consciousness just as Quevedo employs consciousness in his expression of love's unrequited sorrow in the previous sonnet. Whereas Donne is calmly "Inter-assured of the mind," Quevedo is doomed as much by his own perfidious thought, his *ministro sin piedad*, his *fatal persecución del sufrimiento*. The significance of the lover's mental awareness in love indeed mirrors the fundamental cerebral orientation of conceptistic verse. Terms such as Donne's "thinking heart" in "The Blossome" thematically reinforce Donne's and Quevedo's shared introspective and rational approach to an essentially emotional subject.

Just as Quevedo affirms in Poem 472, "Alma a quien todo un dios prisión ha sido . . . / su cuerpo dejará, no su cuidado," so Donne affirms the soul's immortality and its eternal devotion to the beloved. In "Amor constante más allá de la muerte," Quevedo's best known declaration of his passion's immortality and love's invincibility, he refers only to his own devotion to Lisi. In Donne's valediction, however, perhaps his best known affirmation of love's powers, he presents love's mutuality through the union of lovers' souls:

> *Our two soules therefore, which are one,*
> *Though I must goe, endure not yet*
> *A breach, but an expansion,*
> *Like gold to ayery thinnesse beate.*

He reinforces his earlier admonition, "So let us melt, and make no noise," with the metallurgical image of beaten gold which, like their united souls, does not separate as it expands. Like the spheres, their united souls are impervious to the limitations of the material world. Just as the soul is not bound by the limitations of the spatiality of the lovers' bodies, so too does the spiritual quality of their love overcome the spatial limitation of distances that divides those bodies.

In the final stanzas, Donne transcends space by dynamically moving through it as he expresses the spiritual union of the lovers through the compass conceit. He paradoxically employs an object of the material world to symbolize immateriality, just as he argued against the pain of absence in the first stanzas through the metaphor of the ultimate absence of death:

> *If they be two, they are two so*
> *As stiffe twin compasses are two,*
> *Thy soule the fixt foot, makes no show*
> *To move, but doth, if the'other doe.*
>
> *And though it in the center sit,*
> *Yet when the other far doth rome,*
> *It leanes, and hearkens after it,*
> *And growes erect, as it comes home.*
>
> *Such wilt thou be to mee, who must*
> *Like th'other foot, obliquely runne;*
> *Thy firmnes makes my circle just,*
> *And makes me end, where I begunne.*

Through the perfection of the unbroken circle, Donne argues for the unseverable unity of the lovers, who may be separated by space in material terms, but who transcend that space in spiritual terms.

In contrast to the despairing mood of absence and solitude

permeating the majority of Quevedo's Lisi sonnets that express the separation of the lover from the beloved, "A Valediction: forbidding Mourning" is a triumphant declaration of mutual love's conquest of the traditional spatial and temporal separation of lovers.

Whereas Donne's shared love triumphantly transcends all human limitations, love's denial often submerges Quevedo into a world of shadows, solitude, and imponderable grief. We see the absoluteness of this lover's solitude in Poem 359, entitled simply "Soneto amoroso," which, although it is not a Lisi sonnet, deals significantly with the themes of absence, love, and death. As a free imitation of Petrarch's *Rime* No. 226,[5] this sonnet not only demonstrates Quevedo's indebtedness to Petrarch, but also clearly reveals the nature of his metaphysical originality:

> *Más solitario pájaro ¿en cuál techo*
> *se vio jamás, ni fiera en monte o prado?*
> *Desierto estoy de mí, que me ha dejado*
> *mi alma propia en lágrimas deshecho.*

Literally quoting Petrarch in the first two lines, Quevedo views himself as the loneliest of all living beings, lonelier than the solitary bird of the forest or the beast of the mountains. Then replacing Petrarch's final lines ("Ch'i' non veggio 'l bel viso, e non conosco / Altro sol, né quest'occhi hann'altro obietto."), he asserts that he is deserted by his own being, his soul having left him undone by the tears of his sadness. There is none of the self-assuredness with which Donne faces his impending absence from the beloved in "A Valediction: forbidding Mourning."

The fullness of Donne's completed circle contrasts sharply with the utter nothingness, the diminution of the self to the point of extinction, in Quevedo's sonnet. The marvelous spiritual fulfillment which Donne attains in his valediction finds its antithesis in this disintegration of being. Whereas Donne reassures his beloved that their mutual love is, like the soul, beyond the confines of space, Quevedo finds himself abandoned by his own self, his soul undone by the tears he has shed for his unresponsive and distant beloved. In the next quatrain, a complete quotation from Petrarch's sonnet, he foresees the future in terms of more tears, a sharp contrast with Donne's envisioned future reunion:

> Lloraré siempre mi mayor provecho;
> penas serán y hiel cualquier bocado;
> la noche afán, y la quietud cuidado,
> y duro campo de batalla el lecho.

He echoes here Petrarch's interplay of contrasts and paradoxes. That which normally affords the greatest pleasure and joy in life will give him only pain and despair. His solitude invades all potentialities for happiness, transforming them into their opposites. He will lament all happiness and all delights will become sorrows. Serenity will be transformed into apprehension and each night's rest will become an endless struggle.

The contrasts between pleasure and pain emphasize his inner torment in this separation from the beloved:

> El sueño, que es imagen de la muerte,
> en mí a la muerte vence en aspereza,
> pues que me estorba el sumo bien de verte.

Like Petrarch, Quevedo lends an uncommon interpretation to the familiar comparison of sleep and death, but unlike Petrarch, he attributes greater asperity to sleep than to death. For while he sleeps, he forfeits the potential presence of his beloved. Sleep, death's brother, is more insidious than death, for he does not feel its existential restrictions as deeply as he does those of death. They are nevertheless just as powerful and much more paradoxical, for sleep determinedly denies the joys of life and love that may be had were one awake. By its very nature, death eternally terminates this potential for life and love, whereas sleep periodically punctuates it, stealthily and silently taking from men a third of their lives. It is this temporary nature of sleep's denial of life that ameliorates the profound psychological impact of death's permanence.

Quevedo replaces Petrarch's final tercet ("Solo al mondo paese almo, felice, / Verdi rive fiorite, ombrose piagge / Voi possedete, et io piango il mio bene.") devoted to pastoral solitude, praising instead the charms of the beloved:

Que es tanto tu donaire y tu belleza,
que, pues Naturaleza pudo hacerte,
milagro puede hacer Naturaleza.

Lisi is a miracle of nature. Her beauty and charm, which dominate this final tercet, explain the despair that overflows in the quatrains, for the greater the loss, the more intense the consequent suffering and anguish. The pain Quevedo endures in his separation from the beloved contrasts with Donne's argument against such despair in "A Valediction: forbidding Mourning." In the *Songs and Sonnets*, however, Donne also deals with the sorrow of separation and its deathly effects, even on those who share a mutual love.

In "The Expiration," for instance, Donne once again poses as the requited lover who must depart, thrusting the reader into the midst of his dramatic leavetaking. He lovingly chides his clinging beloved as he develops his reasoned analysis of an obviously passionate situation:

> *So, so breake off this last lamenting kisse,*
> *Which sucks two soules, and vapors both away,*
> *Turne thou ghost that way, and let mee turne this,*
> *And let our selves benight our happiest day,*
> *We ask'd none leave to love; nor will we owe*
> *Any, so cheape a death, as saying, Goe;*

Like the self-sufficient love of the courtly lover who deliberately hid his emotion from all outsiders, Donne's requited love is self-contained, owing its existence to no one. Parting and all activities associated with parting cause death. The lovers' "last lamenting kisse" thus disassociates their souls from their bodies and disperses them as irrevocably as the word "Goe" kills both lover and beloved. Donne refers to the beloved as a "ghost," reinforcing the conceit that their kiss did indeed transform her into a disembodied spirit. The separation of lovers who share a mutual love thereby ironically results in death because of a physical expression of that mutuality. Because of his Petrarchan pose, Quevedo never has the fortune of expressing his separation in such intimate terms. Just as Quevedo in his last sonnet declared that all his joys were transformed into agony because he could not see the beloved, so Donne asserts that the separation of lovers will "benight" their "happiest day." Both poets thus contrast love's presence and absence in terms of life and death as they juxtapose the extremes of bright joy and dark sorrow.

The relationship between death and separation becomes more complex in the second stanza as Donne explores the intricacies involved in the parting of lovers:

> Goe; and if that word have not quite kill'd thee,
>   Ease mee with death, by bidding mee goe too.
> Oh, if it have, let my word worke on mee,
>   And a just office on a murderer doe.
> Except it bee too late, to kill me so,
> Being double dead, going, and bidding, goe.

The power of the solitary word is absolute, as one single syllable, "Goe," which begins and ends this stanza, can kill not only the individual toward whom it is directed but the person who utters it as well. Donne presents two equally mortal situations involving the word "Goe," for, because of this word and the reality it signifies, both lovers will ultimately die, either in a mutual murder or a murder-suicide.

The poem ends with the paradox of dying twice, common to Donne's repertoire. In this case, the actual parting from the beloved and his command to her to "goe" have together destroyed all semblance of life in Donne, who recognizes that he is indeed doubly invulnerable to further death, already "Being double dead."

Death and absence are also the significant themes of "A Valediction: of my Name in the Window," in which Donne ponders the relationship of love and lovers to inconstancy and mutability as "Neere death" approaches. In the first three stanzas, using the symbol of his engraved name as his meditative springboard, he reflects on the lovers' firmness, constancy, and union. In the fourth stanza, he presents the fundamental relationship between love and death as he addresses the beloved:

> Or if too hard and deepe
> This learning be, for a scratch'd name to teach,

> *It, as a given deaths head keepe,*
> *Lovers mortalitie to preach,*
> *Or thinke this ragged bony name to bee*
> *My ruinous Anatomie.*

His engraved name may teach several antithetical lessons. In the third stanza, Donne asserts that it may, in its imperviousness to "showers and tempests," proclaim his constancy at "all times." In the fourth stanza, he then declares that if his "scratch'd name" be not capable of proclaiming his love's constancy, it should be preserved at least "as a given deaths head" that would "preach" his own "lovers mortalitie." As in the previous valediction, he attributes primary significance to the unique power of the single, isolated word. The stature of the solitary syllable in these two valedictions derives from its singular power to affect, indeed to effect, the central actions of both poems.

Donne concludes that, if his scratched name is unfit to proclaim constancy and immutability, it may preach the truths of mutability and death. He expands this concept as he vividly alludes to a subject dear to him, the destiny of the body after death. In the context of "mortalitie," "Anatomie," and "deaths head," adjectives such as "ragged," "bony," and "ruinous" strengthen the image of the body's decomposition at death.

In his evocation of physical death, Donne's vocabulary reveals an attitude more macabre and less idealistic than Quevedo's "enamoured dust." In significant contrast to Quevedo's "Amor constante más allá de la muerte," Donne dwells on "Lovers mortalitie," offering little hope for love beyond the grave. As he ultimately declares, his engraved name probably will not demonstrate the lovers' immortality, but rather their inescapable mortality.

In the fifth stanza, Donne expresses the love-death antithesis in terms of the body and the soul:

> *Then, as all my soules bee,*
> *Emparadis'd in you, (in whom alone*
> *I understand, and grow and see,)*
> *The rafters of my body, bone*

> *Being still with you, the Muscle, Sinew,'and Veine,*
> *Which tile this house, will come againe.*

As in "The Expiration," the soul leaves the body when the lovers part. The lover's soul, as well as his physical frame, his "ragged bony name," will remain with the beloved at his parting. As in many of his sermons and *Holy Sonnets*, Donne is obsessed with the body's literal resurrection and reunion with the soul, but he expresses this obsession here in terms of love and the beloved.

In the sixth stanza, he enjoins the beloved: "Till my returne, repaire / And recompact my scatter'd body so." Quevedo also employs images of the dissolution of his body at death, but paradoxically they are images of life. Just as Quevedo insists on continued sentience in the grave in "Amor constante más allá de la muerte," so too does Donne in this valediction plead with the beloved to bestow immortality on him after his deathlike departure. Unlike Quevedo, and because of his love's mutuality, his immortality is totally dependent on the whims and caprices of the beloved.

Love and death define the seventh stanza, as Donne implores the beloved to insure his immortality:

> *So since this name was cut*
> *When love and griefe their exaltation had,*
> *No doore 'gainst this names influence shut;*
> *As much more loving, as more sad,*
> *'Twill make thee; and thou shouldst, till I returne,*
> *Since I die daily, daily mourne.*

The simultaneous "exaltation" of "love and grief" encompasses the grief of parting, made acute by their love, as the strength of their love is made greater by their grief. The two emotions interact, mutually reinforcing and enhancing one another. Words such as "griefe," "mourne," and "die" metaphorically intensify the thematic correlation between death and love's absence.

Recognizing the possibility of his beloved's inconstancy during his absence, Donne implores her to be faithful. The "Lovers mortalitie," which his engraved name must preach, may refer to his own "daily" death while he is separated from the beloved, or her destructive inconstancy, or both. Whatever the interpretation, he is most assuredly mortal and vulnerable to mutability and death.

Donne reverses the death-in-life paradox in the following stanzas as he evokes the concept of life-in-death through the vitality of his "bony name." We have already seen this reversal in both poets' exaltation of the body in death. Donne echoes Quevedo's earlier image of "enamoured dust" in his assertion that his "bony name," his "ruinous Anatomie," retains life and energy. In the eighth and ninth stanzas, he warns the beloved that his "trembling name," which she must recognize as "alive," will "step in" and "hide" the name of any future suitor, thereby countering her attempts to obliterate his memory. The potential for love's mutability and Donne's consequent interest in its permanence exemplify his fundamental obsession with mutability and permanence in life itself. The beloved's fickleness is frightening for the same reasons that mutability and death are frightening. They equally manifest the impermanence of life and its most precious values.

Donne's reference to the etching as "my trembling name" reveals either his actual fragility, his fear of death, or both. In his petition that the beloved imagine "this name alive," he seeks to overcome death and the beloved's fickleness, if only in her mind. His dependence on the beloved again renders him more vulnerable to the mortality of life and love than Quevedo, who can victoriously claim in Poem 475, "iré al sepulcro amando, / y siempre en el sepulcro estaré ardiendo." In contrast, Donne is obsessed with the beloved's possible unfaithfulness after his departure, his demise.

Donne can imagine the worst, of course: that the beloved someday will obliterate the name he hopes will be his incarnation during his absence. He reasons:

> And if this treason goe
> To'an overt act, and that thou write againe;
> In superscribing, this name flow
> Into thy fancy, from the pane,
> So, in forgetting thou remembrest right,
> And unaware to mee shalt write.

This stanza recalls memory's crucial role in the conquest of oblivion throughout Quevedo's poetry. This has a significant precedent in the *Canzoniere*, in which Petrarch's search for immortality, be it through his art or his love, depended primarily on the memory of those yet unborn. The final tercet of *Rime* No. 46, for example, resembles this valediction in its exposition of the interrelationship between death, oblivion, and the search for permanence among things fragile and insubstantial:

> *Questi fuôr fabbricati sopra l'acque*
> *D'abisso, e tinti ne l'eterno oblio;*
> *Onde 'l principio de mia morte nacque.*

Whereas Quevedo usually invokes his own memory, Donne here completely depends on his beloved's memory for immortality. If she should cease to "daily mourne" his absence and if she should someday wish to forget him he then finds his only consolation in the paradox that during her active destruction of his "bony name," the beloved will be forced to remember him.

In the final stanza, Donne abandons this paradoxical argument and attempt at self-consolation, as he recognizes the utter futility of any effort to defeat the powers of mutability through "glasse" and "lines." The extreme mutability of breakable glass and super-scribable lines only accentuates the hopelessness of such an endeavor. He clearly expresses the inextricable relationship between love, parting, death, and mutability:

> *But glasse, and lines must bee,*
> *No meanes our firme substantiall love to keepe;*
> *Neere death inflicts this lethargie,*
> *And this I murmure in my sleepe;*
> *Impute this idle talke, to that I goe,*
> *For dying men talke often so.*

The metaphor of death has so completely taken over this poem about parting that one wonders whether death functions as the metaphor of parting and absence or vice versa. Whether we inter-pret his perception of "Neere death" to be his imminent departure from the beloved or from this life, it is because of death that he asserts the immutability of their "firme substantiall love" through

the clearly mutable means of "glasse" and "lines." This final declaration nevertheless merely echoes his earlier recognition that such
a "learning" might be "too hard and deepe . . . for a scratch'd
name to teach."

The final portion of this stanza likewise repeats the earlier shift
in emphasis as Donne suggests that the beloved consider his name
to be "a given deaths head . . . Lovers mortalitie to preach." Referring to himself as a dying man, he clearly recognizes that he is as
vulnerable to mutability as the scratched bony name that symbolizes his mortal fragility.

The tone of this valediction contrasts significantly with the
optimistic tone of the sonnets and poems discussed in the previous
chapter. Donne does not conclude with love's glorification or with
an affirmation that, in one form or another, love may triumph over
death. After numerous stanzas of intricate reasoning in his typically
quasi-syllogistic approach, Donne undercuts the entire valediction
with the phrase "idle talke." In this final stanza, he belies his
earlier attempts to overcome mutability and wearily surrenders
himself and his argument to encroaching death's invincibility.

In Poem 368, entitled simply "Soneto amoroso," Quevedo also
attaches great importance to the beloved's memory during his absence. Although not from the *Poema a Lisi,* this sonnet reflects the
same mood of desperate isolation that characterizes the Lisi sonnets. The metaphors of death and absence are clearly present as
Quevedo juxtaposes the stark revelations of his agony to the bitter
realization that the beloved for whom he suffers does not even
remember him. His isolation unmitigated, he must endure oblivion
even before his death. As in "A Valediction: of my Name in the
Window," his sensitivity to the beloved's thoughts during his absence is extreme.

The sonnet begins with Quevedo's expression of his misery in
terms of death, suffering, and pain:

> ¿Qué imagen de la muerte rigurosa,
> qué sombra del infierno me maltrata?
> ¿Qué tirano cruel me sigue y mata
> con vengativa mano licenciosa?

He wonders what image of rigorous death, what shadow of hell it is that destroys him, what cruel tyrant pursues and kills him with such a vengeful hand. Composed of six interrogatives, this sonnet first presents the three impersonal questions, "¿Qué?", followed by the personal interrogative, "¿Quién?".

> ¿Qué fantasma, en la noche temerosa,
> el corazón del sueño me desata?
> ¿Quién te venga de mí, divina ingrata,
> más por mi mal que por tu bien hermosa?

Asking what dreadful phantom in the night denies his heart its rest, he invokes the beloved as a harsh, ungrateful goddess whose beauty causes him more despair than it causes her happiness. Who is it, he questions, that inflicts her vengeance on him?

> ¿Quién, cuando, con dudoso pie y incierto,
> piso la soledad de aquesta arena,
> me puebla de cuidados el desierto?

This stanza presents one of Quevedo's most memorable evocations of the solitude and uncertainty that pervade his prose and poetry. Who, he asks, fills my wasteland with anxiety while I tread the solitude of this sand with uncertain and doubtful feet? He juxtaposes the stark image of utter abandonment and desolation with the disturbing image that his desert is peopled by his cares. As in the previous sonnet, the image of the sterility of the lifeless desert accentuates his own spiritual estrangement.

In the final stanza, he introduces the beloved's memory:

> ¿Quién el antiguo son de mi cadena
> a mis orejas vuelve, si es tan cierto,
> que aun no te acuerdas tú de darme pena?

He asks his beloved who it is that has made the ancient sound of his chains return to his ears, since it is certain that she does not even remember him to wish for his suffering. The sound of his chains becomes more haunting in the desolate atmosphere through which they reverberate. His isolation and despair are complete. Although accompanied by his worries, he finds himself utterly alone, wandering in chains through a wasteland of apprehensions and uncertainty. After three stanzas of wondering who could inflict such pain on him in the name of the beloved, the question remains unanswered, as he bitterly realizes that she herself does not even remember him. His sole certainty, therefore, only reinforces his desolation.

Therein lies the harsh irony of his isolated agony. Alone and forgotten by the one person for whom he suffers continually, Quevedo bemoans his unmitigated solitude. In "A Valediction: of my Name in the Window," Donne seeks to avoid this same isolation and oblivion, fearing that his absence from the beloved will result one day in her forgetting to remember him. Whereas Donne suffers through his recognition of the potential loss of memory, Quevedo suffers because of his beloved's *actual* lack of memory. Donne suffers mentally as he imagines a future possibility, while Quevedo suffers in the present, both physically and mentally. Both are nevertheless equally aware of the unavoidable dangers inherent in love's uncertainty and mutability.

In Donne's "A Valediction: of Weeping," which, unlike Quevedo's sonnet and the previous valediction, reflects a mutual love free from the uncertainties and fears of inconstancy, death is nevertheless a significant concern. For love's mutuality itself may present just as much a threat in his departure and absence as the beloveds' indifference in Quevedo's sonnet and the previous valediction. Expanding the conventional tear conceit through witty argument and subtlety of thought, Donne argues that the beloved's tears may conspire to destroy him.

Donne's imagery in the mutuality of sorrow and the tears of parting parallels Quevedo's imagery in Poem 444, entitled "Padece ardiendo y llorando sin que le remedie la oposición de las contrarias calidades." Donne's hyperbolic expansion of Petrarchan tears, sighs, and tempests ultimately leads to death, thereby paralleling Quevedo's use of tears, fire, and floods in his evocation of death. Once again, Donne's valediction reflects the pain of separation for both lovers, while Quevedo's sonnet reveals the sorrows of unrequited passion in terms of absence and isolation.

Donne introduces the tear conceit in the first stanza:

> *Let me powre forth*
> *My teares before thy face, whil'st I stay here,*
> *For thy face coines them, and thy stampe they beare,*
> *And by this Mintage they are something worth,*
>   *For thus they bee*
>   *Pregnant of thee;*
> *Fruits of much griefe they are, emblemes of more,*
> *When a teare falls, that thou falls which it bore,*
> *So thou and I are nothing then, when on a divers shore.*

Donne expresses the relationship of parting to "teares," of love to "griefe," through his innovative imagery. He establishes his union with the beloved in terms of the tears their grief has begotten. When a tear "pregnant of" the beloved falls from his eyes, it suggests the lover's own separation from the beloved. Donne here expresses the notion of sorrowful parting through the multifaceted image of human fertility and the minting of coins. Paralleling the *playas extranjeras* of Poem 473, he extends Quevedo's solitary exile to the beloved as well. Like him, she is reduced to nothingness when on "a diverse shore." Juxtaposing this nothingness with its antithesis in the following stanza, Donne employs the spatial imagery so dear to him as he expresses grief and love through the metaphoric expansion of space:

> *On a round ball*
> *A workeman that hath copies by, can lay*
> *An Europe, Afrique, and an Asia,*
> *And quickly make that, which was nothing, All,*
>   *So doth each teare,*
>   *Which thee doth weare,*
> *A globe, yea world by that impression grow,*
> *Till thy teares mixt with mine doe overflow*
> *This world, by waters sent from thee, my heaven dissolved so.*

The infinitesimal suddenly assumes the measureless qualities of the infinite, as the simple "round ball" of a tear (which was earlier transformed into a minted coin) now "quickly" and effortlessly acquires the qualities that would transform it into the globe of the world. We saw earlier this hyperbolic expansion of the lovers' eyes into global hemispheres, and in "A Nocturnall" Donne will juxtapose spatial extremes in his duality of "quintessence" and "nothingnesse." As he metaphorically expands each tear into global proportions, thereby logically introducing the concept of a deluge, Donne reflects that the beloved's tears, when "mixt" with his own, may easily "overflow" the world itself and dissolve his "heaven" as well. The various interpretations of the word "world," be they metaphorical or literal, contribute to this paradoxical argument so typical of Donne.

As the lovers contemplate their imminent separation, their tears of grief acquire measureless dimensions. In Poem 444, Quevedo presents a similar hyperbole of tears and floods, although, unlike Donne's, his imagery does not venture into such diverse areas as geography and coins. Alone as always, he weeps unconsoled, blinded by his ceaseless tears. The first two stanzas introduce the Petrarchan antithetical elements of fire and water that characterize his passion:

> Los que ciego me ven de haber llorado
> y las lágrimas saben que he vertido,
> admiran de que, en fuentes dividido
> o en lluvias, ya no corra derramado.

> Pero mi corazón arde admirado
> (porque en tus llamas, Lisi, está encendido)
> de no verme en centellas repartido,
> y en humo negro y llamas desatado.

A sense of wonder pervades both quatrains. In the first, Quevedo declares that those who know him and are aware of the many tears he has shed are astonished that his tears have not overflown in a torrential flood. In the second, his heart itself marvels that he is not destroyed by the vigorous flames and black smoke of its own consuming passion.

> *En mí no vencen largos y altos ríos*
> *a incendios, que animosos me maltratan,*
> *ni el llanto se defiende de sus bríos.*
>
> *La agua y el fuego en mí de paces tratan;*
> *y amigos son, por ser contrarios míos;*
> *y los dos, por matarme, no se matan.*

The normally antithetical elements of water and fire are strangely compatible, as the rivers of tears he sheds neither conquer the fire that consumes him nor defend themselves from the vigorous flames. Fire and water ignore their natural antipathies as they join forces in their destruction of the lover.

Air and water, the forces of nature Donne evokes in his final stanza, are not similarly antithetical. The effect their possible union may have on Donne is thus more logical and less paradoxical than the effect of nature's combined forces on Quevedo. In addition, the wind and sea could conceivably conspire the destruction of the beloved in order to forbear her tears and sighs:

> *O more then Moone,*
> *Draw not up seas to drowne me in thy spheare,*
> *Weepe me not dead, in thine armes, but forbeare*
> *To teach the sea, what it may doe too soone;*
> *Let not thy winde*
> *Example finde,*
> *To doe more harme, then it purposeth;*
> *Since thou and I sigh one anothers breath,*
> *Who e'r sighes most, is cruellest, and hasts the others death.*

Representative of this final stanza is Donne's plea, "Weepe me not dead, in thine armes," one of his most beautiful and haunting manifestations of the interrelationship between mutual love, absence, and death. Through his poetic artistry, Donne transforms human sighs and tears into nature's wind and sea, which when violent become tempests powerful enough to kill. These united elements of nature could destroy the lovers, were they themselves to continue grieving with conspicuous tears and sighs. Donne logically arrives at this illogical conclusion by simply taking seriously the medieval notion of the integral relationship between the microcosm and the macrocosm, between human emotions and nature's elements. Central to this conceit, like most of Donne's conceits, is his genius for perceiving, and logically extending to its ultimate extreme, the fundamental unity underlying seemingly disparate aspects of reality. Donne has reversed the priorities of Petrarchan imagery, which often describes the lover's emotions in terms of nature's processes. Here the lover's emotions influence the forces of nature.

Donne and Quevedo have thus created poems which explore the relationship between two apparently different aspects of reality. As the potential alliance between human emotions and nature's elements becomes clarified, both lovers are clearly endangered. The tension between the metaphors applied to human emotions and the logical results of such an application is extreme. As James C. Smith has perceived, the nature of the elements of the metaphysical conceit "must be such that they can enter into a solid union and, at the same time, maintain their separate and warring identity."[6] Although the elements of nature may represent the lovers' emotions, they never lose their own identity, thereby posing a continual threat to each lover. Donne's sea and wind, like Quevedo's floodwaters and flames, remain viable elements of nature despite their metaphorical union with the human manifestations of each lover's personal grief and despair.

The notion of absence in love, so characteristic of the poetry of the Petrarchan tradition, is central to Donne's poetry as well as Quevedo's. The Petrarchan theme of solitary wandering and spiritual estrangement from the beloved acquires a metaphysical intensity in Quevedo's poetry, while Donne's requited love affords him the luxury of expressing absence and mutuality in love from a privileged perspective, usually focused on the actual moment of parting. Despite this mutuality, he nevertheless expresses his parting in terms of death.

Donne's optimistic poems of love's absence, such as "A Valediction: forbidding Mourning," contrast strikingly with Quevedo's pessimistic sonnets of despondent isolation. Donne nevertheless comes quite close to this same pessimistic articulation of absence in love, for the uncertainties of sublunar existence invade the territory of the requited lover as easily and with as much devastation as they envelop the world of love's unrequited wanderer.

Like the human and natural elements, tears, tempests, floods, and sighs, the dimensions of time and space are logical manifestations of spiritual and physical separation, and Donne and Quevedo employ them masterfully through expansion, contraction, logic, metaphor, paradox, and irony. The dominant metaphor in the articulation of love's absence, however, is death itself. Death correlates these various elements of sublunar existence, joining them with the central theme of love. It is the notion of death, then, that unites the aforementioned love poems of Donne and Quevedo. For both the Petrarchan and non-Petrarchan lover, absence from the beloved entails metaphorical death. The intensity of the absent lover's emotion virtually transforms the metaphor, for emotional death is equated with, and often acquires, the qualities of physical death. The consequent grief, despair, and mournful atmosphere further unite the thematic correlation between love, absence, and death.

The time-space and body-soul dualities, through their logical association with absence as well as death, often provide the essential metaphorical link between absence and death. Through self-dramatization, be it in a mood of cynicism, despair, or optimism, Donne and Quevedo enhanced their expression of the sorrows of the absent lover. The power of the lover's thought and imagination to associate death and absence with such diverse notions as the relationship between the past, present, and future, between sleep and death, between being and non-being, increases the metaphysical profundity of Donne's and Quevedo's amorous verse.

As poets of the Baroque, Donne and Quevedo lent to the *amour courtois* association of love's absence with death an interpretation that reveals their abiding obsession with death's existential reality. Indeed, the growing sense of finality that pervaded the Baroque consciousness found one of its most powerful avenues of expression in the poetry of love's absence.

Despite the contrasting love relationships articulated by each poet, the intellectual and esthetic affinities of Donne and Quevedo reflect their shared Baroque vision. The world view revealed in their poetry of absence is one frankly overwhelmed by the consciousness of mortality. Donne's and Quevedo's predilection for expressing amorous loss in terms of finality reflects their kinship as Baroque spokesmen and as Metaphysical poets.

In contrast to the Renaissance writers' comparatively serene approach to loss and absence, Baroque poets expressed its reality with a painful acuteness that allowed little or no room for hope or reconciliation. Whereas the Renaissance expression of absence, either temporary or eternal, was wistful, sad, and melancholic, the Baroque *Weltanschauung* bestowed on the same theme a tragic finality, a sombre tone of despair.

Thus we recall once again Garcilaso's approach in "Égloga III" to his beloved's eternal absence and find a pervading tranquility, a harmonious sense of resignation, indeed, of reconciliation with the death of the beloved. This peaceful reaction to loss in the Renaissance yields to the Baroque's frantic desperation and agonized rejection of loss and absence in love and in life. Because of the intimate relationship between life's most precious commodity, love, and life itself, the absence or loss of love or of the beloved is tantamount, much more for the Baroque mind than for the Renaissance mind, to the loss of life itself. We consequently find that despite contrasting amorous poses, Donne and Quevedo, as Petrarchan or anti-Petrarchan lovers, shared a much deeper affinity than these superficial poetic attitudes. Their fundamental concern with death, an obsession alien to the Renaissance consciousness of poets such as Garcilaso, Sidney, Herrera, and Spenser, overwhelms Baroque spokesmen with an elemental fear due primarily to their intense awareness of its power and its presence.

Renaissance optimism and obsession with life led its poets either to ignore death altogether or, like Garcilaso, to come to terms with it through their art. The volcanic passions of Baroque figures such as Donne and Quevedo, their intense emotion and their acute recognition of the primordial relationship between life and death, resulted in poetry of profound metaphysical implications.

The essential correspondence between life, love, loss, and

death thus was perceived by Baroque poets, perhaps with greater understanding than in any other literary period, and it was men like Donne and Quevedo who articulated the most profound expression to date of the centuries-old poetic association between absence, love, and death.

5

The Omnipotence of Death

Perhaps the most common single attitude articulated directly or indirectly throughout Baroque literature was the fervent certainty of death's omnipotence. As Renaissance confidence in life's supremacy and omnipotence weakened, there grew proportionately a disillusionment with life because of an increasing intellectual and emotional apprehension of finality. A belief in time's fullness and promise, so much a part of the Renaissance vision, yielded to the recognition of time's stealth and destruction. The conviction of life's inherent value and the value of the vital process became in the Baroque an obsession with the final stage of that vital process. Life as a beginning, a constant process of renewal, a bright promise, now becomes life, the accursed temporal condition whose one single goal is its own inevitable destruction. Time is no longer a fulfillment of life, but rather an incessant destroyer of life. It is no longer the purveyor of life; it is instead the accomplice of death.

Recipients of the poetic tradition that for centuries preceded them, Baroque writers often employed inherited imagery and *topoi* in their increasing preoccupation with morbid themes. Donne and Quevedo manipulated and transformed common poetic material, rendering it distinctly their own and typically Baroque. The situations, imagery, and metaphors employed by both poets are not necessarily original. What is unique is their particular attitude, their analytical approach, and the emotional fervor with which they expressed their reaction to death's omnipotence in human

affairs, particularly in their own lives and in the lives of their beloveds.

The smell of death was in the air and it pervaded all aspects of
life. As poets of the Baroque period, Donne and Quevedo shared a
world view quite sensitive to mortality. This acute sensibility led
them to perceive the essence of finality in all realms of existence.

A tragic awareness of death's omnipotence replaced the Renaissance love of life and confidence in humanity. Man was increasingly viewed as a creature of dust, born only to die, whose
every aspiration, insignificant or grandiose, merely magnified the
pitiful brevity of his existence and the futility of his efforts. As
poets of the Baroque, Donne and Quevedo shared a primordial
fear of death's imminence, its omnipresence, and its omnipotence.
As we shall see in this chapter, death, the primary object of their
thoughts, assumed a stifling preponderance reflecting its thematic
supremacy in their love poetry.

As seen in the previous chapter, love, becuase of its inestimable value, is often considered as worthy as life itself and consequently bestows its vitality on all aspects of existence, including
death. When love fails, however, when the beloved ignores or
disdains the lover, or when he loses her through her own physical
death, his love and consequently the lover himself may expire.

The traditional metaphorical expression of dying for love acquires central significance and intensity in the amorous poetry of
Donne and Quevedo. In Poem 473, for instance, entitled "Rendi-
miento de amante desterrado que se deja en poder de su tristeza,"
Quevedo, finding himself the banished victim of love's rigors, surrenders to death:

> *Éstas son y serán ya las postreras*
> *lágrimas que, con fuerza de voz viva,*
> *perderé en esta fuente fugitiva,*
> *que las lleva a la sed de tantas fieras.*

Expressing his anticipated death through vocal anguish and bitter
tears, he envisions the end of the tears that have fed the thirst of
his passion. The ironic dependence of passion on suffering recalls

the conceit in Poem 460 of the lover's death transformed into his love's daughter. The association of love's passion with death and suffering is central to both sonnets. Here the paradox and the wit result from simultaneously accepting the varied meanings of passion. *Pathos*, whose etymological meaning of suffering is now broadened to include any strong emotion, particularly love, literally defines love's paradoxical potential. Passionate love may constitute intense suffering, even unto death. Donne and Quevedo are certainly not the first poets to elaborate the dramatic implications of this etymological fact, for the metaphorical union of love and death is significant throughout literature and legend, Tristan and Iseult being perhaps the most obvious example. Donne's and Quevedo's poetry thus follows a long tradition of the intimate association of love's passion with death's passion.

The second quatrain intensifies the atmosphere of alienation and despair:

> *¡Dichoso yo que, en playas extranjeras,*
> *siendo alimento a pena tan esquiva,*
> *halle muerte piadosa, que derriba*
> *tanto vano edificio de quimeras!*

The distraught lover is the nourishment of an elusive sorrow. Being on foreign shores, he is fortunate enough to encounter pitying death, which destroys his delusions. Death, the great *desengaño*, the final and completely victorious disillusioner, discloses underlying reality through its destruction of the world's appearances.

Donne holds a similar view of death as the great unveiler as he counsels his soul in *The second Anniversarie* (ll. 85–86) to:

> *Think then, my soule, that death is but*
> *a Groome,*
> *Which brings a Taper to the outward*
> *roome.*

Quevedo also expresses this paradoxically positive view of death throughout his works, as he unites the antitheses, birth and death, envisioning death as the entrance to eternal life. In this sonnet, death not only destroys the illusions of this life but also releases the lover from his relentless suffering.

The first tercet expresses the now familiar antithesis of the body and the soul in terms of death and love:

> Espíritu desnudo, puro amante,
> sobre el sol arderé, y el cuerpo frío
> se acordará de Amor en polvo y tierra.

Paralleling Donne's multiple visions of the future in terms of his own death, Quevedo here foresees the separation of his body from his soul. Love's passion will nevertheless continue to rule both his body and spirit. As in his "Amor constante más allá de la muerte," Quevedo asserts a continued semblance of life by declaring that memory's power will remain with his cold, dead body.

The imagery employed in the final tercet bears a remarkable resemblance to two of Donne's three following poems, as Quevedo claims:

> Yo me seré epitafio al caminante,
> pues le dirá, sin vida, el rostro mío:
> "Ya fue gloria de Amor hacerme guerra."

He envisions himself as an epitaph to pilgrims, his lifeless face attesting to his glorious destruction by love's hostility.

In "The Paradox," Donne presents the same belligerent relationship between love and lover, the same startling image of the lover as epitaph. "The Paradox" treats the life-in-death, death-in-life theme, so crucial to Quevedo's poetry and philosophy. As in the Lisi sonnets, love is the cause of this paradoxical living death:

> No Lover saith, I love, nor any other
> > Can judge a perfect Lover;
> Hee thinkes that else none can nor will agree,
> > That any loves but hee:
> I cannot say I lov'd, for who can say
> > Hee was kill'd yesterday?

The paradox again arises as Donne takes seriously commonplace and inherited metaphors and images. Here he deals with the Elizabethan correlation between sexual love and metaphorical death. Donne follows this metaphor to its logical conclusion, finding that no one can love and then boast of his deeds because dead men do not talk.

We saw earlier love's ability to kill through the beloved's murderous disdain for the lover. The passionate heat of love's actualization, however, is as fatal as the coldness of death or the passionate suffering caused by love's denial. Donne's contrast of the heat of *love's* destruction with the coldness of *death's* destruction recalls Quevedo's duality of the lover's flame and death's ashes, "sobre el sol arderé, y el cuerpo frío / se acordará de amor en polvo y tierra." Both requital and non-requital may ultimately destroy the lover. In "The Paradox," however, Donne deals with the perils of love's consummation instead of the danger of its denial.

> Love with excesse of heat, more yong then old,
>   Death kills with too much cold;
> Wee dye but once, and who lov'd last did die,
>   Hee that saith twice, doth lye.

Through the Elizabethan conceit of sexual death, Donne logically establishes that life and love are mutually contradictory. The supreme paradox of "The Paradox," then, is that love's requital, not love's denial, causes the lover's death. The logical result of this metaphorical event is that the lover will thereafter be immune to death. Metaphorical death through sex has acquired the reality of physical death.

Donne acknowledges the disparity between appearance and reality in the following lines, as the lingering effects of life belie death's hidden actuality:

> For though hee seeme to move, and stirre a while,
>   It doth the sense beguile
> Such life is like the light which bideth yet
>   When the lights life is set,
> Or like the heat, which fire in solid matter
>   Leaves behinde, two houres after.

In this analysis of death-in-life, we see the same living death central to many of Quevedo's sonnets expressed in terms of temporal disparities between cause and effect.

Donne employs the imagery of fire and ashes, of major significance in Quevedo's "Amor constante más allá de la muerte," but to a different purpose. Quevedo compares his earthly remains to sentient, glowing ashes which would eternally manifest life and love despite physical death. Conversely, Donne employs the metaphor of hot ashes to describe the nature of a living death inflicted by love. The body may remain, as do the semblances of life, but the fire has gone out and the afterglow will also eventually fade.

> Once I lov'd and dyed; and am now become
> Mine Epitaph and Tombe.
> Here dead men speake their last, and so do I;
> Love-slaine, loe, here I lye.

Because of love, whose inevitable result is death, Donne now finds that his own words are his "Epitaph," his own body his "Tombe." As in Quevedo's sonnet, love has undone that subtle knot uniting body and soul.

Because of the shared metaphor of the lover as epitaph, "The Paradox," devoted to subtlety, wit, and sexual puns, bears a thematic and imagistic relationship to Quevedo's loftier Poem 473. The images of Quevedo's lifeless face and Donne's sepulchral body share the metaphor of battle, through which both lovers communicate their defeat by love to others. Donne's "Love-slaine, loe, here I lye" parallels Quevedo's "Ya fue gloria de Amor hacerme guerra." Be it through the requital or non-requital of their passion, love victoriously destroys both lovers.

The death-by-love imagery was also a part of Petrarch's poetic apparatus, as seen, for instance, in *Rime* No. 82. Petrarch asserts his constancy in love and belligerently demands a grave beautiful and white, inscribed with the name of his tormentor:

> Io non fu' d'amar voi lassato unquanco,
> Madonna, né sarò mentre ch'io viva;
> Ma d'odiar me medesmo giunto a riva,
> E del continuo lagrimar so' stanco;

E voglio anzi un sepolcro bello e bianco,
Che 'l vostro nome a mio danno si scriva
In alcun marmo, ove di spirto priva
Sia la mia carne, che pò star seco anco.

In their particular articulations of love's violence, Donne and Quevedo nevertheless undercut its destructive results through their mellifluous expressions of their respective fates. The predominance of liquid sounds in the final words of both poems, the l's in Donne's poem and the r's in Quevedo's sonnet, ameliorates the harshness of their meaning. Love's triumph over each lover, although irrevocable, is gentle, as both stoically endure their defeat.

In "The Paradox," Donne's body remains a testament to his metaphorical death and a "Tombe" for his spirit. He is in Quevedo's terms "vivo con la muerte" (Poem 337). The interrelatedness of body and soul in life is severed in death and in living death as well. The body is dead, but the spirit is trapped within its confines. The spirit, once it flees its metaphorical tomb, will cause actual physical death. The image of the soul entombed within the body, therefore, furthers the argument that Donne's death, like smoldering embers, is a living death that "doth the sense beguile."

Many other poems in the *Songs and Sonnets* portray a distinctly pessimistic relationship between love and death. The image of the epitaph appears again, for instance, in "A Nocturnall upon S. Lucies Day, being the shortest day." Donne was no doubt intrigued for many reasons by S. Lucies day, but perhaps the most significant reason is the one he mentions in the title itself. The shortest day of the year emphasizes the notions of darkness and temporal brevity. The shortness of S. Lucies day is simply a microcosmic reflection of the brevity of man's existence as a whole.

The same sombre mood and oppressive atmosphere that characterize Quevedo's Poem 473 pervade "A Nocturnall." But whereas love's denial destroys Quevedo, the lady's actual death destroys Donne. Both are nevertheless vulnerable, their anguish acute, because of the intensity of their emotion. The imagistic manifestation of their sorrow is the same also, as Donne declares that his loss has transformed him into an "Epitaph":

'Tis the yeares midnight, and it is the dayes,
Lucies, who scarce seaven houres herself unmaskes,
    The Sunne is spent, and now his flasks
    Send forth light squibs, no constant rayes;
        The world's whole sap is sunke:
The generall balme th'hydroptique earth hath drunk,
Whither, as to the beds-feet, life is shrunke,
Dead and enterr'd; yet all these seeme to laugh,
Compar'd with mee, who am their Epitaph.

The psychological precision and intensity with which Donne and Quevedo express their despair and isolation from the world of men characterize their religious poetry and prose works as well as much of their love poetry. Both transform psychological truth into a physical, palpable reality. Images of unrelieved solitude, despondence, and emptiness, which mutually reinforce and intensify each other, thereby create a physical atmosphere of subdued horror. Nothingness paradoxically assumes a spatial reality as each poet expresses his own physical progression through it.

In "A Nocturnall," darkness, sterility, and bleakness reflect the pervasiveness of death and nothingness. The withering of life, which is "Dead and enterr'd," reflects a desolate atmosphere similarly found in Quevedo's Poem 480, entitled "Muestra haber seguido el error de otro amante que había sido primero." Quevedo is thrown into an alien and quietly hostile world and, like Donne, finds no solace in external reality.

Por yerta frente de alto escollo, osado,
con pie dudoso, ciegos pasos guío;
siga la escasa luz del fuego mío,
que avara alumbra, habiéndome abrasado.

He dares to scale the rigid face of a dangerous peak, guided only by his own unsure and blind steps. The scant light of his love's flame gives him little help, for it has almost expended itself in his destruction. As in "A Nocturnall," "The Sunne is spent" and his inner fire only sends "forth light squibs, no constant rayes." The love that burdens him takes much and gives little in return, debilitating him and drawing him into a world of cold shadows. Because of his unrequited passion, he must endure a virtual living death, imprisoned in an atmosphere of mortality. The lover's isolation, pilgrimage, and ultimate destination are simply intensified metaphors for the general human condition. Man is born alone, dies alone, and, in the interim, journeys blindly and painfully through a world of shadows and sorrow. Donne and Quevedo keenly perceived the irony of man's brief, uncertain, and all too mortal existence, and shared a poetic genius for expressing the tensions arising from such an acute awareness. Life's solitude ultimately culminates in death's final and irrevocable solitude, and as such can be viewed as a foreshadowing of this inevitable mortal isolation.

The relationship between the sacred and the profane, previously seen in the religious images and themes of "The Canonization" and "The Relique," characterizes the association of love and death in "A Nocturnall." Louis L. Martz comments on this correlation between sacred and secular love, between love and death, noting that in Donne's poetry "human love is exalted to the religious level, notably in 'A Nocturnall upon S. Lucies Day,'" and that Donne employs "the ancient ecclesiastical usage of the term 'nocturnal'" in his commemoration of "the death of his beloved— his saint. . . . In any case, the Nocturnall vividly illustrates the way in which Donne's poetry, throughout his career, moves along a Great Divide, between the sacred and the profane, now facing one way, now another, but always remaining intensely aware of both sides."[1]

We have also seen the correlation between the sacred and the secular in *Poema a Lisi* in Poems 460 and 474. In "A Nocturnall," Donne suffers a living death because physical death has claimed his beloved, his saint. In Poem 473, Quevedo also suffers a living death, but at the hands of "Love" itself. Both lovers are equally bereft of love, however, and consequently view themselves as living images of death, as death's epitaphs. Donne considers himself an "Epitaph" of all that is "Dead and enterr'd" because of love and the death of his beloved, whereas Quevedo sees himself as an "epitafio al caminante" who would warn all those that follow of his defeat by love. In the second stanza of "A Nocturnall," Donne also discusses the effect his living death will have on those who would love in the future:

> Study me then, you who shall lovers bee
> At the next world, that is, at the next Spring:
>   For I am every dead thing,
>   In whom love wrought new Alchimie.
>   For his art did expresse
> A quintessence even from nothingnesse,
> From dull privations, and leane emptinesse:
> He ruin'd mee, and I am re-begot
> Of absence, darknesse, death; things which are not.

Love's miraculous alchemy has effected his rebirth from "things which are not." This image of the birth of nothingness and of death recalls Quevedo's musings in Poem 460 on the paradox of his own death being the begotten child of his love. In both poems, the antithetical themes of birth and death are united through the theme of love. The irony of the lover's situation is accentuated by the fact that his is a re-birth, which in Christian terms indicates the renewal of life in the glorious fullness of *Agape*, implicitly contrasted here with the "leane emptinesse" of *Eros*.

This second stanza of "A Nocturnall" also resembles in many ways the following two stanzas of Quevedo's Poem 480:

> Cae del cielo la noche, y al cuidado
> presta engañosa paz el sueño frío;
> llévame a yerma orilla de alto río,
> y busco por demás o puente o vado.
>
>   En muda senda, obscuro peregrino,
> sigo pisadas de otro sin ventura,
> que para mi dolor perdió el camino.

Quevedo creates the same atmosphere of sterility and emptiness that characterizes "A Nocturnall." The utter desolation of the environment evoked in the first quatrain becomes more intense in the second, as night falls, bringing cold sleep and deceptive peace to the lover stranded on the dry banks of a high river. He is utterly alone, hopeless, and lost. Quevedo sustains the impression of darkness and coldness in the following tercet. Retaining the image of darkness, and therefore of coldness, he strengthens the mood of desolation with the *muda senda*, the 'silent path' he treads. In his death-like journey, love's pilgrim finds himself bereaved, surrounded by companions of the grave: lifelessness in all of its primordial manifestations—chaos, darkness, coldness, aridity, and fearful silence.

Whereas love places Quevedo in this elemental, lifeless atmosphere, Donne in "A Nocturnall" claims that love rebegets his very being out of this elemental world "Of absence, darkness, death; things which are not." While death's attributes merely surround Quevedo, Donne poignantly affirms his total identification with death through his assertion, "I am every dead thing."

In "A Nocturnall" and Poem 480, Donne's and Quevedo's predilection for contrasts and antitheses reflects their shared recognition of the essential oneness of all things. In his paradoxical phrase "A quintessence even from nothingnesse," Donne juxtaposes the most antithetical of all antitheses. In Quevedo's sonnet, this juxtaposition occurs through the stark contrast between the first three stanzas and the final tercet. Lisi appears as the embodiment of the qualities of life which have been denied the distraught lover throughout the sonnet. She is also the living antithesis of the moribund lover in "A Nocturnall":

> cuando elocuente, Lisi, tu hermosura
> califica en tu luz mi desatino
> y en tus merecimientos mi locura.

In contrast to the silence which has enveloped Quevedo, Lisi's beauty assumes not only the qualities of sound, but eloquence, the quintessence of sound. She brings light as well, driving out the darkness which had shrouded the first three stanzas. Confronted with the eloquence and brilliance of her beauty, the lover comprehends his immersion in such madness. Quevedo juxtaposes the bleakness of his world with Lisi's virtues, just as Donne contrasts the abstract terms "nothingnesse" and "quintessence." Lisi's very existence is the cause of Quevedo's agony, whereas the death of

Donne's beloved motivates his agony and conviction that he is the epitome of nothingness. The brilliance and eloquence of the unresponsive Lisi have paradoxically submerged Quevedo in a dim, elemental atmosphere. Whatever the cause, both lovers find themselves alone in a dark, lifeless world in which they themselves reflect the madness of chaos and the sterility of nothingness. Quevedo's isolation is more extreme than Donne's because of the unrequited nature of his purely Petrarchan stance. Even in the unrelieved desolation of "A Nocturnall," Donne's solitude is mitigated by his memory of the love and suffering he once shared with his beloved.

The isolation and uncertainty of both are also intensified by the juxtaposition of each lover's solitude with past or future lovers. Somehow they can only relate to unknown lovers whose presence is felt, but not real. Quevedo is following the footprints of an earlier lover who wandered alone and lost. Donne would seek to be the antithesis of that lover in "the next world, that is, at the next Spring," to warn future lovers of the dangers he, like Quevedo, knows all too well. The contrast between the new life of the Spring and the yet unborn lovers with the mid-winter of S. Lucie's day and the now spent lover is implicit.

Each beloved is once again important not because of herself, but rather because of the emotions she evokes in the lover and the opportunity she thereby gives him for self-analysis. Instead of emphasizing the nature of the departed lady, "A Nocturnall" thus presents Donne's own despair and consequent living death as he reacts to her death. Quevedo similarly devotes three stanzas to his sorrow's intensity and only one tercet to the beloved's charms. Just as Donne's interest is rarely in his assorted ladies, Quevedo's concern is not really with Lisi but with the emotions she evokes in him, the despair of his passion, the psychological and metaphysical significance of his sorrow.

The third stanza of "A Nocturnall" continues the elemental and morbid mood established in the preceding stanzas as well as Donne's obsessive self-concern. Only in the second portion does it provide the poem's major reference to the beloved. Donne recalls love's mutuality, but, in keeping with the nature of the poem, he does so in negative terms. He employs "Chaosses," "absences," and "carcasses," images dear to Quevedo also, in his evocation of love's deathly nature:

> All others, from all things, draw all that's good,
> Life, soule, forme, spirit, whence they beeing have;
>   I, by loves limbecke, am the grave
>   Of all, that's nothing. Oft a flood
>   Have wee two wept, and so
> Drownd the whole world, us two; oft did we grow
> To be two Chaosses, when we did show
> Care to ought else; and often absences
> Withdrew our soules, and made us carcasses.

Quevedo parallels Donne's extreme concern with the disastrous effects of love and death in Poem 485, entitled "persevera en la exageración de su afecto amoroso y en el exceso de su padecer." In this sonnet, he asserts that love's wound destroys him physically (in the quatrains) and psychologically (in the tercets). In his own way, Quevedo articulates many of the ideas expressed in "A Nocturnall":

> En los claustros de l'alma la herida
> yace callada; mas consume, hambrienta,
> la vida, que en mis venas alimenta
> llama por las medulas extendida.

Quevedo repeats the concept presented in Poem 472, that the very essence of life is contained in the soul, veins, and marrow. We again see his obsession with silence, as he declares that love's wound lies (as in the grave) silent in the cloisters of his soul. Such silence is insidious, for it consumes his life, his veins, his marrow. Quevedo neither optimistically envisions his own transcendence of death nor evokes the image of death's piteous release. He is too occupied with the actual process of love's consumption of him. In "A Nocturnall," Donne is not eaten alive, but his very being is destroyed and he is rebegotten out of "things which are not." His *soul* is not the grave of his love's wound as in this sonnet, but *he himself* is transformed into "the grave / Of all, that's nothing."

Whereas in "A Nocturnall" Donne contrasts himself with "All others" who draw "life, soule, forme, spirit, whence they beeing have," Quevedo expresses his being in terms of what is taken from him:

> Bebe el ardor, hidrópica, mi vida,
> que ya, ceniza amante y macilenta,
> cadáver del incendio hermoso, ostenta.

Like Donne's "hydroptique earth," which imbibes the "generall balme," his hydroptic life yields to his love's ardor, leaving his body a "cadaver." Withered ashes, smoke, and darkness remain the only manifestations of his existence. The words *cadáver* and *macilenta*, 'withered,' provide another metaphoric comparison with the third stanza of "A Nocturnall," in which Donne recalls that "often absences / Withdrew our soules, and made us carcasses." While Quevedo wastes away alone because of the ardor of his unrequited passion, Donne reveals that previous "absence" one from the other has often transformed the beloved herself, as well as Donne, into a carcass. Unlike the aloof Lisi, Donne's lady suffers in love also.

In his description of the capacity of their mutual absence to "withdraw" their "soules," Donne attributes to absence the power of death, the power to separate the body from the soul, to render the body a lifeless carcass. While Donne recalls his periodic physical absence from love's mutuality, Quevedo has always suffered the absence of love's mutuality, the spiritual, as well as physical, absence of the beloved.

> La gente esquivo y me es horror el día;
> dilato en largas voces negro llanto,
> que a sordo mar mi ardiente pena envía.
>
> A los suspiros di la voz del canto;
> la confusión inunda l'alma mía;
> mi corazón es reino del espanto.

Poem 485 ends as Quevedo discloses the intensity of his despair through the antithesis of his *largas voces* which are heard only by a *sordo mar*, a 'deaf sea.' Quevedo accentuates the strength of his cries through the spatial connotations of *dilato* and *largas*. The second antithesis that characterizes his despair is *negro llanto* and *ardiente pena*. He appeals to our visual, instead of our aural, sense with the extreme contrast between his black tears and his flaming, burning sorrow. He reflects his emotional strain through the metaphorical tensions of this first tercet.

These tercets evoke a sense of horror, of utter solitude, of chaos and dark, unmitigated suffering. The solitary lover avoids people and is terrified by the light of day, while his dark cries are heard by no one but the deaf sea. His soul is filled only with confusion; his heart is a kingdom of terror. With his characteristic genius for capturing the psychological essence of fear and desolation, Quevedo cooperates in his own immersion in death's kingdom by avoiding the world of the living and the light of day. His unending cry, magnified in length and in volume, is hauntingly ineffective as he juxtaposes it to a world of emptiness.

The spiritual absence of Quevedo's unrequited love results in horror and desolation as assuredly as the physical absence of requited love converts Donne into a "grave," an "Epitaph," and an amalgam of "absence," "darknesse," and "death."

> But I am by her death, (which word wrongs her)
> Of the first nothing, the Elixir grown;
> Were I a man, that I were one,
> I needs must know; I should preferre,
>   If I were any beast,
> Some ends, some means; Yea plants, yea stones detest,
> And love; All, all some properties invest;
> If I an ordinary nothing were,
> As shadow,'a light, and body must be here.

In this stanza, Donne vehemently asserts the quintessence of his nothingness. He is neither man, animal, vegetable, mineral, nor "an ordinary nothing" such as a shadow. He has no physical body, and even if he did, there is no light with which to cast his shadow, it being the "yeares, and the dayes deep midnight." The shortest day of the year, the day of minimum light and maximum darkness, thereby temporally reinforces the concept of the lover as a spatial non-entity. Donne's insistent elaboration on his nothingness, like Quevedo's hopeless presentation of his desolation, reflects his extreme "anthropological pessimism," an attitude common to both poets and a signficant contrast to their grand "transcendental optimism" seen earlier.[2] Because of love's loss, both lovers are incapable of vanquishing the horror and nothingness that invade their souls, mortally overwhelming them and their world.

Donne maintains the mood of darkness that has prevailed throughout "A Nocturnall" as he prepares himself for death in the final stanza:

> But I am None; nor will my Sunne renew.
> You lovers, for whose sake, the lesser Sunne
>   At this time to the Goat is runne
>   To fetch new lust, and give it you,
>   Enjoy your summer all;
> Since shee enjoyes her long nights festivall,
> Let mee prepare towards her, and let mee call
> This houre her Vigill, and her Eve, since this
> Both the yeares, and the dayes deep midnight is.

The emptiness and despair with which "A Nocturnall" began is unrelieved throughout. Utter hopelessness invades Donne's spirit because of his bitter recognition that love is not invincible, that death may conquer it. His hopelessness acquires cynical overtones as Donne, bitterly envious of new lovers, attributes no spirituality, only crude sexuality, to their young love.

The perils of requited love are explicit and overwhelming and curiously similar to the horrors of unrequited love. The danger of placing one's faith in a mortal, mutable being lies in mortality itself. To do this is to die spiritually, for to bind one's self totally to the uncertain earth is to lose all hope of ever transcending mutability. Loss of the physical object of adoration paradoxically results in the second death of the lover.

Quevedo's Poem 479, entitled "Lamentación amorosa y postrero sentimiento de amante," resembles "A Nocturnall" in its powerful description of death-in-life. Quevedo again grieves, not because of the physical death of the beloved, but rather because of his own intense suffering of love's non-requital.

Whereas Donne declares only in the sixth stanza, "Let mee prepare towards her," Quevedo immediately affirms his willingness to die:

No me aflige morir; no he rehusado
acabar de vivir, ni he pretendido
alargar esta muerte que ha nacido
a un tiempo con la vida y el cuidado.

As in "A Nocturnall," death assumes various forms. Both Donne and Quevedo contemplate the ultimate physical separation of the body from the soul as part of their immediate future. Their present death-in-life nevertheless plagues them and also motivates their desire for physical death. In "A Nocturnall," Donne refers to himself as an "Epitaph" and as a "grave." Quevedo here declares that dying does not trouble him and that he has never tried to lengthen his living death, which was born simultaneously with life and its cares. The unabashed fear that overwhelmed him in Poem 485 is absent in this sonnet. There is no grief or despondence because of physical death's imminence.

Just as various forms of death prevail in this sonnet, so too does Quevedo manifest contradictory attitudes toward it. After announcing his lack of concern regarding his physical death in the first quatrain, he reveals his concern for the fate of his body after death in the second quatrain. We have already seen this concern for the body in each poet's attitude toward death. Quevedo respects his body because of its role in love, albeit a sexually unfulfilled love:

Siento haber de dejar deshabitado
cuerpo que amante espíritu ha ceñido;
desierto un corazón siempre encendido,
donde todo el Amor reinó hospedado.

He feels intense remorse in deserting the body which housed his love, the heart which was ruled by love. He thus admits that the physical aspects of death do cause him grief. The sundering of soul from body is a bitter future to contemplate, but the actual departure from this life of sorrows, from this living death, causes him no grief.

Donne, in contrast to this sonnet and to many of his own poems, expresses no such despair in "A Nocturnall" because he has denied his own corporality. Having already experienced this aspect of physical death, he has found himself to be a disembodied spirit, abandoned by all forms of life. Much of the bitter remorse expressed in "A Nocturnall" is indeed due to the results of physical death; the lover bereft of his corporality is the "quintessence of nothingness."

The totality of Donne's despair reflects his inability to contemplate life after death or any form of spiritual transcendence. He not only endures the horrors of physical death, but must also face irrevocable spiritual death. The utter nothingness of his vision contrasts sharply with Quevedo's optimistic projection into his unrequited love's future.

The intensity of mutuality, of earthly requital, determines the strength of despair once the lover is deprived of the beloved's presence. Conversely, the acuteness of Quevedo's death-in-life, due to his eternal denial of this same requital, determines the intensity of his ultimate glory, his life-in-death. Physical death is not final for Quevedo, as it is for Donne. He declares in the first tercet:

> Señas me da mi ardor de fuego eterno,
> y de tan larga y congojosa historia
> sólo será escritor mi llanto tierno.

His flame will be eternal, he asserts, due to the strength of his love. Life will continue after death through love, just as, in life, love caused his death. The antipathy between fire and water evident in other sonnets becomes a sympathetic union of elements that in their diverse ways reflect the lover's eternal anguish. The tears of despair and the eternal ardor of his passion, asserts Quevedo, will forever define the nature of his unrequited love.

In the final tercet, he affirms:

Lisi, estáme diciendo la memoria
que, pues tu gloria la padezco infierno,
que llame al padecer tormentos, gloria.

Quevedo's predilection for word play and conceits is obvious here. "Gloria" may mean worldly glory or heavenly glory, and in this tercet it means both. He thereby extends the tension between heaven and earth to include heaven and hell. Recognizing that he suffers hell because of Lisi's "gloria," he asserts that the endurance of such torments should also be called "gloria." The dichotomy between the glory of the beloved and the glory of the suffering lover is as great as the abyss between the splendors of paradise and the torments of hell. As Quevedo extends the concept of death-in-life, expressed in the first quatrain, beyond the realm of this world, it becomes an amalgam of heaven-in-hell and hell-in-heaven.

In this sonnet, Quevedo has considered the deathly nature of this life in the first quatrain, actual physical death in the second quatrain, and has declared in the tercets that even after physical death the lover's passion will continue to rule his being. The life-death dichotomy becomes a heaven-hell duality because in death, as in life, his unrequited passion will control his being.

This achievement of glory through the suffering of a kind of metaphorical hell contrasts with the dark nothingness of Donne's dispirited night. Like Donne in "A Nocturnall," Quevedo suffers intensely and will eternally endure the infernal torments of his love. The beloved's qualities nevertheless paradoxically transform this hell into "gloria." Quevedo envisions his suffering as glorious, ironically transforming his despair into a kind of hope. In "A Nocturnall," however, not even the faintest glimmer of hope or light relieves the sterility and emptiness of Donne and his world.

Quevedo's Poem 492, entitled "Laméntase, muerta Lisi, de la vida, que le impide el seguirla," also deals with the same themes as "A Nocturnall." It culminates Quevedo's expression of the life-love-death relationship found in the Lisi sonnets. As in "A Nocturnall," the beloved is dead, and because of his love for Lisi, Quevedo's life is now a burden. The intensity of the relationship between death and love in "A Nocturnall" reflects Quevedo's torment in this sonnet. The lover's extreme idealization of the beloved intensifies his reaction to her earthly frailty. Death's power is total, as it destroys the best that this earth possesses.

In the first quatrain, Quevedo recognizes the inevitability and the impartial universality of death as he asks when his own death will occur.

> ¿Cuándo aquel fin a mí vendrá forzoso,
> pues por todas las vidas se pasea,
> que tanto el desdichado le desea
> y que tanto le teme el venturoso?

As Metaphysicals, Donne and Quevedo shared the capacity for simultaneously maintaining contradictory views as equally valid interpretations of reality. As he recognizes the validity of man's divergent views of death, Quevedo exercises a kind of Baroque perspectivism, perceiving reality from myriad vantage points. Those who only suffer desire death as an escape, while those who live happily have much to lose and therefore fear death's arrival.

Quevedo's poetry as a whole, like Donne's, presents attitudes regarding death which contradict each other. In this sonnet, he does not express fear of death; nor does the desire for freedom from human nescience motivate his plea for death's release; nor does he seek out death because of the pain of loving and the denial of love's requital. As in "A Nocturnall," the beloved's death compels him to seek her beyond the realm of the living. Just as Donne recognizes that his "Sunne" will not "renew" and, therefore, "abjures" life's "Springtime" to "prepare towards" his lady, the symbol of "the yeares, and the dayes deep midnight," so too does Quevedo seek his *sepulcro perezoso*, his 'indolent sepulchre':

> La condición del hado desdeñoso
> quiere que le codicie y no le vea:
> el descanso le invidia a mi tarea
> parasismo y sepulcro perezoso.

But disdainful fate requires that he eagerly desire Lisi while being unable to see her. Although he desires death and the ease of the tomb, he finds no rest from his efforts. He seeks death as a means of again seeing the beloved and as a release from his earthly miseries without her.

In the first tercet, Quevedo expresses the dichotomies of life and death, of appearance and reality, through his concern with time:

> Quiere el Tiempo engañarme lisonjero,
> llamando vida dilatar la muerte,
> siendo morir el tiempo que la espero.

Time in this life is virtual death for the lover whose beloved is dead. It seeks to deceive him by claiming that the conditions of his living death are manifestations of life. As time's movement continues, he also must continue to endure his living death. Time and life in this world are merely appearances that would deny the reality that the lover is continually dying. What appears to be life is really a living death endured while he awaits his release through actual physical death.

He believes that destiny is jealous of his love for Lisi because it does not allow physical death to overtake him:

> Celosa debo de tener la suerte,
> pues viendo, ¡oh, Lisi!, que por verte muero,
> con la vida me estorba el poder verte.

He longs to die so that he can see Lisi, but fate forces him to endure physical life, living death. Throughout Quevedo's poetry, the concept of death alternates between the actual moment in which the soul leaves the body and the continual process of dying that begins at birth. Death is so much a part of life that it is never separated from it.

Donne reflects this philosophy in "A Nocturnall" when he declares, "and I am re-begot / Of absence, darknesse, death; things which are not." As in Quevedo's sonnet, the beloved's death causes the paradoxical amalgam of opposites. Like Quevedo, Donne expresses the ominous alliance between life and death in terms of love.

In Quevedo's Poem 488, entitled "Desea, para descansar, el

morir," love similarly imparts significance to the death-in-life and life-in-death paradoxes. As in "A Nocturnall," the lover longs for death:

> Mejor vida es morir que vivir muerto,
> ¡oh piedad!; en ti cabe gran fiereza,
> pues mientes, apacible, tu aspereza
> y detienes la vida al pecho abierto.

Like Donne in "A Nocturnall," Quevedo endures a deathly existence and remonstrates that it would be a better life to die than to continue living as a dead man. This quatrain also presents the contrast between appearance and reality. Pity is paradoxically fierce and rough despite its outer appearance of gentleness. For pity is not gentle if it detains life "al pecho abierto," if it denies the peace of death to those defenseless against the tortures of life and love. Just as "flattering Time" sought to deceive the lover in the previous sonnet, so too does pity disguise its asperity with a show of mildness.

Quevedo continues:

> El cuerpo, que de l'alma está desierto
> (ansí lo quiso Amor de alta belleza),
> de dolor se despueble y de tristeza:
> descanse, pues, de mármoles cubierto.

The pain of unrequited love has already fulfilled death's function by separating the soul from the body, just as Donne in "A Nocturnall" claims that "often absences / Withdrew our soules, and made us carcasses." As Donne envisions the transformation of his living death into actual death, so too does Quevedo plead that his deserted body be allowed to rest in peace, freed of its pain and sadness.

The first tercet clarifies the paradoxical relationship between cruelty and pity:

> En mí la crueldad será piadosa
> en darme muerte, y sólo el darme vida
> piedad será tirana y rigurosa.

Quevedo establishes the conceptual antithesis between *crueldad* (*piadosa*) and *piedad* (*tirana y rigurosa*). Death's cruelty would be merciful to the distraught lover, while life's blessings would only be rigorous tyranny. He seeks death as a release from the agony of living, from the torments of loving. In contrast to "A Nocturnall" and Quevedo's previous sonnet, the beloved's indifference, not her death, motivates the lover's plea for release. Physical death can release him from living death, by far the worse of two evils, thereby becoming a positive force because of its contrast with living death.

The final tercet provides a resolution now familiar in the Lisi sonnets:

> Y ya que supe amar esclarecida
> virtud, siempre triunfante, siempre hermosa,
> tenga paz mi ceniza presumida.

He finds peace in the knowledge that he has loved such noble virtue and beauty. A curious paradox inextricably links love and death; for love impels the lover to seek death, yet ultimately triumphs over its rigors.

"The Dissolution" deals with the same problem found in "A Nocturnall" and in Quevedo's sonnet written at the death of Lisi. Donne must face the reality of the beloved's physical death:

> Shee'is dead; And all which die
> To their first Elements resolve;
> And wee were mutuall Elements to us,
> And made of one another.

In this poem, Donne expresses love's mutuality, not as the union of souls, as was seen in "A Valediction: forbidding Mourning," but as the union of bodies. He claims that before his beloved's death, the elements of both lovers' bodies were mutual.

Following the syllogistic logic of his argument, his own actual physical elements have thus doubled since her soul abandoned her body:

> My body then doth hers involve,
> And those things whereof I consist, hereby
> In me abundant grow, and burdenous,
> And nourish not, but smother.

Such an increase in elements is detrimental, not salutary, for the increased elements his body inherits from his beloved's body stifle his own physical existence. The contrast with "A Nocturnall" is obvious. While in "A Nocturnall" he speaks of the utter destruction of his own spiritual, as well as physical, reality because of his beloved's death, the opposite is the result in "The Dissolution." In "A Nocturnall" Donne does not even possess the corporality necessary to cast a shadow, and in "The Dissolution" he is overwhelmed by the "Elements" left him:

> My fire of Passion, sighes of ayre,
> Water of teares, and earthly sad despaire,
>   Which my materialls bee,
> But neere worne out by loves securitie,
> Shee, to my losse, doth by her death repaire,
>   And I might live long wretched so
> But that my fire doth with my fuell grow.

Whereas in "A Nocturnall" he expresses his grief because of his beloved's death in terms of sterility and "nothingnesse," in this poem he manifests through grief and sorrow his increased, not diminished, physical elements. His "fire of Passion" and "Water of teares" resemble many of Quevedo's Petrarchan sonnets, in which fire and water typically characterize his emotions. Similarly, the line "And I might live long wretched so" recalls Quevedo's sonnet concerning Lisi's death, in which he bemoans his living death.

Donne, however, continues the arguments made possible by the conceit of the elements, victoriously envisioning his own physical death, a death for which Quevedo does not dare hope:

> This death, hath with my store
>   My use encreas'd.
> And so my soule more earnestly releas'd
> Will outstrip hers; As bullets flown before
> A latter bullet may o'rtake, the pouder being more.

Through the metaphor of a swift bullet, which has more powder than one previously shot, he ingeniously determines that the speed of his soul's flight will enable him to overtake his beloved's soul.

Just as the lovers' bodies were united in this life, so too does he desire his soul's union with the beloved's in death.

In addition to his concern with the relationship between the body and the soul, Donne also presents the situation in terms of the time-space continuum. He expresses death's separation of the soul from the body through the metaphor of the bullet's flight. He explores this conceit, pursuing the logic of the bullet's movement through time and space. This journey through space is perhaps the swiftest ever described by either Donne or Quevedo. The intricate relation between time and space is implicit in Donne's syllogistic reasoning that he can regain the time lost through his own soul's swifter movement through space.

The envisioned reunion of the lovers' souls contrasts significantly with the lover's fate in Quevedo's sonnet. The forces of destiny compel him to grieve Lisi's death in this world, for his desire of joining her in death is thwarted. Whereas Quevedo must solitarily combat the "dilatory" forces of "Time," Donne envisions his love's victory over life and death through the mutuality of corporal, as well as spiritual, love. If his body did not "hers involve," such a victory of love over life and death could never be possible. This triumph of mutual love contrasts with Quevedo's sonnet of sorrow. Although death will not release him, the despairing lover is consoled by his recognition of the transcendence of his unrequited love for the elusive Lisi.

In "A Nocturnall," Quevedo's Poem 492, and "The Dissolution," the themes of love and death are inseparably fused as death strikes the beloved. Donne's "A Feaver" also deals with the beloved's physical death as he pleads with her not to die, yet ultimately resigns himself to this inevitability. Donne effects the idealization of the beloved in this poem in terms of time and mutability, of eternity and infinity. He invokes his beloved:

> Oh doe not die, for I shall hate
>   All women so, when thou art gone,
> That thee I shall not celebrate,
>   When I remember, thou wast one.

He employs the antithetical emotions of hate and love in this stanza to describe his adoration of the beloved. His hatred of all women is a curious manifestation of his love for the beloved, for it is an emotion that begrudges all women life if the one lady he adores is denied life. Donne elaborates on this understandable human reaction, however, as he pursues the irony that the beloved, as a member of the hated female sex, would consequently not merit his celebration of her.

In the following stanzas, we see Donne's predilection for images of spatial expansion. He introduces the metaphor of the world and ultimately perceives the beloved as the world's soul:

> But yet thou canst not die, I know;
>   To leave this world behinde, is death,
> But when thou from this world wilt goe,
>   The whole world vapors with thy breath.

He argues against death through wit and ingeniousness, asserting that the world would evaporate with the beloved's last breath; for instead of remaining behind, it would simply follow her and, like her, cease to exist. The beloved's metaphysical significance is paramount. Just as Donne has associated her with all women, he now equates his sorrow with the grief and destruction of the entire world.

We see Donne's obvious concern with the body-soul duality in the following stanza:

> Or if, when thou, the worlds soule, goest,
>   It stay, 'tis but thy carkasse then,
> The fairest woman, but thy ghost,
>   But corrupt wormes, the worthyest men.

As the world's soul, the beloved may leave the world, her body; but as in death, it will become a lifeless body, a "carkasse." The world would be rendered as lifeless as the lover in Quevedo's Poem 489, who will describe his moribund self in terms of ashes left by his love's flame: "Yo soy ceniza que sobró a la llama." Donne furthers the material-spiritual duality as he envisions the dead world in terms of the soul after death ("The fairest woman, but thy ghost") and in terms of the body ("But corrupt wormes, the worthyest men.").

The last stanza presents the final hyperbole through which Donne reveals the extent of his love:

> Yet 'twas of my minde, seising thee,
>   Though it in thee cannot persever.
> For I had rather owner bee
>   Of thee one houre, then all else ever.

Utilizing the *amour courtois* concept of *pleroma*, he expresses time's relativity through his love for the beloved, for she has the power to bestow eternity and infinity on a single hour. This expansion of measurable time to measureless eternity parallels the expansion of space in "The Good-morrow," in which love transforms "one little room" into the inconceivable inclusiveness of "everywhere."

Donne's consummate devotion to the beloved recalls Poem 473, in which Quevedo declares that his own non-existence is a joy if it is for love: "Y el no ser, por amar, será mi gloria." Quevedo's contrast between existence and non-existence is comparable to Donne's contrast of one hour in man's finite time with the vast reaches of infinity, as seen in "The Legacie": "And Lovers houres be full eternity."

Donne and Quevedo idealize their ladies in the most metaphysical of terms. "A Feaver," like Quevedo's sonnet which began this chapter ("Ya fue gloria de Amor hacerme guerra."), reveals its author's tendency toward anthropological pessimism and transcendental optimism. Like Quevedo, Donne is immersed in the seriousness of his own *rapprochement* with death.

Yet, not all of Donne's and Quevedo's poems regarding the relationship between death and love are sad and despondent. The satirical, perhaps cynical, quality of "The Paradox," for instance, does not deny the lover's playful wittiness. Quevedo's Poem 489, entitled "Artificiosa evasión de la muerte, si valiera; pero, entretanto, es ingeniosa," like "The Legacie," is a witty investigation of the interrelationship between death and love:

> Pierdes el tiempo, Muerte, en mi herida,
> pues quien no vive no padece muerte;
> si has de acabar mi vida, has de volverte
> a aquellos ojos donde está mi vida.

The poems recently discussed concerned moribund lovers seeking the transformation of their living deaths into actual death because love's sorrows had metaphorically separated their bodies from their souls. Quevedo here playfully employs the same argument to evade true physical death. Asserting that "he who does not live can not suffer death," he declares that he no longer lives and if death wants him, it must seek his life in his mistress' eyes. This is an ingenious argument based on the conventional metaphors of the optics of love.

He then claims that death would fail in such an endeavor:

> Al sagrado en que habita retraída,
> aun siendo sin piedad, no has de atreverte;
> que serás vida, si llegase a verte,
> y quedarás de ti desconocida.

In its search for the lover, death itself would change if his beloved were to look at it. Her eyes would miraculously transform death into life, so that even death could not recognize itself.

He describes his own complete destruction by love's fires:

> Yo soy ceniza que sobró a la llama;
> nada dejó por consumir el fuego
> que en amoroso incendio se derrama.

He is only *ceniza*, 'ashes.' Being dead already, he has nothing to offer death and could declare with Donne in "A nocturnall" that he is "every dead thing." Death can do no more than what love has already accomplished. As in the previous poems, death and love are closely allied in their shared power to destroy the lover.

In the final tercet, Quevedo advises death to return to those who seek it as a release from their suffering, for having already been killed by love, he has nothing to offer it:

> Vuélvete al miserable, cuyo ruego,
> por descansar en su dolor, te llama:
> que lo que yo no tengo, no lo niego.

Love's strictures have rendered him immune to death's powers and threats. In ironic contrast to many of the poems in Chapter

Three, the lover feels immune to death because of the harshness of unrequited love, not because of the transcendent powers of an all-consuming love. Instead of elevating him to a state that transcends this world, mutability, and death, love has killed him.

In contrast to the earlier poems of this chapter, Quevedo employs the metaphor of living death to avoid, rather than attract, actual physical death. Resembling the requited Donne in "The Computation" ("Can Ghosts die?"), the unrequited Quevedo defies death, by similarly extending traditional metaphors through witty syllogism.

Thus, we have seen that Donne and Quevedo present varied approaches to what is essentially an anthropological pessimism in love, in life. Through shared images and traditions, wit, perverse logic, metaphysical conceits, and an acute sense of loss, they express a deep-seated alienation with spatial-temporal existence. Love provides no salvation from their profound despondence, plunging both instead into a deep despair from which escape either through death or within life is virtually impossible.

The concept of a living death, the image of the slain lover as an epitaph for others, and the *chiaroscuro* imperceptibility between appearance and reality characterize the first poems discussed. The chaotic solitude of the bereft lover, the desolation and hopelessness of his physical and psychological world, and his own metaphorical alliance with carcasses, the grave, and death's horror typify the following group of poems. The final set presents the ingenious and paradoxical manifestations of the body-soul and time-space dualities. Each lover seeks death as a release, as an escape from the horror of living after his beloved has died.

We have been immersed in a suffocating atmosphere in which death clearly prevails over love, the lover, and the beloved. Be it actual physical death or a spiritual living death, the lover, because of his love, must contend with his own desolation and mortality as well as the mutability of a world that reflects his morbid physical and psychological state. Death's omnipotence reigns supreme in the darkened soul of the solitary lover. The irrevocable loss of love immeasurably magnifies his essential solitude as he confronts his life's decay, his death's ultimate sovereignty.

Perhaps in this chapter, more than in any other, we have approached the fundamental relationship between the Baroque *Weltanschauung* and the Metaphysical style. As Warnke perceived it, the Metaphysical style encompasses theme as well as technique. Certainly, a fundamental concern with ultimate matters characterizes the Metaphysical style which, through its complex and seemingly far-fetched conceits, reveals its ironic vision and propensity to view reality as a host of multi-faceted phenomena.

Because of this metaphysical approach to reality, the consequent vision of the close relationship between death and absence, further emphasized through the fundamental Baroque obsession with death, thus contributes to a body of poetry which cries out in desperation at life's tragic truth.

The intellectual capacity to perceive the tragic in the trivial and the commonplace and the overpowering emotional commitment to the exploration of life's mysterious finality thus characterize the Metaphysical poetry of these two outstanding Baroque poets. In their intellectual and emotional apprehension of the omnipotence and ubiquity of mortality, Donne and Quevedo mirror the fundamental preoccupations of their age. In their poetic expression of the metaphysical correspondences between existence and nonexistence, between presence and absence, between life and death, between possession and loss, they reveal the intellectual and emotional attitudes that characterize the Baroque *Weltanschauung*.

The solemn tone that permeates their articulation of absence, loss, solitude, and death differs profoundly from Renaissance and *amour-courtois* expressions of absence. The Baroque obsession with death has invaded this realm of human relationships with perhaps its most appropriate results; for absence, solitude, and loss, although they be merely temporary situations, presage the eternal absence, solitude, and loss that await mankind. It is the compelling legitimacy of this metaphysical correspondence that bestows upon the artistry of Donne and Quevedo its irrepressible vigor—its vehement passion—and reflects its tenacious engagement with life's tragic actuality.

6

Love, Murder, and Death: Dreams and Shadows

As Renaissance clarity and precision yields to the shadows and tenebrous uncertainties of the Baroque, so too does Renaissance serenity and tranquility yield to an esthetic expressivity reflecting the turbulence of the Baroque period. The peaceful pastoral mood of the poetry of Garcilaso and San Juan de la Cruz is replaced by an atmosphere of inquietude and tension that often erupts in thematic or esthetic violence.

The action, mood, and imagery of the Baroque drama is similarly dominated by violence, by a physical violence that mirrors the internal tensions and psychological strain that pervade the age. The metaphorical and physical violence with which Calderon's *La vida es sueño* opens, for instance, is sustained in imagery and in action throughout the play:

> *Hipogrifo violento*
> *que corriste parejas con el viento,*
> *¿dónde, rayo sin llama,*
> *pájaro sin matiz, pez sin escama,*
> *y bruto sin instinto*
> *natural, al confuso laberinto*
> *destas desnudas peñas*
> *te desbocas, arrastras y despeñas?*
> *Quédate en este monte,*
> *donde tengan los brutos su Faetonte;*

que yo, sin más camino
que el que me dan las leyes del destino,
ciega y desesperada
bajaré la aspereza enmarañada
deste monte eminente
que arruga al sol el ceño de su frente.
Mal, Polonia, recibes
a un extranjero, pues con sangre escribes
su entrada en tus arenas,
y apenas llega, cuando llega a penas.

Likewise, the imagery, action, and theme of Shakespeare's greatest tragedies are dominated by a primordial violence. Human relationships are often psychologically, if not physically, violent. We have only to recall Lear and his daughters; Hamlet and his mother, Ophelia, and almost everyone in his world; Macbeth and his countless victims; and finally, the Moor and Desdemona. In the amorous poetry of the Baroque, the relation between lovers is likewise often expressed in violent terms. Indeed, a kind of animosity between lovers frequently characterizes tone, imagery, theme, and action.

We find, however, that the Baroque differs from preceding literary periods not so much in the incidence of thematic and imagistic violence, but rather in its overwhelming preponderance. Donne and Quevedo, as poets of amorous violence, and at times of amorous murder, echo the ancient cry of lovers hopelessly defeated by their beloveds or by Love itself. Violence in amorous relationships is indeed a well-worn poetic *topos*, which includes the notion of the embattled lover, the beloved triumphant in the war of love, and the beloved-assassin's murder of the lover. Petrarch himself was an articulate heir to many of these images inherent in the courtly love experience. He expressed numerous, often contradictory, reactions to the beloved's violent attitude. We encounter in *Rime* No. 172, for instance, a submissiveness and dedication to Love, despite the lover's ceaseless destruction by the beloved:

Né, però che con atti acerbi e rei
Del mio ben pianga e del mio pianger rida,

Poría cangiar sol un de' pensier mei.

Non, perché mille volte il dí m'ancida,
Fia ch'io non l'ami, e ch'i' non speri in lei;
Che s'ella mi spaventa, Amor m'affida.

In contrast, in *Rime* No. 256 Petrarch expresses an alienation from
the hostile beloved who has violently provoked his vengeance. In
her every action she slays him, and hour by hour she consumes his
weary soul:

Far potess'io vendetta di colei
Che guardando, e parlando, mi distrugge,
E per piú doglia poi s'asconde e fugge,
Celando li occhi, a me sí dolci e rei.

Cosí li afflitti e stanchi spirti mei
A poco a poco consumando sugge;
E 'n sul cor, quasi fiero leon, rugge
La notte allor quand'io posar devrei.

This same beloved-as-murderer motif, so much a part of the
amour courtois–Petrarchan tradition, acquires an articulation in the
Baroque which reflects an underlying urgency and desperation.
The prevailing preoccupation with death resulted in a new profundity of inherited motifs, in a more somber, sinister, and awesome
expression than in preceding literary periods. Thus the change
from the Renaissance to the Baroque world view was often due to a
slight shift in perspective, to a sharpening of existent emotional
and intellectual perceptions, or to the sharp confrontation of Renaissance values with the insurgent metaphysical preoccupations
of the Baroque. Hence we find that through the inherited motif of
the beloved-assassin, the metaphorical expression of death at the
hands of the beloved or of Love itself acquired a morbid specificity
and a metaphysical intensity suggested in the poetry of previous
periods yet never before explored with the intensity and profundity
so typical of Baroque writers.

Donne and Quevedo portrayed their ladies as purveyors of
death, a metaphorical death that acquired actuality in its specificity,
in its morbidity, and in the lover's profound desperation. This motif

is perhaps the most common manifestation of the growing predilection for violence as a valid expression of human relationships. The contemporaries of Donne and Quevedo likewise articulated their psychological interest in a potentially explosive relationship between lovers, a relationship which, in fact, paralleled the increasingly tense relationship between man and his physical environment, between man and his universe, between man's consciousness and his tragic destiny. The outlet for such pent-up emotions and existential despair was often the dramatization of violence and of murder itself, be it actual as in the drama or metaphorical as in the lyric. In the Baroque lyric, the metaphorical death of the lover acquired a compelling authenticity never before seen in the amorous lyric of Western Europe.

The loss of artistic proportion and harmony, of stylistic balance, of visual symmetry or metrical regularity in the painting and literature of the Baroque are esthetic parallels of the political, economic, and religious disorder of the age. Similarly, this stylistic distortion mirrors the thematic violence dominant in the drama, prose, and lyric of the period. Extreme sensitivity to the violent upheavals in the institutions and attitudes of their times is often reflected in the seriousness with which Baroque poets articulated inherited themes of violence in intimate amorous relationships and in the excesses and distortions which they imposed on traditional forms and images.

The violent confrontation between intellect and emotion, a psychological phenomenon particularly pertinent to the Baroque, is another manifestation of the disorder and tumultuous nature of their age. In the Middle Ages, for instance, the intellectual recognition of finality was accompanied by the emotional acceptance of, or resignation to, mortality. In the glorious Renaissance luminosity of confidence and clarity, both the intellectual and emotional confrontations with death faded into thematic and imagistic insignificance. As the Renaissance assuredness receded, however, both the intellectual and emotional confrontation with temporality and mortality resurged with increased vigor, and it is the equal strength of both that created the emergent violence and distortion in Baroque literary themes, tone, and style.

The theme that competes most successfully with the theme of death for prominence in Baroque literature is the illusion-reality antithesis. The darkness that prevails in so many Baroque paintings, making indistinguishable the precise point in which background becomes foreground, in which the subject merges into his surroundings, has its literary counterpart. It is in the literature of the Baroque, more than any other period, that one of the dominant features is a twilight atmosphere which exaggerates man's fundamental inability to actually distinguish between reality and the world of illusion, fantasy, and dreams.

Shakespeare's tragedies again come to mind as we observe Hamlet's great metaphysical dilemma regarding the relative value of being and non-being or Othello's tragic uncertainty as to Desdemona's guilt or innocence. Truth is most elusive in the Baroque, and few are the protagonists who remain unscathed in their encounter with reality, following their numerous deceptions by life's prevailing illusions. Don Quijote, the protagonist most deceived in Baroque literature, or in any other literary period for that matter, succumbs and dies upon his encounter with reality. This tragic clash between illusion and reality, as observed at the end of the *Quijote*, is nevertheless a rare phenomenon. More frequent instead are the countless experiences in which doubt prevails. Such experiences constitute the bulk of *Don Quijote* or *La vida es sueño* and the major portion of *Hamlet*, *Othello*, or *King Lear*, in which the protagonist is incapable of distinguishing between illusion and reality.

This theme, of all themes, is certainly not unique to the Baroque, or to any other literary period. As we noted earlier, it is the essence of both comedy and tragedy. This dual nature of the illusion-reality antithesis was never more brilliantly manifested, however, than in the greatest novel of the Baroque, *Don Quijote*. Here again, we note the particular Baroque capacity of simultaneously expressing divergent, yet equally valid, aspects of reality, of maintaining disparate attitudes in a constant and unresolvable tension. The ineffable mystery and majesty of Cervantes' novel arise from this comic-tragic duality. The Knight of the Sad Countenance, who simultaneously elicits our tears and our laughter, represents, as no other protagonist does, the Baroque genius for perceiving and expressing the fundamental confusion between reality and illusion. This same inability to distinguish between the phenomena of the worlds of fantasy and reality characterizes a good portion of the Baroque lyric as well. Indeed, this basic imperceptibility is a significant thematic ingredient of the Baroque drama, prose, and lyric.

Thus the motif of the beloved-as-murderer, like the theme of the imperceptibility between illusion and reality, acquires in the literature of the Baroque a unique poignancy, an unprecedented profundity, and an unparalleled expressive power. The poetry of Donne and Quevedo provides numerous examples of both themes, so much a part of the Baroque *Weltanschauung*. The physical or metaphorical death of lovers, or of love itself, for instance, often acquires a far more skeptical and cynical tone in Donne's poetry than we have seen thus far. Similarly, although his now familiar lamentations of unrequited love virtually define Quevedo's *Poema a Lisi*, he is far better known for his satirical poetry.

In his presentation of the eventual destruction of love itself, Quevedo expresses existential mutability through Lisi's elusiveness. In Poem 463, entitled "Recuerdo que de la felicidad perdida atormenta," he presents a form of death in life—the loss of love, which proves to be as painful as death itself. He realizes that the loss of love is simply a prelude to the ultimate and inevitable loss of all through death.

Mutability and solitude are the corollary themes which appear in this exploration of the relationship between love and death. Throughout his poetry and prose, Quevedo articulates powerfully and effectively the absoluteness of man's metaphysical isolation. As in previous sonnets, he presents in a most penetrating, poignant, and haunting manner the utter loneliness the sensitive individual feels as he contemplates his solitary existence and inevitable death. Like Renaissance poets before him, he finds himself in an ideal pastoral setting:

> *Aquí, donde su curso, retorciendo,*
> *de parlero cristal, Henares santo,*
> *en la esmeralda de su verde manto*
> *ya engastándose va, y ya escondiendo.*

Echoing Góngora and the *culteranistas*, Quevedo employs the polished and cultivated terms *cristal* and *esmeralda* to evoke the idyllic qualities of the river and the countryside. In the second quatrain, however, this idealized setting will only emphasize his awareness of his own misery, and in the final tercet the loveliness of this pastoral setting will intensify the bitterness of its loss.

Quevedo continues:

> sentí, molesta soledad viviendo,
> de engañosa sirena docto canto,
> que, blanda y lisonjera, pudo tanto,
> que lo que lloro yo, lo está riendo.

The word *soledad* occurs but once, its solitary uniqueness thereby enhancing its meaning and lending greater effectiveness to the sonnet's message. The laughter of the *engañosa sirena*, contrasting cruelly with his tears, stresses his solitude and sorrow caused by an unresponsive lady.

> Luego mi lira y voz al monte hueco
> tu nombre, Lisi esquiva, le enseñaron,
> y fue piadoso en repetirle el eco.

The only sound that accompanies him in his isolated sorrow is the echo of his own voice beseeching his absent beloved. Its haunting sadness contrasts with the sweet, illusory quality of the siren he had found so alien to his sorrow. His love for Lisi, valuable to him in and of itself, nevertheless evokes the bittersweet quality of these first three stanzas. Despite Lisi's elusiveness, his only conceivable solace is the sound of her name echoed back to him by the merciful mountains.

The irrevocable loss of this small happiness provokes his despair in the final stanza:

> Ya todos estos bienes se pasaron
> y a mis labios dejaron sólo en trueco
> un "¡Ay, que fueron!" "¡Ay, que se acabaron!"

Despair caused by the invincible forces of mutability has replaced the sorrow caused by Lisi's evasiveness. Abandoned and desolate,

Quevedo laments that all his former joys have fled, leaving behind only the anguished echo of his cry of loss, "¡Ay, que fueron!" "¡Ay, que se acabaron!" The irretrievable loss of love, the undeniable finality of life's joys, and the individual's utter solitude before the caprices of time and mutability are the themes interacting in this sonnet. Love and all its manifestations are subject to mutability and death. Bereft even of his former bittersweet laments, Quevedo woefully realizes that they will never return.

This sonnet bears a strong resemblance in theme and a significant contrast in tone and resolution to the Renaissance sonnets and eclogues of Garcilaso. Once again, "Égloga III" provides a particularly interesting parallel because Garcilaso submerged his loss in myth, in a profound resignation to nature's mysteries, and in the esthetic distance of his presentation. In contrast, the first-person immediacy of Quevedo's sonnet lends a desperate urgency to his lament. Unlike the prevailing harmony of Garcilaso's Renaissance works, a frank lack of serenity or restraint characterizes this typically Baroque sonnet. Representative of the Baroque sonnet in theme and in mood, it reflects the period's haunting emotional and intellectual recognition of loss.

The tone, plaintive and sorrowful, reflects the theme of the death of love itself. The similarity of theme and the stark contrast of tone with Donne's "The Will" is of interest. In "The Will," another of Donne's self-dramatizations in which he anticipates his own death, but nevertheless desires the retention of some kind of contact with the world, he requests, "Before I sigh my last gaspe, let me breath, / Great love, some Legacies."

Like Quevedo's satirical poems, his *Sueños* and *Buscón*, "The Will" is primarily a vehicle for satirizing the abuses of many professions and trades of the day. The first five stanzas present this satire, and only in the final stanza do we see that an unhappy experience in love motivates the poem. Donne declares:

> *Therefore I'll give no more; But I'll undoe*
> *The world by dying; because love dies too.*
> *Then all your beauties will bee no more worth*
> *Then gold in Mines, where none doth draw it forth;*

> *And all your graces no more use shall have*
> *Then a Sun dyall in a grave.*
> *Thou Love taughtst mee, by making mee*
> *Love her, who doth neglect both mee and thee,*
> *To'invent, and practise this one way, to'annihilate all three.*

In his previous sonnet, Quevedo spoke with an awareness that mutability and death had overcome him, thereby destroying his past love. This submission to death and its accomplices contrasts with the sonnets in which he asserts that his love will triumphantly reign in death. In the previous sonnet, however, he mourned the virtual death of love. In contrast to Quevedo's lamentation, Donne here boasts that he will die himself in order to kill love and his beloved. His belligerence and aggressiveness are the antitheses of Quevedo's passivity and helplessness.

The tone of "The Will" is cynical and vengeful, whereas the tone of Quevedo's sonnet is melancholic and nostalgic. *Despite* Lisi's unresponsiveness, Quevedo mourns the loss of the days when his love was alive. *Because of* the beloved who "neglects" him and love itself, Donne threatens to "undoe / The world by dying," for in so doing "love dies too." He will, through his own death, "Annihilate" love and the beloved. Donne actively seeks the destruction of "all three," including himself, whereas Quevedo submissively laments, "¡Ay, que fueron!" "¡Ay, que se acabaron!"

Death will come to the beloved, declares Donne, through his death and her consequent loss of his love for her. Her beauty and charm will no longer elicit his love, which has died, and, consequently, death's darkness will condemn them. Her beauty will be buried in a "mine" and her graces in a "grave." The visual impact of a sundial in a grave, where there is neither light nor time, is haunting and paradoxical. The intensity of its visual impression corresponds to the intensity of the aural impact that Quevedo's sonnet achieves as the word *eco*, in conjunction with *hueco* and *trueco*, resounds against the plaintive cry, "¡Ay, que fueron!" "Ay, que se acabaron!" Through his artistic sensitivity to death's severity, each poet creates the impression of utter desolation. In neither poem is there either a hint at, or an expressed hope for, an abiding, eternal love. The mood of both is distinctly nihilistic, in sharp contrast with the highly optimistic mood of preceding Renaissance poetry. Despite the contrast between the tone of the lovers, the visual or aural manifestations of solitude intensify the final impression of nothingness.

Quevedo's plaintive tone, although clearly absent from "The Will," does appear in other poems in the *Songs and Sonnets*. "Twicknam Garden," for example, reflects the passive, lamenting quality observed in so many of Quevedo's sonnets. After three stanzas of describing his bitter torments and tears, Donne cries out:

> *O perverse sexe, where none is true but shee,*
> *Who's therefore true, because her truth kills mee.*

The beloved's *constancy* ironically denies him love. In "Twicknam Garden," that same inimical constancy which Donne found so unbearable in "The Blossome" kills the lover, whereas in "The Will," he is the one who acts, resolving to kill himself, the beloved, and love itself.

In "The Will," Donne asserts that "Love" taught him the way "to'annihilate all three." The active role he attributes to love, and its direct association with death and murder, characterize another poem by Donne, entitled "Loves Exchange," in which he chides love for its rough, unjust treatment of him:

> *Love, any devill else but you,*
> *Would for a given Soule give something too.*

Having given his soul to love, he now feels himself cheated in the outcome, for he has received nothing in return.

In the third stanza, he reveals the torment love causes him:

> *Give mee thy weaknesse, make mee blinde,*
> *Both wayes, as thou and thine, in eies and minde:*
> *Love, let me never know that this*
> *Is love, or, that love childish is.*
> *Let me not know that others know*
> *That she knows my paine, least that so*
> *A tender shame make me mine owne new woe.*

He ironically pleads for ignorance in a world in which nescience already defines the human condition. He actively seeks life's deceptions and its constant confusion between appearance and reality. In his continued derision of love, he ironically seeks love's "weaknesse" and blindness, the negative attributes typical of the lover in Quevedo's dolorous sonnets.

Quevedo's Poem 475, entitled "Amante desesperado del premio y obstinado en amar," like "Loves Exchange" presents an individual denied love's requital. He describes his condition as one of blindness and nescience. The mood of uncertainty pervading Quevedo's love sonnets is also clearly evident here. The impossibility of ever distinguishing truth from illusion defines the lover's inherent limitations:

> ¡Qué perezosos pies, qué entretenidos
> pasos lleva la muerte por mis daños!
> El camino me alargan los engaños
> y en mí se escandalizan los perdidos.

Death, which appears in "Loves Exchange" only in the final stanza, establishes itself here as the central theme in the first stanza. Quevedo complains that death is cruel in its lazy journey towards him. The phrases *perezosos pies*, 'lazy feet,' and *entretenidos pasos*, 'entertained footsteps,' introduce the notion of movement through space. Time is also an important consideration, for death's unhurried, lazy, and entertained movement through time and space tortures him. Death's leisurely approach contrasts with the bullet-like rapidity of the lover's envisioned death in "The Dissolution."

In this sonnet, movement through space is expressed through the metaphor of *El camino*. The deceptions and losses that surround him unhappily lengthen the road of life on which he journeys:

> Mis ojos no se dan por entendidos;
> y por descaminar mis desengaños,
> me disimulan la verdad los años
> y les guardan el sueño a los sentidos.

Paralleling Donne's plea in "Loves Exchange" for love to "make mee blinde . . . in eies and minde," Quevedo recognizes that darkness and ignorance already unavoidably limit his existence. He finds himself in a world in which his eyes, like his other senses, no longer function. The years deceive him and truth is unattainable, for time's passage, which should proclaim death's advent, dissimulates it instead. Time, then, is not merely the vehicle of death; it also deludes man into ignoring its relevance. Quevedo's adjectives of silence often modify time and its passage in his emphasis on the effectiveness of its delusive powers. Death, however, remains inevitable, despite the powerful illusions that would deny him the truth.

In this sonnet Quevedo has not as yet revealed the significance of love, whereas in "Loves Exchange" Donne addresses "love" throughout. Conversely, he introduces death only in the final stanza of "Loves Exchange," while it permeates Quevedo's sonnet from the very first line. Each poet emphasizes a different aspect of the love-death antithesis, firmly establishing the interrelationship between death, love, and life.

In his third stanza, Quevedo succinctly and poignantly expresses this correlation:

> *Del vientre a la prisión vine en naciendo;*
> *de la prisión iré al sepulcro amando,*
> *y siempre en el sepulcro estaré ardiendo.*

For Quevedo the world is a prison which he must endure in his journey from the womb to the grave. The immutable essence of love will nevertheless rule his being in life and in death, for this eternal quality will always inflame him. His transcendental optimism thus transforms the anthropological pessimism of the first two quatrains.

The final tercet nevertheless undercuts a bit the idyllic quality of this one by returning to the subject of his distress in this world. As in "Loves Exchange," the sorrows of unrequited love cause that distress. Donne's poem, however, allows no idyllic declarations concerning the immortality of the lover's passion. The cynicism characterizing the final stanza of Donne's poem will provide a striking contrast to the optimism of this tercet.

After describing life in this world as dark and illusory in the first two stanzas and as a prison in this third stanza, Quevedo equates it with death in the final stanza. Death, whose spirit has pervaded the entire sonnet, ultimately appears in terms of the familiar death-in-life paradox:

> *Cuantos plazos la muerte me va dando,*
> *prolijidades son, que va creciendo,*
> *porque no acabe de morir penando.*

He complains once again of death's slow movement toward him, recognizing that its postponements are actually death's own tedious prolongation of itself. Death, actual physical death, is love's accomplice in this sonnet. Unrequited love immerses the lover in ceaseless pain and living death, while physical death, his only release from this suffering, delays its arrival and his rescue.

Lovers such as Quevedo, his predecessor Petrarch, and even Donne at times find their release from love's pains in a kind of hopeful anxiety. While they await the true release of either death or requital, they often remain in a state of ecstatic suffering. Petrarch's *Rime* No. 130 provides a significant precedent to this sonnet:

> *Poi che 'l camin m'è chiuso di mercede,*
> *Per desperata via son dilungato*
> *Da gli occhi ov'era (i' non so per qual fato)*
> *Riposto il guidardon d'ogni mia fede.*
>
> *Pasco 'l cor di sospir, ch'altro non chiede,*
> *E di lagrime vivo, a pianger nato:*
> *Né di ciò duolmi, perché in tale stato*
> *È dolci il pianto piú ch'altri non crede.*

Petrarch here articulates with disarming honesty the joy of suffering in love, the excitement of amorous anticipation. The way of mercy being denied to Petrarch and the arrival of death being denied to Quevedo, both are ironically thrust into the same situation, Petrarch reacting in the typically *amour courtois* fashion while his Baroque successor is overwhelmed by death's ominous presence.

In "Loves Exchange," death again prevails as a weapon even more obviously controlled by "Love." In this poem, love itself can kill the lover. The dichotomy between actual and metaphorical death creates the tension in this poem. In the final stanza, Donne eventually gives this accepted quality an unexpected and shocking twist. He asserted earlier that in "loves warfare" he had, like a "small towne" stood "stiffe" and made "Love" reveal its true "face." In the final stanza, then, the interrelationship between love and death is clear:

> For this, Love is enrag'd with mee,
> Yet kills not. If I must example bee
>   To future Rebells; If th'unborne
> Must learne, by my being cut up, and torne:
>   Kill, and dissect me, Love; for this
>   Torture against thine owne end is,
> Rack't carcasses make ill Anatomies.

The stark specificity of Donne's poem differs significantly from Quevedo's use of general terms to describe his misery. Words such as *daños*, *perdidos*, *engaños*, and *penando* contrast with Donne's directness and bluntness; words such as "cut up," "torne," "Kill," "dissect," and "carcasses" create a more bitter tone than Quevedo's innocuous terms of despair. The situation is nevertheless the same, for love's powers and the pains of unrequited love utterly overwhelm both lovers who submit to death.

The analogy ends here, however, for Quevedo pleads for physical *death* to release him from the pains of a living death caused by love. Donne, on the other hand, dares *love* to destroy him through physical death. He dwells on the gory details of physical death, leaving no room for doubt that love's powers extend beyond the metaphorical realm of death. In Quevedo's sonnet, physical death is a means of escaping love's living death, while in Donne's poem love also controls physical death itself.

The contrast between the ultimate end of each lover is striking indeed. Whereas Quevedo's love will be eternal and immutable, remaining aflame even in the tomb, love will murder Donne, leaving behind his "Rack't carcasse." He asserts that this should not be the "example" love gives its "future Rebells." As in "The Canonization" and "The Relique," we see Donne's interest in the effect his own love might have on future generations. His immortality will likewise depend on the memory of future generations. In contrast, and as in previous sonnets, Quevedo is assured of his love's immortality within the tomb itself, independent of the mutable world of the living.

The themes of unhappiness in love, the powers wielded by the beloved over the lover, and the consequent consideration of metaphorical and physical death, combined with the use of the concept of murder to further the poet's purposes, appear in other poems by Donne and Quevedo. "The Dampe," for instance, addresses the beloved, as does Quevedo's Poem 366, a "Soneto amoroso," one of Quevedo's many love sonnets addressed to women other than Lisi. In both poems, the lover accuses the beloved of murdering him either in a dream, as in Quevedo's sonnet, or at some hypothetical time in the future, as in Donne's poem.

"The Dampe" begins with Donne's insistent obsession with the future that will follow his eventual death:

> When I am dead, and Doctors know not why,
>   And my friends curiositie
> Will have me cut up to survay each part,
> When they shall finde your Picture in my heart,
>   You thinke a sodaine dampe of love
>   Will thorough all their senses move,
> And worke on them as mee, and so preferre
> Your murder, to the name of Massacre.

This first stanza strongly resembles the final stanza of "Loves Exchange" as he envisions his "cut up" body. This interest in anatomy, dissection, and exploration pervades Donne's work, as seen, for instance, in "The Legacie" ("When I had ripp'd me,' and search'd where hearts did lye") and in *The first Anniversary*, subtitled "An Anatomie of the World." Donne's interest in physiology is indeed, as Joan Bennett has observed,

the counterpart of his delight in the life of the senses. He is as medieval in his insistence on the grave and the narrow margin that divides the skeleton from the living face, as he is in his scholastic delight in the processes of reasoning. . . . Realistic and familiar treatment of the physical facts of death is not peculiar to Donne; it is the mark of his age, it stamps the pages of Webster, of Burton, of Jeremy Taylor no less than Donne's own. . . . The more the life of the senses is valued, the more terrible and insistent the fact of its transience becomes and also the physical incidence of death. One may thrust these down into the unconscious, but this was never Donne's way nor the way of his contemporaries. With him as with them a full rich physical life brought into prominence the fact of mortality, in a way which is perhaps less morbid than its opposite, the 'hush! hush!' attitude to disease and death.[1]

We could further elaborate on Ms. Bennett's observations by noting that this "full rich physical life" was a significant holdover of the Renaissance attitude toward earthly existence. Indeed, the frank openness towards death in the Baroque, which reveals a morbidity, indeed a pathological excessiveness, is also a paradoxical result of Renaissance exuberance and passionate love of life.

The aggressive approach toward death in the Baroque parallels the often belligerent attitude toward love itself. The lover's aggressive attitude toward the beloved in this poem is similar to the attitude toward Love itself in "Loves Exchange." The woman addressed is the disdainful, heartless kind that would murder the lover with her cruelty. In contrast to "The Relique" and "The Canonization," she and Donne do not enjoy a mutual love that would ultimately overcome death itself and perhaps become the object of devotion in future times. Quevedo's idealization of love in sonnets such as "Amor constante más allá de la muerte" also reflects an attitude toward the beloved and love itself that contrasts with Poem 366.

In Poem 366, as in "The Dampe," Quevedo deals with his relationship to the beloved and her powers to murder him:

> Soñé que el brazo de rigor armado,
> Filis, alzabas contra el alma mía,
> diciendo: "Éste será el postrero día
> que ponga fin a tu vivir cansado."

Quevedo's concern with the soul in this sonnet counters Donne's obsession with the body at death in "The Dampe." Donne hypothesizes that the curiosity of his friends will motivate the dissection of his corpse; Quevedo tells Filis that he dreamed that she had "raised the hand of armed might" against his soul. Both situations take place in the lovers' minds, and neither poem relates actual fact. Donne *imagines* that it will be his beloved who ultimately kills him while Quevedo *dreams* that Filis puts an end to his tired life.

The majority of the poems discussed heretofore have concerned death and love, but the active role of the beloved was not very important. The lovers suffered actual or metaphorical death because of their beloveds' disdain or because of their absence; or death's arrival was simply a natural event providing the proper perspective for the lovers' thoughts regarding love. In this sonnet and in "The Dampe," however, both poets envision the beloved herself, not the rigors of love or Love personified, as a murderess. Quevedo equals the visual impact of the beloved's "Picture" in Donne's "heart" through the supernatural quality he attributes to the beloved, who can kill him by merely raising her arm.

Echoing Donne's phrases "Your murder" and "your conquest," Quevedo in the second stanza envisions the actual death blow with which the beloved kills him:

> *Y que luego, con golpe acelerado,*
> *me dabas muerte en sombra de alegría,*
> *y yo, triste, al infierno me partía,*
> *viéndome ya del cielo desterrado.*

With one swift blow, the beloved kills him in a "shadow of happiness." Finding himself banished from her heaven, he sadly departs for hell. Quevedo's reliance on certain antitheses is obvious. In the tercets, the more pervasive antithesis of appearance and reality will follow this tension between heaven and hell, between sadness and happiness. The duality characterizing "The Dampe" also emerges in the final stanzas, as Quevedo explores the male-female antithesis.

In the first tercet, he establishes the relationship between appearance and reality, as he awakens to learn that the seeming reality of his agony was only a dream:

> *Partí sin ver el rostro amado y bello;*
> *mas despertóme deste sueño un llanto,*
> *ronca la voz, y crespo mi cabello.*

His voice hoarse and his hair curled from fright, the anguish of his own weeping awakens him. This stanza, then, portrays the effect of the dream world on the lover's waking reality. There is ultimately no fixed barrier to prevent dreams or illusions from invading and affecting reality because of the "Baroque conviction that the phenomenal world is illusion."[2]

Most frightening for Quevedo is his realization that what had so powerfully overwhelmed his spirit and caused him so much torment was partially a dream:

> Y lo que más en esto me dio espanto
> es ver que fuese sueño algo de aquello
> que me pudiera dar tormento tanto.

The quality of reality which dreams so often acquire has produced actual physical changes in him. His weeping, hoarse voice, and curled hair provide tangible evidence that appearances and dreams can and do affect reality. Such a melding of the world of appearances and the world of reality ultimately results in the troubled realization that these two realms are often indistinguishable one from the other. Quevedo endures his greatest *espanto*, his most powerful fear, because of this fundamental recognition.

The intrusion of dreams into waking reality also has its counterpart, for the reality of the beloved's disdain initially motivated his nightmare. Quevedo recognizes this when he affirms that it was "sueño algo de aquello / que me pudiera dar tormento tanto." The cause of his terror, he asserts, was only partly his dream. The beloved may not be as powerful as he dreamed, but she still has the power to intrude her reality into his dream world. The tension between his *imagined* or *dreamed* power of the beloved to kill and her *actual* power constitutes the final pair of contrasts that define this sonnet.

In "The Dampe," Donne is likewise concerned with the nature of the beloved's powers over his life and well being. In the final two stanzas, he establishes the contrast between the strength of the beloved, who is "armed" with the weapons of "*Disdaine*" and "*Honor*," and her power when she is bereft of these forces. In her natural "Naked" state, the lady's power over him is as great as is the lady's in Quevedo's sonnet before his dreams intensify her disdain. The beloved's strength increases in "The Dampe" through the accouterments of *"Disdaine"* and *"Honor"* and in Quevedo's sonnet through the lover's own frenzied visions.

In the second stanza of "The Dampe," Donne employs the conventional image of love as warfare, as he challenges the beloved to create a semblance of equality between opponents by putting down her weapons of conquest:

> *Poore victories! But if you dare be brave,*
> *And pleasure in your conquest have,*
> *First kill th'enormous Gyant, your* Disdaine,
> *And let th'enchantresse* Honor, *next be slaine,*
> *And like a Goth and Vandall rize,*
> *Deface Records, and Histories*
> *Of your owne arts and triumphs over men,*
> *And without such advantage kill me then.*

Just as Quevedo's awakening to reality ultimately countered his dream, so too is the lady's hypothetical murder of Donne countered by a return to the present and to the reality of his relationship with the beloved. After his own individual foray into the unknown, each poet returns to the tangible present. While Quevedo is astonished by the power that dreams wield on waking reality, Donne demands the alteration of the reality that besets him. He challenges the beloved first to strip herself of her "arts" and "advantage" and only then attempt his murder.

The final stanza of "The Dampe" presents Donne's capacity for interjecting sexual connotations into whatever subject he may be exploring. He furthers the tension between himself and the beloved through the contrast of his own "Gyants" with those of the beloved mentioned in the previous stanza:

> *For I could muster up as well as you*
> *My Gyants, and my Witches too,*
> *Which are vast* Constancy, *and* Secretnesse,
> *But these I neyther looke for, nor professe;*
> *Kill mee as Woman, let mee die*

> As a meere man; doe you but try
> Your passive valor, and you shall finde than,
> Naked you'have odds enough of any man.

His "Gyants" and "Witches," which are his Petrarchan "*Constancy*" and "*Secretnesse*," will not take part in the contest, just as he admonishes her not to use her "*Disdaine*" and "*Honor*" against him. The struggle will be between the individuals as unarmed representatives of their sex. In such a match, the beloved need not actively perform, for her "passive valor" can alone destroy him. Donne then reinforces the contrast between the beloved's active courage, described in the first stanza, and her passive valor, disarmed in the second stanza.

In this final stanza, Donne argues that any active effort to destroy him is unnecessary when her "Naked," "passive valor" can easily do so. He twists the argument in the very last line of this poem through the word "Naked," reinforcing the possible sexual interpretations of the words "die" and "Kill." Woman, in her unadorned state, affirms Donne, can easily conquer "meere man." He thereby wittily divests the beloved and himself of any emotional obstacles that might prevent the sexual union for which he argues in these final lines.

We find that "The Dampe" compares significantly with Petrarch's *Rime* No. 256, which could have easily served as the model from which Donne forged out in his own revolutionary direction:

> Far potess'io vendetta di colei
> Che guardando, e parlando, mi distrugge,
> E per più dogli poi s'asconde e fugge,
> Celando li occhi, a me sí dolci e rei.
>
> Cosí li afflitti e stanchi spiriti mei
> A poco a poco consumando sugge;
> E 'n sul cor, quasi fiero leon, rugge
> La notte allor quand'io posar devrei.
>
> L'alma, cui Morte del suo albergo caccia,
> Da me si parte; e di tal nodo sciolta,
> Vassene pur a lei che la minaccia.

> *Meravigliomi ben, s'alcuna volta,*
> *Mentre le parla, e piange, e poi l'abbraccia,*
> *Non rompe il sonno suo, s'ella l'ascolta.*

The aggressive, vengeful attitude shared by Donne and Petrarch dominates their respective poems. Similarly, both ladies treat their lovers with consummate disdain. What distinguishes "The Dampe" from Petrarch's sonnet is Donne's frank dramatic monologue addressed toward a beloved whose presence contrasts significantly with Laura's cruel absence. Whereas Donne speaks *to* his beloved, Petrarch can only speak *of* his beloved, who sleeps peacefully, unaware of his violent anguish. Donne, in contrast, lies in bed with his lady, and as the final lines of "The Dampe" reveal, his love contrasts with the spiritual idealizations of Platonic love. We also observe Petrarch's frank divergence from Platonic ideals, however, for his love plaints, like those of Quevedo, although discreet and circumspect, are clearly not those of the lover whose love is purely spiritual and seeks no physical recompense whatsoever.

The numerous sexual connotations or explicit references to physical love in Donne's poetry contrast with the muted *amour courtois* of the *Canzoniere* and *Poema a Lisi*. For a clear reference to sexual love in Quevedo's poetry, as an expression of his frank anti-Petrarchism, we must look beyond *Poema a Lisi*. Poem 337, addressed to Floralba, is clearly sexually oriented. The interrelationship between life and death is an important consideration also, as is the correlation between dreams and reality.

In this sonnet, as in many of Donne's witty poems, Warnke's observation regarding the playfulness of Baroque love poetry is significant. He notes that this playfulness

> shows itself in four distinct but related features: the imposition of a double view, through which the speaker simultaneously voices his personal passion and distances himself from it in a half-amused way; the formulation of the speaker's relation to the beloved in quasi-dramatic terms; the use of comic hyperbole; and the practice of insulting or showing aggression toward the beloved, with the consequent creation of a kind of amorous agon, or erotic flyting.[3]

Quevedo employs the dramatic monologue that Donne often uses for humorous purposes:

> *¡Ay, Floralba! Soñé que te . . . ¿Dirélo?*
> *Sí, pues que sueño fue: que te gozaba.*
> *¿Y quién, sino un amante que soñaba,*
> *juntara tanto infierno a tanto cielo?*

After debating whether or not to divulge the content of his dream, he decides that he can do so because it was merely a dream. The frank provocativeness of a dream in which he sexually enjoys Floralba echoes Donne in his most erotic of moods.

As in his previous sonnet, Quevedo's use of the dream-reality antithesis reveals the effect that the world of illusion, appearances, and dreams may have on reality. For the Baroque artist, the material world was often only a world of illusion, its tangibility disintegrating the instant one tried to penetrate its inner core, much as a dream vanishes upon waking. In Baroque literature, reality is often indistinguishable from dreams and from the illusions that constantly shroud it.

Instead of dreaming that he is murdered by the beloved, Quevedo dreams that he delights in the physical ecstasy of his own passion's consummation. In his use of the explicitly coarse verb *gozar*, he denies any possibility of spiritual connotations. In contrast to the mutuality of physical passion reflected in "The Canonization" or "The Extasie," he only physically possesses or "enjoys" Floralba. There is no specific indication that Floralba reciprocates his passion. Even in dreams, Quevedo cannot clearly establish a relationship of mutual affection with the beloved. He alludes to this harsh reality in the last two lines of the first stanza by rhetorically questioning, "Who but a lover would dream of the union of so much hell with so much heaven?" The dualities of heaven and hell, observed in Quevedo's previous sonnet, once again appear as the first in a series of antitheses that characterize this sonnet.

Echoing the traditional antitheses of fire and snow, he continues describing his dream's paradoxes:

> *Mis llamas con tu nieve y con tu yelo,*
> *cual suele opuestas flechas de su aljaba,*
> *mezclaba Amor, y honesto las mezclaba,*
> *como mi adoración en su desvelo.*

The mixture of contraries and their interrelationships creates the unresolvable tension that defines this sonnet. Love's antitheses, his passion's fire and her disdain's coldness, unite in his dream just as love has often united his adoration and consequent anxiety.

Finding himself in possession of the unattainable, Quevedo recalls that he objectively stood off from his dream to analyze his happy situation:

> Y dije: "Quiera Amor, quiera mi suerte,
> que nunca duerma yo, si estoy despierto,
> y que si duermo, que jamás despierte."

The probability of his dream being reality is of little concern to him. He prefers neither reality nor the illusion of his dream, desiring only the continuation of whatever state he may be in. If this great conquest is only a dream, may he continue dreaming and never awaken. If it is in truth reality, may he never sleep. The mutually contradictory natures of sleeping and waking intensify the dramatic tension of this tercet, foreshadowing the paradox of the final tercet.

Just as sleep is often compared to death, wakefulness is comparable to life. The mutually contradictory nature of sleeping and waking established in this tercet intensifies the paradox of living with death established in the final tercet:

> Mas desperté del dulce desconcierto;
> y vi que estuve vivo con la muerte,
> y vi que con la vida estaba muerto.

He understands that the dream of absolute happiness, of complete possession of the beloved, is a *dulce desconcierto*, a 'sweet illusion.' Awakening from the dreams of appearances to the truth of reality, he expresses his new awareness in terms of sight, declaring, "And I saw that I was living with death, / and I saw that with life I was a dead man." Because of love's fervor, this sonnet is one of Quevedo's most memorable and eloquent expressions of the intensity of disillusionment, one of his most haunting declarations of the interrelatedness of life and death. The gulf which seemingly divides illusion from reality, life from death, is itself an illusion. Death and its accomplices limit, define, and ultimately terminate life. Quevedo finds himself overcome by death's powers because the illusion of requited love no longer seems to be a reality. As he awakens from the loveliness of his dream, reality's harshness signifies his death.

It is more than death, however, for it is a living death, a death he must endure in total consciousness. This living death, which so overwhelms him, lacks the one saving grace that final death possesses—the loss of consciousness, the loss of awareness. Quevedo's repetition of the verb *vi* emphasizes the visual intensity of his awareness as the veil of sleep's illusion falls from his awakening eyes. His is a most cruel disillusionment, for he is denied the blindness to reality that, like Donne in "Loves Exchange," he would have preferred. Quevedo paradoxically suffers in this sonnet because reality's clearness is thrust upon him, whereas in many other sonnets, such as Poem 475 ("Mis ojos no se dan por entendidos"), he suffers because of the darkness of the deceptions that shroud his world.

He never accuses Floralba of being his murderess, as he accused Filis in the preceding sonnet. His awakening to reality in the previous sonnet, however, was much more propitious than in this sonnet. Just as the dreams of each lover are diametrically opposed in content, so too is the reality to which they awaken. Filis' lover awakens to life, albeit in a shattered condition, whereas Floralba's lover awakens to a metaphorical, but nevertheless psychologically painful, living death.

He recognizes that he is dead to life. It holds no joys, no meaning, no happiness for one deprived of the illusion of love and, therefore, of the will to live. The contrast is clear, the tension overwhelming, and the paradox undeniable. Life and death are one and the same for the lover bereft of all hope for requited love.

In his "Image and Dream" Donne deals with this same interrelationship between illusion and reality, between man's dreams and his waking reality. Donne recognizes that the gulf between illusion and reality is all but non-existent and presents his argument in terms quite similar to Quevedo's:

> So, if I dreame I have you, I have you,
> For, all our joyes are but fantasticall.

> *And so I scape the paine, for paine is true;*
> *And sleep which locks up sense, doth lock*
> *out all.*

The joys of this life are but diverse fantasies, while its pains are a
very real constancy. The intense anguish Quevedo must endure
when he awakens to reality certainly supports Donne's assertion.
Dreams' pleasures have as much reality as the pleasures of one's
waking moments, for, awake or asleep, the "joyes" of this world
"are but fantasticall."

Donne repeats this concept later in the elegy when he affirms:

> *Alas, true joyes at best are dreame enough;*
> *Though you stay here you passe too fast away:*
> *For even at first lifes Taper is a snuffe.*

Reality's pleasure, the conquest and possession of the beloved, is
illusory like his dreams, he declares, for the beloved is as fleeting
and ephemeral as life itself. Donne's comparison of "lifes Taper" to
a mere "snuffe" metaphorically compresses infancy and old age
into a single image, a single instant. This emphasis on life's ephemeral nature dramatizes his earlier assertion that "all our joyes are
but fantasticall" and reflects the Baroque preoccupation with life's
precariousness. Due to the intensity of this vision, Donne experiences life's pleasures with a penetrating sense of desperation, for
they all savor of finality.

Donne and Quevedo thus agree that all of life's joys, be they
experienced in dreams or in waking reality, are ephemeral and
illusory. They also agree nevertheless that "paine is true" and that
the dream world of joyful illusions is a most satisfactory means of
escaping it. Donne asserts, however, that waking reality is most
cruel and unsympathetic, for "sense" can no longer "lock out all."
Quevedo would disagree with Donne in this assertion that pain
cannot enter man's dream world. As seen in the lover's dream of
his own murder in Poem 366, pain may also invade man's dreams.

Quevedo's two sonnets presenting the relationship between
dreams and reality deal with a beloved whose elusiveness and
disregard for him actually motivate his dreams. In one sonnet, he

awakens to a living death because of the reality of her disdain, while in the other, the cruel beloved condemns him to death in his dream. The beloved-as-murderer is a theme in other poems by both Donne and Quevedo, each poem differing in tone, image, and thematic resolution. The alliance between religion and the beloved who destroys the lover creates interesting metaphorical possibilities for both poets. Donne's "The Funerall," for example, recalls "The Relique" in its use of the concept of idolatry. It parallels portions of Quevedo's Poem 484, to be discussed later, but it bears the greatest resemblance to Poem 377, which is not a Lisi sonnet.

Like so many of Donne's poems, "The Funerall" begins as he hypothesizes events following his death. The title is again specifically related to death, and Donne articulates utmost concern for his corporality:

> Who ever comes to shroud me, do not harme
> 	Nor question much
> That subtile wreath of haire, which crowns mine
> 	arme;
> The mystery, the signe you must not touch,
> 	For 'tis my outward Soule,
> Viceroy to that, which then to heaven being gone,
> 	Will leave this to controule,
> And keepe these limbes, her Provinces, from dis-
> 	solution.

Donne gives the body-soul duality a bizarre twist as he explains that the wreath of hair which he wears on his arm is his "outward Soule." He intensifies the paradox of the soul's acquisition of corporal properties through his declaration that its function will be the prevention of his own bodily "dissolution." The wreath, serving as the "viceroy" to his inner soul, already gone from this world, will perform an impossible task, but one which is of utmost importance to Donne—the maintenance of his corporal integrity after death.

The second stanza presents his own rationalization regarding the power of the beloved's hair to, as he says, "make mee one of all":

> *For if the sinewie thread my braine lets fall*
> > *Through every part,*
> *Can tye those parts, and make mee one of all;*
> *These haires which upward grew, and strength and art*
> > *Have from a better braine,*
> *Can better do'it; Except she meant that I*
> > *By this should know my pain,*
> *As prisoners then are manacled, when they'are con-*
> > *demn'd to die.*

The first part of this stanza, complimentary toward the beloved and the miraculous capacities of her hair to prevent his dissolution, is followed by the quasi-syllogistic reversal, so typical of Donne, as he questions the beloved's motivations in her gift of the wreath. Instead of viewing it as a means of his protection from death's results, he sees it as an omen of his destruction by the beloved.

The final stanza reflects Quevedo's Poem 377 and portions of Poem 484, addressed to Lisi, as Donne weaves religious imagery into the dominant themes of love and death:

> *What ere shee meant by'it, bury it with me,*
> > *For since I am*
> *Loves martyr, it might breed idolatrie,*
> *If into others hands these Reliques came;*
> > *As 'twas humility*
> *To'afford to it all that a Soule can doe,*
> > *So, 'tis some bravery,*
> *That since you would save none of mee, I bury some*
> > *of you.*

He intricately intertwines the three themes of love, death, and religion, referring to himself as "Loves martyr," who dies for love as others have died for their religious beliefs.

The body-soul duality is central to the resolution. Donne counters his earlier reference to the wreath with a more mundane and macabre assertion that since the beloved contributed to his murder, he will return the favor by burying at least "some of" her. The wreath, no longer the "Viceroy" to his soul, is merely part of the

beloved's body. As in previous poems, we see a continually changing perspective of the reality Donne encounters. As in many of the
Songs and Sonnets, his mood likewise changes from optimism and
love to pessimism, doubt, and sarcasm.

The final line, in which he directly accuses the beloved of
responsibility for his death, echoes the first stanza of Quevedo's
Poem 484 to Lisi:

> Lisis, por duplicado ardiente Sirio
> miras con guerra y muerte l'alma mía;
> y en uno y otro sol abres el día,
> influyendo en la luz dulce martirio.

The tone of this sonnet, however, differs from the belligerent cynicism that eventually overwhelms "The Funerall," yet has the same
result. The lover finds himself condemned to martyrdom by the
beloved's consummate beauty, not the cruelty or disdain seen in
"The Funerall." Lisi's mere gaze causes his "sweet martyrdom."
The idyllic quality of this first quatrain contrasts significantly with
the insistent realism of Donne's first stanza, in which he considers
the shrouding of his lifeless body at death. Donne's typical realism
maintains a paradoxical tension between metaphorical death and
literal death, much more extreme than the tension that defines
Quevedo's Lisi sonnets. His gory insistence on dissection and
physical decay contrasts with Quevedo's less repulsive descriptions
of death's effects, for Quevedo in the *Poema a Lisi* does not counter
metaphorical interpretations of death with possible literal interpretations of his martyrdom.

In the final stanza of "The Funerall," Donne alludes to another
religious concept, idolatry, which also appears in Quevedo's Poem
484:

> Amo y no espero, porque adoro amando;
> ni mancha al amor puro mi deseo,
> que cortés vive y muere idolatrando.

Quevedo asserts the purity of his love, which lives and dies in the
worship of his beloved, free from the blemishes of physical desire.
The practice of idolatry here contrasts with the interpretation of

idolatry in "The Funerall." Donne employs the conceit that he is "Loves's martyr" and that, consequently, his "Reliques," his arm, and the wreath of hair, should be buried with him in order to prevent future generations from idolizing them. He foresees his own possible deification, in which others would commit idolatry in their worship of his martyrdom and his relics. Quevedo in Poem 484, on the other hand, declares that he himself is the idolater because of his worship of Lisi.

Quevedo makes the same assertion in Poem 377, which he addresses to a nameless lady:

> Aunque cualquier lugar donde estuvieras,
> templo, pues yo te adoro, le tornaras
> ídolo hermoso, en cuyas nobles aras
> no fuera justo que otra ofrenda vieras.
>
> Templo fue del señor de las esferas
> donde sentí las dos primeras jaras
> que afiló Amor en esas luces raras,
> bastantes a que más valor vencieras.

As they reinforce the connotation of an idolatrous worship, the terms *templo* and *ídolo* disclose the nature of his adoration of the beloved. In the first stanza, he deifies the beloved, whom he calls a "beautiful idol," by affirming that her presence would transform any place she might be into a "temple."

He then asserts that he first experienced the emotions of idolatrous devotion in the "temple of the lord of the spheres." The first tercet reveals his deeper involvement in idolatry:

> Volví la adoración idolatría,
> troqué por alta mar seguro puerto;
> vi en la iglesia mi muerte en tu hermosura.

Adoration of God becomes idolatry of the beloved in his exchange of the port's safety for the high seas' danger. The perilous results of such a foolhardy act would come not from God's wrath, but from the beloved's beauty. In the final line, the beloved kills him, not with her disdain or cruelty as in "The Funerall," but with her beauty, as in Poem 484.

The final stanza of Poem 377 reflects the interest in burial seen throughout "The Funerall":

que entonces a los dos nos convenía:
por retraída a ti, que me habías muerto,
y, como muerto, a mí, por sepultura.

The church is convenient for both the murdered lover and the murdering beloved. Having committed a murder, the beloved may find refuge within its walls, while he, having died, may find a burial sepulchre. Quevedo discusses his clearly metaphorical death in a mood of peaceful acceptance. The death Donne envisions, however, is a vital experience in which morose and practical details such as shrouding are important.

In contrast to the idyllic peacefulness with which Quevedo submits himself to the high seas of love and to his own destruction by the beloved, Donne ultimately discloses a cynical attitude that manifests itself in his own form of retaliation against the beloved. His reasons for desiring his burial with the wreath vary throughout the poem. Originally, he seeks to prevent his bodily dissolution; secondly, he would prevent the establishment of an idolatrous religion after his martyrdom; finally, his request for burial with the wreath is a witty attmept to retaliate against the beloved's disdain by at least burying "some of" her. Resembling the final lines of "The Will," in which he determines to "annihilate all three," Donne affirms that his will not be a solitary death.

We observe this theme of ingenious revenge in another of Donne's love poems, whose title, "The Apparition," typically alludes to an aspect of death. It is a witty variation of an idea central to Petrarch's own assertion that Laura visits him after her death. In significant contrast to the vengeful lover of "The Apparition," in *Rime* No. 342, Laura, full of pity, visits Petrarch's bed, wipes his eyes, and, in his conception, gives him all the happiness that a mortal can possibly experience in this world. Donne, in contrast, is a repulsed lover who imagines the future after the lady's disdain has murdered him:

When by thy scorne, O murdresse, I am dead,
And that thou thinkst thee free

From all solicitation from mee,
Then shall my ghost come to thy bed,
And thee, fain'd vestall, in worse armes shall see.

As in previous poems, Donne's predilection for dramatizing his own death characterizes his argument. This tendency is evident not only in his poetry but also in his sermons and other prose works. His dramatic posing in his shroud for the statue that stands in St. Paul's reflects the obsession with which he continually envisioned his eventual demise. Such dramatic tendencies reveal Donne's own personal reflection of the dramatic atmosphere in which he and Quevedo lived and wrote. As Warnke has noted,

> the Baroque is one of the few supremely great ages of drama in the history of world literature. It is the age in which, by common consent, the theatre reached its finest flowering in England, France, Spain, and Holland. . . . The drama itself, primitive and ritualistic in its origins, retains always something of the character of those origins: the ludic and agonistic elements which are its essence—roleplaying and contest—imply a conviction, no less operative for being possibly below the level of consciousness, that ultimate reality, never to be determined by the appearance of things, has the shape of the conflict of opposites.[4]

In his establishment of the dramatic conflict, Donne's bizarre and macabre look into the future creates a spectral atmosphere intended to frighten his lady. As in previous peoms, he refers to her as a "murdresse" who kills him with her "scorne." As in "The Funerall," the possibilities for a metaphorical interpretation of his death are minimized by his specificity. He envisions the return of his ghost to the bed of the woman who scorns him.

Quevedo at times struck this same threatening pose before an unyielding lady. The title of his Poem 338, "Venganza de la edad en hermosura presumida," reveals his vengeful attitude toward a lady once presumptuous because of her beauty but now scorned because of her age and contempt for the lover. The line of argument is different from the macabre dramatization of "The Apparition," but the purpose is the same—the wrathful reproach of a disdainful woman. Whereas Donne employs the spectre of his own ghost to punish his lady, Quevedo threatens his beloved with time's decay.

He employs the familiar *carpe diem* argument, but with a bitter vengeance:

> *Cuando tuvo, Floralba, tu hermosura,*
> *cuantos ojos te vieron, en cadena,*
> *con presunción, de honestidad ajena,*
> *los despreció, soberbia, tu locura.*
>
> *Persuadióte el espejo conjetura*
> *de eternidades en la edad serena,*
> *y que a su plata el oro en tu melena*
> *nunca del tiempo trocaria la usura.*

Like Donne in "The Apparition," Quevedo addresses his lady with scorn, as he disdains his own eyes for having once gazed upon her vain, presumptuous, and immodest beauty. Quevedo sardonically reverses the optics of love from the *amour courtois* tradition. This is not a Lisi sonnet, and Quevedo is therefore free to reveal the same cynicism in love that Donne often expresses in the *Songs and Sonnets*.

In the second quatrain, time is his personal accomplice in this contempt for her beauty, just as Donne's own death aids in the persecution of his scornful "murdresse." Quevedo recognizes that her mirror had once persuaded Floralba of the immutability of her reflected youth. Like the lover in Poem 475, who laments "me disimulan la verdad los años," Floralba was beguiled by her youth into believing that time would never fade and that its usury would never transform her golden hair to silver. The deceptive present effortlessly deludes the unwary into ignoring the frightening reality of time's passage and mutability. Donne's vengeance occurs in the imagined future, Quevedo's in the recollected past. Just as Donne's ghost will someday mockingly approach his lady's bed, so too have time's ravages already mocked Floralba's vanity and coldness.

Donne continues the imaginative encounter between his ghost and his murderess with obvious delight, foreseeing her dismay and fright:

> *Then thy sicke taper will begin to winke,*
> *And he, whose thou art then, being tyr'd before,*

> *Will, if thou stirre, or pinch to wake him, thinke*
> > *Thou call'st for more,*
> *And in false sleep will from thee shrinke,*
> *And then poore Aspen wretch, neglected thou*
> *Bath'd in a cold quicksilver sweat wilt lye*
> > *A veryer ghost then I.*

The bitterness of Donne's prediction also characterizes his motivation for writing the poem. Since the lady has already rebuked his entreaties, it is only fitting that his ghost visit her while she is bestowing her charms on someone more fortunate. It is also appropriate that his ghost should frighten her to death, since it was she who killed him.

He intends to maintain the lady in dread suspense by not divulging the nature of his future reprimand as he wittily transforms the traditional role of the courtly lover's secrecy:

> *What I will say, I will not tell thee now,*
> *Lest that preserve thee;'and since my love is spent,*
> *I'had rather thou shouldst painfully repent,*
> *Then by my threatenings rest still innocent.*

Now that he no longer loves her, her remorse must consist of a ceaseless apprehension of the future. This same bitter heartlessness with which Donne addresses his lady characterizes Quevedo's sonnet, as he joyfully dwells on time's cruel transformation of his lady's beauty into unattractive old age:

> *Ves que la que antes eras, sepultada*
> *yaces en la que vives; y, quejosa,*
> *tarde te acusa vanidad burlada.*
>
> *Mueres doncella, y no de virtuosa,*
> *sino de presumida y despreciada:*
> *esto eres vieja, esotro fuiste hermosa.*

With time's passage, Floralba is forced to see herself as she is: old and withered, no longer young and beautiful. She must recognize that her youth and beauty are forever entombed within her aged body. The past, like her youth, is dead. For that matter, the present is dead also, for she is nothing more than an animated corpse, virtual living death. Wounded vanity accuses her much too late of the reality of her failing youth, beauty, and life. She is dying and her youth and virginity with her; yet she dies not for virtue, but for her past presumptions and presently-endured scorn. Like Donne in "The Apparition," Quevedo stands back and calculatingly observes the lady in her unique distress.

Whereas Donne imagines that he can torment his lady through *his* own death, Quevedo torments his lady with time's passage, which strips her of her youth and beauty and draws *her* nearer to death. Both poets nevertheless seek revenge through the mental torment of their ladies, whose disdain has transformed their devotion into unmitigated hatred. Death and time's movement toward death are their most powerful instruments of vengeance.

In contrast to previous poems in which time, mutability, and death conspire against the lovers' happiness, they are here the scornful lovers' instruments of mental torture. Indeed, throughout Donne's and Quevedo's love poetry, the relationship between mutability, death, and love assumes varied and contradictory manifestations. Donne's "Farewell to Love," for instance, reveals the same disillusionment expressed in Quevedo's Poem 463 ("¡Ay, que fueron!" "¡Ay, que se acabaron!"), but the tone is much more cynical, reflecting instead the bitter scorn of the lover in "The Apparition" or Quevedo's Poem 338. Donne employs the religious imagery observed in earlier poems, contrasting it ironically with love's reality and, through it, introducing the notion of death.

As the title indicates, Donne is quite disenchanted with love. The strength of his *desengaño* reveals the power of his earlier confidence in love. His apparent disregard for permanence in this world indicates the actual urgency of his need for material permanence and consequent disillusionment with actual mutability.

> *Whilst yet to prove,*
> *I thought there was some Deitie in love,*
> *So did I reverence, and gave*
> *Worship, as Atheists at their dying houre*
> *Call, what they cannot name, an unknowne power,*
> *As ignorantly did I crave:*
> *Thus when*

> *Things not yet knowne are coveted by men,*
> *Our desires give them fashion, and so*
> *As they waxe lesser, fall, as they rise, grow.*

Donne will eventually assert that the "Deitie" he has sought in love does not exist. The comparison of "Atheists at their dying hour" with the lover who fervently seeks love's transdcendence establishes love's relationship with death and religion. He compares the "Atheists'" frantic, last-minute desire for the unknown, for union with the absolute, and for immortality after death with the lover's craving for permanence and meaning in love. Yet, the love he explores is ironically quite physical. Spiritual love and an evergrowing mutual affection are conspicuously absent. Donne thereby denies any possibilities of permanence by imposing on love the limitations of materiality and the fleetingness of the physical.

Whereas the lovers in "The Apparition" and Poem 338 become disenchanted with their ladies, the lover in "Farewell to Love" is disillusioned with love itself. This poem, like Quevedo's sonnet, asserts that love is purely destructive, as it reveals the lover's consequent attempts to abandon such a deathly pursuit.

In the second stanza, Donne recognizes that love's passion, like all other aspects of man's existence, is vulnerable to decay and mutability:

> *But, from late faire*
> *His highnesse sitting in a golden Chaire,*
> *Is not lesse cared for after three dayes*
> *By children, then the thing which lovers so*
> *Blindly admire, and with such worship wooe;*
> *Being had, enjoying it decayes:*
> *And thence,*
> *What before pleas'd them all, takes but one sense,*
> *And that so lamely, as it leaves behinde*
> *A kinde of sorrowing dulnesse to the minde.*

Physical love, despite the anxiety and passion with which men seek it, once enjoyed, loses its original value. In his assertion that "Being had, enjoying it decayes," Donne's choice of words is significant. Ironically, physical love decays because it is fulfilled. Material actualization leads ineluctably to material destruction, just as birth leads inevitably to death.

Emotional decay is a psychological corollary to the realities of the physical world. As man and other creatures or elements in nature grow and mature, they eventually reach the zenith of their powers. Thereafter, all change is a movement away from this achieved ideal. Physical decay then begins as men age, flowers wither, and all eventually die. Like physical decay, psychological decay also begins at the moment of supreme fulfillment and ripeness.

The paradoxical simultaneity of supreme fulfillment and incipient decay characterizes the waxing and waning of the moon, the changing of the seasons, the sun's daily arrival and departure. Emotions also wax and wane, rise and fall, grow and decay. In "The Apparition," Donne declared, "My love is spent," and in Poem 338, Quevedo dealt with the transformation of a great passion into contempt and scorn because of nonrequital. Curiously, in "Farewell to Love," requital does not transform passionate desire into scorn but into intense disillusionment. For the moment of actualization does not necessarily measure up to desire's imagined bliss. In contrast to these two previous poems, his love diminishes not because the beloved spurns his entreaties, but rather because she acknowledges them. Donne laments the reality of "A kinde of sorrowing dulness" which overwhelms "the minde" following sexual union. The death of passion, of what was once such an all-consuming drive, poignantly reflects the inevitable termination of all of man's actions and endeavors, foreshadowing the physical death of man himself.

This paradoxical result of the possession of that which is so passionately desired reflects the poignant nature of life's evanescence. M. M. Mahood has observed that this uncomfortable reality accounts for much of the cynicism with which Donne describes free love:

> This defence of free love recurs throughout the Elegies, Songs and Paradoxes. At the root of its fashionable cynicism lies a deep frustration, revealed from time to time in an unexpectedly melancholy phrase, an echo of *'post coitum omne animal tristis est.'*[5]

This same recognition of the dangers of fulfillment are central to Quevedo's philosophy. Otis Green has noted, for instance, that Quevedo realized that the gulf between desire and fulfillment is a salutary one: "Quevedo proclama: 'Hay muchas bondades que duran con la pretensión y se acaban en poseyendo. Uno es el que pretende y otro el que goza.' 'No hay cosa tan grosera para los deleites humanos como la posesión de ellos.'"[6] The most destructive characteristic of human pleasure is the achievement of one's desires. The disenchantment is overwhelming because achievement can never equal the fervor of striving. The result is the paradoxical indestructability of the courtly lover's passion, for he will never suffer that final disappointment. He will never have to wonder why love's fulfillment is so unfulfilling. His imagination remains boundless, unfettered by reality, and all the universe is his domain. Once love is actualized, the mind's limitless perspectives are drastically restricted by the reality of a single event, bound by space, time, and all other manner of specificities. Despite his overwhelming despondence due to his nonrequited passion, Quevedo enjoys the mental freedom to strive and hope for future bliss through exquisite requital. Donne, in his requital, is despondent because he can only look back to the disillusionment of fulfillment. Imagination is replaced by knowledge, dreams give way to reality, and the requited lover must forever live imprisoned by the disillusionment of the actualized past. The unrequited lover remains free to enjoy the torments and failures of a love whose bliss, ecstasy, and passion remain in the boundless potential of the future, free from the all-too-disappointing reality of actualization.

As in the *amour courtois*–Petrarchan tradition, Quevedo's *Poema a Lisi* reflects a tension between love's desire and love's denial, somewhat akin to Donne's "Farewell to Love." Obviously, neither the extreme cynicism of "Farewell to Love" nor its frank discussion of the psychological and physical effects of coitus characterize Quevedo's expressed desire for love's requital. Whereas Quevedo does suffer the exquisite torments and boundless intensity of unrequited desire, Donne in "Farewell to Love" suffers love's requital and the consequent loss of the anxious joys of desire and anticipation. He recognizes, in his own way, the value of a love like Quevedo's *amour courtois* adoration of Lisi, a constant longing, an endless quest, a love which is never fulfilled and therefore never decays:

> *Ah cannot wee,*
> *As well as Cocks and Lyons jocund be,*
> *After such pleasures? Unlesse wise*
> *Nature decreed (since each such Act, they say,*
> *Diminisheth the length of life a day)*
> *This; as shee would man should despise*
> *The sport,*
> *Because that other curse of being short,*
> *And onely for a minute, made to be*
> *Eager, desires to raise posterity.*

Donne's logic inextricably unites sex, disillusionment, time, and death. He agrees that the sex act may literally hasten man's physical death. As such, it is an accomplice of time, mutability, and death and for this reason depsondency and disillusionment overwhelm man after each sexual encounter. Passion and desire conspire to shorten his life, thereby making him an accomplice in his own death. Time is of utmost importance, for the passion of "a minute" erases "a day" from the lover's future. Paradoxically, however, it may also result in the birth of a new life. Desire's "curse of being short" thereby prevents man from literally killing himself, while his eagerness simultaneously insures the birth of future generations.

The paradox inherent in this view of the sex act, of one moment in time that affects birth and death alike, parallels Quevedo's vision of the simultaneity of human birth and death and reflects Donne's own declaration in "Image and Dream" that "even at first lifes Taper is a snuffe." Nowhere in the *Songs and Sonnets* is the interrelationship between time, love, birth, and death more vividly expressed than in this compression of the concepts of birth and death into a single instant, the moment of sexual consummation. Donne concludes that, since permanence cannot be found in sexual love, he will cease to pursue it, for in the end he only hurts himself in such encounters.

In the final stanza, Donne assumes one of his most naturalistic and cynical stances:

> *Since so, my minde*
> *Shall not desire what no man else can finde,*
> *I'll no more dote and runne*
> *To pursue things which had, indammage me.*
> *And when I come where moving beauties be,*
> *As men doe when the summers Sunne*
> *Growes great,*
> *Though I admire their greatness, shun their heat;*
> *Each place can afford shadowes. If all faile,*
> *'Tis but applying worme-seed to the Taile.*

The absolute is not to be found in the ecstatic moments of physical union with one's beloved, for that moment is fleeting and leaves behind it the seeds of disillusionment. Like life, it exhausts itself in its own being. Man cannot have it without inevitably losing it.

In "Salmo XIX" of his *Heráclito cristiano*, Quevedo echoes Donne's declaration that "all our joyes are but fantasticall":

> *¡Oh condición mortal! ¡Oh dura suerte!*
> *¡Que no puedo querer vivir mañana*
> *sin la pensión de procurar mi muerte!*

Reflecting on man's "mortal condition" and his bitter destiny, he realizes that he himself cannot wish to live another day without also soliciting his own death. To wish for the future necessitates the corollary wish for all that the future brings, including decline, decay, and death. To wish for anything in this world of change is paradoxically to desire its inevitable loss, for man cannot hold onto life or the heights of sexual passion forever.

Declaring that he will no longer "pursue things which had, indammage me," Donne recognizes that in the pursuit of his desires he has unwittingly pursued his own death. Consequently, he will henceforth shun love's passionate heat while still admiring its greatness from a distance in the cool, safer shadows. He will, in a sense, imitate the unrequited lover of the Lisi sonnets, preferring to forgo fulfillment of his desires rather than experience the ephemeral joys of possession.

The final line of this poem is one of Donne's most scabrous, and its highly naturalistic terminology echoes the savage realism of

Quevedo's satirical poems, his *Sueños*, and his picaresque novel, the *Buscón*. It parallels the anti-Petrarchan Quevedo, the fiercely naturalistic Quevedo not seen in *Poema a Lisi*. In the final line of "Farewell to Love," Donne provokes his own repulsion from sex by expressing its reality in the crudest manner possible. The term "worme-seed" echoes many of his sermons expressing his obsession with man's mortality and ultimate destination, the grave. The image of the worm also recurs throughout Quevedo's works, for he often expresses his horror over the decomposition of the body at death with an eloquence similar to Donne's. In *La cuna y la sepultura*, for instance, he reflects on death's separation of the body from the soul, noting that the soul has true value while the body must ultimately surrender itself to the earth and its worms. The horror of the body's fate at death is so disgusting that even the memory of having once lived in it is a severe punishment:

> y cuando llega la hora postrera, que en forçoso apartarse el vno del otro, hallas que el cuerpo te dexa y que tu mejor parte es el alma; y para pena tuya conoces entonces que te dexaste a tí, viuiendo por lo que es mortal y ceniza; y ves tu cuerpo, causa de tus delitos y tus culpas y hierros, que—depositado en tierra y en poder de gusanos—desengaña la estimación en que le tuviste; tan feo y disforme, que la memoria de auer viuido en él te castiga.[7]

In his sermon "Death's Duel," Donne similarly reflects on the nature of man's physical death and decomposition, as he imagines the day when

> these bodies that have been the children of royall parents, and the parents of royall children, must say with Job, Corruption thou art my father, and to the Worme thou art my mother, and my sister. Miserable riddle, when the same worme must bee my mother, and my sister, and my selfe. Miserable incest, when I must bee maried to my mother and my sister, and bee both father and mother to my owne mother and sister, beget and beare that worme which is all that miserable penury; when my mouth shall be filled with dust, and the worme shall feed, and feed sweetely upon me. . . .[8]

Like Quevedo, Donne is concerned with the body's fate at death, as he imagines all the horrors of the grave, the worms' emergence from, and consequent destruction of, the corpse. Since man's body is the seed for worms, any sexual encounter resulting in the birth of another human being would ultimately and inevitably create future "worme-seed." The sex act, crudely expressed, is no more than the application of "worme-seed to the Taile," for the child that may result from the father's seed will eventually die and himself become the seed for worms.

There is no hint whatsoever at man's transcendence of his earthly existence and mortality through love as seen in "The Canonization" or in "Amor constante más allá de la muerte." On the contrary, love is death's accomplice, for it hastens its inevitable arrival and spawns future food for the worms of death. "Farewell to Love," oriented towards the material world alone, specifically emphasizes the negative aspects of existence. The metaphor of the atheist at the beginning established the hopeless, nihilistic tone that permeates the poem and overwhelms it in the final line.

In *Poema a Lisi*, Quevedo's poems of despair in love express in more spiritual terms his despondent attempts to extricate himself from love's agony. In Poem 478, entitled "Exhorta a los que amaren, que no sigan los pasos por donde ha hecho su viaje,"[9] for instance, Quevedo discusses love in terms of death, but there is no room for crudeness or even for a concern with physical love. Instead, the burden of love's emotion overwhelms him. The title reflects the concern Quevedo shared with Donne regarding the impact his own love may have on future lovers as he exhorts them not to follow his footsteps:

> Cargado voy de mí: veo delante
> muerte que me amenaza la jornada;
> ir porfiando por la senda errada
> más de necio será que de constante.

One of Quevedo's most compelling lines, "Cargado voy de mí," the antithesis of "Desierto estoy de mí" in Poem 359, is paradoxically expressive of the same emotional tension. Quevedo articulates the oppressive burdens of love and life through the image of the speaker overwhelmed by his very existence, by mental and emotional burdens which somehow have acquired the qualities of the material world. He is overcome by an exhaustion similar to that which prompted Donne to admit in "A Valediction: of my Name in the Window" that "Neere death inflicts this lethargie." Like the lover in Donne's valediction, he is weary of life, obsessed by death.

Quevedo immediately presents death as a corollary, relating it to love's errors. It threatens his journey through life, and he recognizes that to continue on the road toward inevitable death is more imprudence in love than virtuous constancy. Like Donne in "Farewell to Love," he finds himself struggling against a love he recognizes to be an instrument of death itself. He presents this strife through the metaphor of a journey, of movement through space, whereas Donne expresses his struggle with an unabashed sexual specificity. While Donne seeks to overcome or forestall mutability in his world, Quevedo recognizes that his own inconstancy would be a virtue. Change would paradoxically be for the better, for he could then cease his relentless movement down love's mistaken path toward death. Donne has also presented change and inconstancy as preferable alternatives to immutability, notably in "The Blossome," and "Twicknam Garden."

Quevedo continues:

> Si por su mal me sigue ciego amante
> (que nunca es sola suerte desdichada),
> ¡ay!, vuleva en sí y atrás: no dé pisada
> donde la dio tan ciego caminante.

He admonishes other blind lovers who may take the same road he took to turn back, for they should not repeat the heedless mistake he has made. He pleads with them to see and learn from the errors of his past. Like Donne in "Loves Exchange," he views himself as an example to others, to potential victims of love's harshness. His disillusionment with love, like his obsession with its inevitable result, death, reflects the fundamental kinship between this sonnet and Donne's "Farewell to Love."

As in "Farewell to Love," Quevedo clearly associates his experience in love with sorrow and death:

> Ved cuán errado mi camino ha sido;
> cuán solo y triste, y cuán desordenado,
> que nunca ansí le anduvo pie perdido;

> *pues, por no desandar lo caminado,*
> *viendo delante y cerca fin temido,*
> *con pasos que otros huyen le he buscadoo.*

His path in love has been sad, lonely, chaotic, and he finds himself utterly lost. In the final tercet, he reveals that his actions are the opposite of those he has exhorted others to follow. He continues his mortal journey, although he sees death before him, and quite near. With the energy other men employ to elude death, he consciously and steadily moves towards it. In "Farewell to Love," Donne specifically tries to avoid such a fate. Love's power over Quevedo, however, is overwhelming, and he can only continue his suicidal journey through time and space towards death. In Quevedo's sonnets and "Farewell to Love," the lovers' exhaustion arises from the psychological tension of time's endless movement forward, as both, clearly spent, submit to the conquest of time, mutability, and death.

Donne's naturalistic obsession with sex and its consequent "sorrowing dulnesse" contrasts with Quevedo's revelation of inner torment through the metaphor of a lonely pilgrim overwhelmed by love and death. The resolution of each poem differs, as Donne asserts that he will desist from loving because it can "indammage" him and Quevedo laments the Petrarchan nature of his love, which to his despair "más de necio será que de constante." Each poet expresses in his own way a deeply-felt obsession with the alliance between love and death.

In both poems, time is the significant link between love and death. Donne is concerned with mutability, the relationship between "each such Act" and the consequent shortening of "the length of life a day." Quevedo has added the dimension of space to the well-known relationship between time and life. He has externalized time by translating it into spatial dimensions, thereby allowing it to acquire physical identity through the metaphor of the road. The pilgrim's movement through time toward his inevitable destiny becomes actual movement through space along this road.

"A Lecture upon the Shadow" similarly reflects Donne's concern with time and space as he lectures his beloved on the danger of love's mutability. Quevedo's Poem 141, "El reloj de sol," although not expressly concerned with love, bears an important thematic and imagistic correlation with Donne's "Lecture" and many of the poems previously discussed. These final two poems bring us full circle back to the first themes discussed much earlier in "The Blossome" and Quevedo's Poem 446: mutability, time, and movement through space. The situation, however, is much graver. The playful wittiness of "The Blossome" and the idealization of Quevedo's beloved now yield to the sombre metaphor and theme of the shadow as well as the intensity of both poets' awareness that the threat of death and decay is constant and inescapable. The antitheses of reality and appearance, life and death, and time and space pervade both poems.

In these final poems, both poets express their mutual obsession with life's inconstancy in terms of the sun and the movement of its shadow. They are haunted by mutability, by a deep sense of the uncertainty implicit in the visual reflection of time's silent movement. The shadow is a perceivable, yet intangible, manifestation of time's elusive and mysterious nature: it is a visual assertion of the paradoxical simultaneity of the realization and loss of human potential through love, through time.[10]

The first half of Donne's "Lecture" is as follows:

> *Stand still, and I will read to thee*
> *A Lecture, Love, in loves philosophy.*
>   *These three houres that we have spent,*
>   *Walking here, two shadowes went*
> *Along with us, which we our selves produc'd;*
> *But, now the Sunne is just above our head,*
>   *We doe those shadowes tread;*
> *And to brave clearnesse all things are reduc'd.*
>   *So whilst our infant loves did grow,*
>   *Disguises did, and shadowes, flow*
> *From us, and our care; but, now 'tis not so.*
>
> *That love hath not attaine'd the high'st degree,*
>   *Which is still diligent lest others see.*

Comparing the infancy of their love to the shadows which they produced while walking, he declares that now that disguises and shadows no longer "flow" from the lovers and their "cares," their love has "attain'd the high'st degree." The clarity of the noonday sun reflects the openness and the purity of their fullgrown love, which, unlike love in the *amour courtois* tradition, requires no secrecy. The lecture continues:

> Except our loves at this noone stay,
> We shall new shadowes make the other way.
>   As the first were made to blinde
>   Others; those which come behinde
> Will worke upon our selves, and blind our eyes.
> If our loves faint, and westwardly decline;
>   To me thou, falsly, thine,
> And I to thee mine actions shall disguise,
>   The morning shadowes weare away,
>   But these grow longer all the day,
> But oh, loves day is short, if love decay.

> Love is a growing, or full constant light;
> And his first minute, after noone, is night.

"Loves day is short, if love decay," Donne declares, equating decay and mutability with death. The imagery of lightness and darkness, which logically pervades this poem, corresponds to the dualities of life and death, of growth and decay. He recognizes that the shadows of the afternoon grow longer as time passes, whereas the shadows of the morning grow shorter with each passing moment. Darkness descends upon false love much more swiftly, however. Its "first minute, after noone, is night," Donne warns, as he envisions the immediate envelopment of love's "full constant light" at the first instant of deception.

The sun's movement is man's natural means of measuring time's passage. When viewed metaphorically, the morning shadows it produces reveal the future yet to be lived, as its afternoon shadows reflect the past already lived. Noon symbolizes the shadowless "brave clearness" of the present, free from the deceptions of the past and the future's uncertainty. In his argument for love's continued truthfulness, Donne also desires the retention of the present, the transcendence of time's passage, eternity itself. As love grows, lovers' deceptions wane like morning shadows. But if love should then continue to follow the example of time and the sun, at that moment of its greatest brilliance and perfection, all change would be inevitably negative and the shadows of the lovers' deceptions would return and ultimately destroy their love. Decay overwhelms a love that suffers from the shadows of deception, just as darkness begins to envelop the day after it passes its noontime brilliance.

The first half of the "Lecture" dealt with the growth of love and the gradual abatement of morning shadows, ultimately culminating in the clarity and fullness of shadowless love. But just as the sun rises in the east and ultimately sets in the west; just as the infant eventually achieves his adult height and capacity, only to decline in the dusk of his later years; so too can the fullness of the lovers' adoration decline and decay, its brightness darkened by the ever-growing shadows of the setting sun.

This recognition of the intrusiveness of mutability and death in love's domain creates the despondent tone characteristic of much of Donne's and Quevedo's love poetry. In this poem particularly, Donne is obsessed by human love's precarious situation in this world, by its extreme sensitivity to decay and mutability. His affirmation in "The Anniversarie" that "none can doe / Treason to us, except one of us two" is implicit in this lecture. Love must be free from the shadows of "Disguises," for if the lovers prove untrue, love will "decay" and its "constant light" will become the blackness of "night."

In the final couplet, Donne expresses the possibilities for love's transcendence in terms of eternity's clearness, as he envisions its freedom from the limitations of time and space. He speaks of love in terms of darkness, for time's obscurity can all too easily overcome the eternity of love's "full constant light." In this final couplet, Donne presents the antithetical concepts of love which characterize the different poems included in this study. He recognizes that love is potentially transcendent and eternal, free from the limitations of time and space. Yet, it is also potentially mortal and subject to the limitations of the time-space continuum, to time's darkness which inevitably shrouds man's life as stealthily as it envelops the light of day:

> *Love is a growing, or full constant light;*
> *And his first minute, after noone, is night.*

This final couplet thus provides a microcosm of the antitheses regarding love, life, and death that define Donne's *Songs and Sonnets* and Quevedo's *Poema a Lisi*.

In "El reloj de sol," Quevedo repeats the haunting image of the afternoon's growing shadow which irrevocably brings night's darkness. Like Donne, he presents mutability, death, and darkness in terms of the movement of the sun's shadow. The sun itself ironically causes shadows, just as life causes death.

In "El reloj de sol" Quevedo deals specifically with his awareness of the instability and uncertainty of life, of man's material world and physical existence. In the same didactic tone as Donne's "Lecture," he admonishes a friend to heed the sun dial's lesson by applying its example to his own life. Beginning with line 15, he uses the imagery of the shadow to present the duality of life and death:

> *pues tu vida, si atiendes su doctrina,*
> *camina al paso que su luz camina.*
> *No cuentes por sus líneas solamente*
> *las horas, sino lógrelas tu mente;*
> *pues en él recordada,*
> *ves tu muerte en tu vida retratada,*
> *cuando tú, que eres sombra,*
> *pues la santa verdad ansí te nombra,*
> *como la sombra suya, peregrino,*
> *desde un número en otro tu camino*
> *corres, y pasajero,*
> *te aguarda sombra el número postrero.*

He advises his friend that his own life marches along at the same pace as the passage of the sun's light on the dial. Its movement symbolizes his encroaching death, as the dial represents his life. As time moves, the sun dial's shadow darkens one number after another, only to leave behind it an ever-growing shadow. This image of continually increasing darkness that ultimately engulfs the light of day parallels human life. Man's past grows with each passing day that he lives, while his future decreases proportionately. Like the movement of the sun's light on the dial, man eventually completes his own movement through time and space. The light of his future is unavoidably snuffed out as the shadows of the past ultimately define the completed circle of his life.

Whereas Donne deals with deception and sincerity in love and with love's consequent exposure to the darkness of death, Quevedo deals directly with man's existential vulnerability to encroaching death. Death hastens toward him with every minute that passes and with every inch of the sun's brightness that is replaced by the growing shadow of its movement. As in his previous sonnet, Quevedo interrelates space and time so closely that spatial movement is a significant manifestation of time and mutability. Just as afternoon shadows increase in length in Donne's lecture, so too does Quevedo warn his friend that, with each hour that passes, the shadow on the sun dial grows in its insistent pursuit of light. Death and time are as persistent in their pursuit of life as is the shadow in its destruction of light.

For Quevedo, time does not "stand still," nor is there any attempt as in Donne's "Lecture" to suggest that it could. Love's transcendence does not appear as a possible escape from the time-space continuum. Just as Donne warns against love's "decay" in terms of time, however, so does Quevedo warn against life's decay because of time's swift movement.

Each poet's obsession with mutability—its relationship to the sun and its shadows, its alliance with time—has motivated his particular lecture. Whereas Quevedo's lesson dwells on mutability itself and its direct influence on the lives of men, Donne compares this reality to love, recognizing that even the clarity of love's candor is prey to the deceptions that continually threaten truth and reality. Each lecture reflects its author's attempt to impress upon the individual addressed a sense of disillusionment with the world of time, shadows, and appearances. They emphasize a cautious approach because both recognize that the shadows of existence—appearance, time, and mutability—can all too easily destroy the light of life or of love. In both poems, the spatial movement of the sun's shadow portrays time's advance as the purveyor of the death of love in

Donne's "Lecture" and the purveyor of the death of life in Quevedo's lecture.

Thus we have seen that Donne and Quevedo employ similar themes and images to relate their disenchantment with love. In the first poems discussed, a kind of nihilism prevails. Both poets deal with the death of love or lover, the beloved-as-murdrer, and the deliberate prolongation of the lover's suffering by love or by death. Love and death are partners in a cruel conspiracy against the unfortunate lover.

In his search for a *rapprochement* with his disdainful lady, each resorts to the powerful sub-conscious world of dreams and imagination. Whatever form their attempted escape takes, Donne and Quevedo clearly establish the inextricable alliance between appearance and reality as they explore the mysterious power that intangible illusions and dreams wield in the tangible world.

The beloved-as-murderer likewise assumes a role associated with religion, as the themes of martyrdom and idolatry are woven into each poet's presentation of his grand disillusionment and incredible suffering because of love. The traditional concept of the religion of love acquires a very personal connotation, for through their shared intensity of emotion and fervent belief in death's dominance in all aspects of man's life, including love and religion, Donne and Quevedo lend a vigorous uniqueness of expression to familiar themes and metaphors.

Both poets similarly seek ingenious revenges on their disdainful ladies through the auspices of time, mutability, and death as well as through their own wit and ingenuity. Their disillusionment with love, be it Petrarchan or non-Petrarchan, acquires a vivid psychological authenticity. Finally, the relationship between time and space, the sun and its shadows, appearance and reality, and love and death preoccupies Donne and Quevedo alike in their unifying exploration of life's inherent contradictions, of the profound disparities between desire and fulfillment, and of the nature of disillusionment in love and in life.

The prevailing shadows of the Baroque consciousness, evident in its art, as in its literature, epitomize the world view of the late sixteenth and early seventeenth centuries. Like their contemporaries in art and literature, Donne and Quevedo recognized that shadows are one of nature's most haunting visual representations of time's passage, of the arrival of the absolute darkness of death, as well as the inherent potential for an incipient and ever-growing obscurity in human relationships.

The brilliant noontime lucidity of Renaissance optimism and self-confidence ultimately yielded to this antithetical view of the world and of man's place in it. No longer the omnipotent paragon of virtue or the confident ruler of his universe, man became in his own eyes the terribly vulnerable victim not only of time and its hostile shadows but also of the fatal hostility of other individuals. The mood of doubt and uncertainty prevailed in the realm of human relationships as much as in the realm of metaphysics. Baroque literature, like Baroque art, frequently presented the lengthening shadows cast by the afternoon sun as the full and constant light of the Renaissance faded, while it stressed man's consequent tragic consciousness of the approach of the absolute darkness of night, of amorous hostility or infidelity, and of physical death itself.

Conclusion

In the literary period known as the Baroque, men of letters expressed with greater emotional intensity than in any other literary period their intellectual perception of the tragic irony of the human condition. The Baroque world view was characterized by a prevailing sadness and melancholy because of its headlong confrontation with the most sinister and haunting forms of reality. Donne and Quevedo expressed with tragic intensity their individual and quite personal reactions to the chaos of their times, to the tumultuous changes in political, religious, and scientific thought, and to the critical change in man's position in the universe. The reactions of both poets, although very much their own intimate emotions, were nevertheless constituents of the prevailing *Weltanschauung* of their age. As men of their age, Donne and Quevedo were necessarily influenced by the emotional and intellectual climate surrounding them. Similarly, however, the emotional and intellectual reactions of Donne and Quevedo, like the reactions of other sensitive men of their age to their changing world, contributed to the pervading mood of despondence and apprehension.

The Baroque period, following as it did the Renaissance, in many respects articulated an intensified version of inherited Renaissance and Medieval themes and expressions. The Baroque *Weltanschauung*, like the Metaphysical style, which so well reflected the preponderant obsessions of the age, often resulted from the extreme exaggerations of traditional *topoi* and styles. The existential situation and the consequent metaphysical awareness of Baroque man reverberated in all artistic forms of expression, distorting and deforming Renaissance themes and styles.

We find, for instance, that the great thirst for knowledge in the Renaissance, particularly man's renewed interest in himself and his world, became in the Baroque period a morbid form of self-interest and a profoundly dolorous encounter with a world that no longer reflected his felicitous vitality and mirrored instead his mortality in its own decay and mutability. The quest for self-knowledge, the ceaseless urge toward introspection, so typical of the Baroque and so much a part of its painting and its literature, was simply the final twilight manifestation of the explosive burst of inquisitive energy and humanistic investigations at the dawn of the Renaissance. A painting such as Caravaggio's Narcissus, for instance, or any of the numerous Rembrandt self-portraits, of dark, somber, analytical intensity and tragic introspection, expresses the same obsessive self-interest that we have observed in the poetry of Donne and Quevedo. As seen in Petrarch's *Canzoniere* or in the poetry of *amour courtois*, the frank articulation of self-interest was not unique to the Baroque. Nevertheless, in the Baroque, poets expressed more than ever a fundamental self-concern, overwhelmed by a pervasive and haunting awareness of transience, of the flux of being, of the human personality that is defined by constantly changing psychological states.

Similarly, the Renaissance zest for living, in its confrontation with the increasing Baroque disillusionment with this life, cursed by its own inherent temporality, resulted in an anguished cleaving to existence which assumed many stylistic and thematic manifestations. We observe these contrasting forms, for instance, in the Baroque styles, Metaphysical and High Baroque. The lean, analytical Metaphysical style and its complementary opposite, the ornate, flamboyant style of High Baroque, constitute the major duality in Baroque style. While the Metaphysical style reflects the direct, unadorned approach to reality of men like Donne and Quevedo, the High Baroque style of excessive adornment reflects other men's search for refuge from the truth which Donne and Quevedo so audaciously sought. The High Baroque style, an extreme expression of Renaissance imagery and themes, stressed the superficial beauty of nature and art, deliberately ignoring the great metaphysical problems which beset those who dared confront them. It differed from the Renaissance styles and themes in this excessiveness and in its revelation through a melancholic mood or through fleeting impressions of the underlying impermanence and uncertainty which originally provoked the attempt to conceal decay and loss through excessive ornamentation and embellishment. These same impressions, no longer fleeting but instead powerfully accentuated, also dominate the Metaphysical style through which other Baroque poets probed, analyzed, and explored extensively the tragic realities of human limitation, temporality, and loss.

The constant articulation of the obsession with death by Metaphysical poets such as Donne and Quevedo was, in essence, a literary form of therapy, an attempt to purge their elemental terror by bringing it out in the open, to fear it less and to prepare psychologically for its inevitability by dwelling on its omnipotence in all realms of life. In contrast, the preceding Renaissance quest for knowledge was a quest which probed very little into the hidden mysteries of existence. Rather, its interests, like the interests of the High Baroque, remained above the metaphysical and psychological surface.

Despite their emotional and intellectual apprehension of immanence, the fundamental urge toward transcendence resounds throughout the love-death poetry of Donne and Quevedo. As Metaphysical poets, they possessed an inherent impulse toward the union of disparate phenomena, including the extremes of immanence and transcendence. At times they succeeded in their search for the transcendence of their own immanence, but as we have seen, they failed much more often than they succeeded. We usually find in their love poetry either their frank recognition of transitoriness and death or a deliberate rebellion against these undeniable facts of existence. Death, the ultimate and the definitive truth of life, ignored by most Renaissance writers, became for the Baroque poet the measure of all things—of birth, life, and love, of human aspirations, triumphs, and failures.

Donne and Quevedo occupy a unique position in the tradition of European love poetry. Quevedo, the traditionalist (in the *Poema a Lisi*), and Donne, the iconoclast, represent the divergent amorous attitudes possible in their age and symbolize the dualistic nature of the Baroque. Indebted to the centuries of poetic tradition that preceded them, they simultaneously express the Baroque interpretations of that tradition. Among the final European poets to be influenced by the Petrarchan mode, whether in continuation of or retaliation against it, they nevertheless view inherited themes through the somber lenses of Baroque preoccupations. Their highly complex, paradoxical, and cerebral style derives from the Baroque deformation, the emotional and intellectual intensification of traditional metaphors and images. This intensity of style reflects their shared tragic consciousness of the relationship between love and death.

We have seen in the love-death poetry of Donne and Quevedo the "distinctly recognizable patterns of thought and artistic expression"[1] that, in Segel's words, distinguish one literary period from another. We have found that the love-death poetry of Donne and Quevedo, despite their significantly different attitudes toward Petrarchan motifs, imagery, and themes, nevertheless shared a fundamental thematic similarity. We found that the Baroque obsession with death thematically dominated their love poetry, but that it acquired differing, at times contradictory, manifestations. The themes of their love-death poetry, be they Petrarchan or anti-Petrarchan, thus assumed the aforeseen divisions: love's relationship to time, mutability, and old age; love's transcendence of death; the thematic and metaphoric relationship between absence, love, and death; the confident assertion of love's omnipotence over death; the articulation of the inherited themes of amorous assassination and violence; and the imagistic significance of dreams and shadows in the articulation of the illusion-reality antithesis.

Time's passage, mutability, and consequent old age were dominant Baroque themes that had rarely accompanied the heroic and glorious themes of Renaissance literature. Transcendence through love is a rare phenomenon in the poetry of Donne and Quevedo, occurring only rarely. It appears, however, always in terms of the transcendence of temporality and mortality. Much more common is the theme of death's omnipotence, as the Renaissance confidence and optimism faded and the Baroque spirit gained dominance. Donne and Quevedo keenly felt the sharp edge of death's reality. Despite their heroic attempts at reconciliation with its inevitability, they nevertheless feared its arrival. The prominence of the notion of death's omnipotence in the Baroque was a simple, psychological attempt at conciliation with the unspeakable and the unavoidable. The fact that John Donne slept in his own coffin, for instance, provides an existential parallel to this literary attempt to purge the fear of the unknown through the frank confrontation with its physical manifestations.

Absence in love and in death, a traditional *amour courtois* theme, acquires in the Baroque and in the poetry of Donne and Quevedo a particularly haunting articulation. Absence, be it physical or spiritual, is a powerful metaphor for death, and is consequently one of the most significant aspects of the love-death poetry of the Baroque. It expresses the fears of requited lovers as powerfully as it reflects the sorrow of the unrequited lover of Petrarchan tradition.

The omnipotence of death and the beloved's murder of the lover are themes which received little emphasis in the Renaissance. Because of the increasing Baroque disillusionment with life and with love, these totally negative themes acquired a haunting, and at times, a morbid expression. Like the themes of love's omnipotence or love's absence, they had their Petrarchan antecedents. Donne in his anti-Petrarchan pose and Quevedo in his Petrarchan stance revivified traditional themes through the intensity of their Baroque vision and the vigor of their Metaphysical style.

The prevailing obscurity of the Baroque world view and the consequent difficulty of distinguishing illusion from reality also characterize the love-death poetry of Donne and Quevedo. Like the beloved-assassin motif, the dominance of hostile shadows and the occurrence of violent dreams threaten the protagonists of the poetry of Donne and Quevedo with physical and metaphysical annihilation.

Thus we conclude that Donne and Quevedo shared much more than a coincidental contemporaneousness. They participated with the same intellectual fervor and spiritual anguish in the Baroque orientation to life and death, just as they employed the Metaphysical style to express through their passionate reasoning the major dilemmas of the human condition. Donne and Quevedo shared the essentially tragic vision of the Baroque, a vision overwhelmed by the consciousness of loss and by an accompanying aspiration for transcendence, which was nevertheless usually doomed to failure.

The love-death poetry of Donne and Quevedo is distinguished by the validity and profundity of its intellectual and emotional perception of the metaphysical paradox of existence. Metaphysical style similarly thrived on paradox. In its conceits it reflected the unique Baroque vision of the world—a vision which recognized the simultaneous validity of disparate, often contradictory phenomena. The unifying vision of the Baroque and the unifying Metaphysical style were self-complementary, just as the Renaissance vision of a world composed of harmonious constituents was complemented by the accompanying style of balance, symmetry, and proportion. As in other literary periods, style mirrored vision and attitude in the Baroque.

Helmut Hatzfeld has observed that the threat of death and the feeling of insecurity is "lo que origina la inquietud espiritual, lo que produce la 'tension' interna y el anhelo de paz del hombre barroco."[2] The obsession with death, the spiritual restlessness, the internal tension, and the consequent search for inner peace that Hatzfeld discovers in "Baroque man" pervade the love poetry of John Donne and Francisco de Quevedo.

Although the concerns that they shared were of intense interest in their day, they were not unique to their age. As I. A. Richards has noted, throughout the history of literature "the most incomprehensible and inexhaustible objects for meditation" have been:

    i. Man's loneliness (the isolation of the human situation).
    ii. The facts of birth, and of death, in their inexplicable oddity.
    iii. The inconceivable immensity of the Universe.
    iv. Man's place in the perspective of time.
    v. The enormity of his ignorance.[3]

The profundity of Donne's and Quevedo's perception and exploration of these "objects for meditation" characterizes their love poetry, their prose, and their religious poetry; for both poets perceived from different, and often contradictory, perspectives the problems of time and space and of man's inescapable solitude in birth and death. Their love poetry provides a wide range of positive and negative attitudes, mental and emotional, toward love and death, which both poets express through the diverse manifestations of the antitheses of the body and the soul, time and space, and appearance and reality.

Donne and Quevedo were psychological, as well as metaphysical, poets who, like their *amour courtois*–Petrarchan predecessors, were interested as much in their own emotions regarding reality as their intellectual comprehension of that reality. As psychological poets, they expressed with intensity and fervor their own reactions to terrene limitations, their fears over the loss of life and love, and their consequent recognition of the inexpressible alliance between human love, life, and death. They feared death with a visceral intensity, while simultaneously approving its destruction of the temporal, spatial, and corporal limitations of their sublunar existence. Thus their contradictory expressions of the relationship between the temporal and the eternal, between the spatial and the infinite, and between the material and the spiritual imbue their love poetry with a constant dynamism, an internal tension, reflected in theme and in style. The *Songs and Sonnets* and *Poema a Lisi* reflect the vigorous vitality of the Metaphysical style through each poet's search for the reconciliation of the dualities that define the human condition. Their reconciliation thus resulted in each poet's own manifestation of Western Europe's philosophical heritage: the mystical and the intellectual concept of unity-through-diversity.

Donne and Quevedo transformed the inherited tradition of Augustinian-Petrarchan introspection into a dramatic scenario in which the lover-poet himself nevertheless remained the major object of interest. Through the externalization of their innermost selves, they sought clarification of their own existential situation and of their psychological and intellectual reactions to that situation. In the expression of their profound inner reality by means of the substantive world, the dualities of existence—the body and the soul, the material and the spiritual, appearance and reality, the time-space continuum and the timeless—consequently assumed dominance. While abjuring the physical limitations of this world, they paradoxically sought meaning through the tangible, the sensible, the corporal.

Quevedo, like Donne, covered the whole range of possible reactions to Petrarchan tradition, although within the *Poema a Lisi* his pose as Lisi's long-suffering servant was unswerving. In poems outside this self-contained sonnet sequence, however, Quevedo's amorous spectrum was as broad as Donne's. Even their extreme anti-Petrarchan poems, however, revealed both poets' indebtedness to the *amour courtois*–Petrarchan tradition through their vehement denial of its conventions.

Within this wide range of possible approaches to love, the intensity and vibrance of Donne's and Quevedo's poetry, combined with their shared obsessions of time, mutability, and death, disclose their similar perceptions of life as well. Warnke has noted that "the unity of a period style appears not in the dominance of a set of identical techniques but in the way in which differing, even contrasting techniques articulate a common group of preoccupations and emphases."[4] This common group of preoccupations, reflective of the Baroque *Weltanschauung*, unites the poetry of Donne and Quevedo, while their "concrete particularity and intellectual complexity . . . [and] persistent urge to unify experience"[5] reflect their Metaphysical style.

Through their perception of the kaleidoscopic nature of life and their simultaneous apprehension of varied and contradictory aspects of its reality, Donne and Quevedo insistently sought permanence and the transcendence of an all-encompassing unity. The antitheses that define their poetry reveal this recognition of reality's disparateness, its continual change, and the interrelatedness of all aspects of existence.

Donne and Quevedo spent their lives in a ceaseless quest for truth and unity—a quest that reflected their awareness of the inexpressible alliance between death and time, between life and love. Their originality and authenticity lie not so much in the selection of these themes, which have always been of universal interest and magnitude. They reside rather in the artistry with which Donne and Quevedo portrayed the intensity of their feelings and the complexity of their thought. Through their poetic genius, they transformed their emotions and their thought into poetry that pulses with the vitality of their passions and the intensity of their obsessions. Donne's *Songs and Sonnets* and Quevedo's *Poema a Lisi* reflect not only the "unity of a period style," but also the artistic integrity and essential uniqueness of each poet's solitary search for his own reconciliation of the limitations of the human condition with the aspirations of the human spirit.

Notes

INTRODUCTION

1. All statements regarding the life of Donne are based on R. C. Bald, *John Donne. A Life*.

2. All statements regarding the life of Quevedo are based on Antonio Papell, *Quevedo: su tiempo, su vida, su obra* and James O. Crosby, *En torno a la poesía de Quevedo*.

3. The chronology of Quevedo's vast work, earlier established by Clara Campoamor, *Vida y obra de Quevedo*, has been more reliably documented by James O. Crosby, *En torno a la poesía de Quevedo*, and important articles.

4. *European Metaphysical Poetry*, p. 3. In his later study of the Baroque, *Versions of Baroque: European Literature in the Seventeenth Century*, Warnke amplifies this earlier theory to include the term Mannerist, which he considers to be the proper designation for the Metaphysical manifestations of the Baroque period, as seen in the poetry of Donne, Herbert, Marvell, Sponde, Quevedo, Huygens, and Fleming. In this study, however, we shall retain the term Metaphysical for the designation of Donne's and Quevedo's poetry. Warnke continues characterizing the second "option" of the Baroque attitude, or the "quintessential Baroque" of Crashaw, Gryphius, Marino, d'Aubigné, Góngora, and Vondel, as "High Baroque."

5. Frank J. Warnke, *Versions of Baroque*, p. 12.

6. I am here in particular agreement with Harold B. Segel, *The Baroque Poem*, pp. 21–22, who has further amplified Warnke's view of the Baroque in his assertion that "a period term and concept such as Renaissance, Classicist, Romantic, Symbolist, or Baroque connotes not only a time segment but a way of looking at the world (*Weltanschauung*) and an aesthetic proclivity characteristic of the period and distinguishable in important respects from those of the preceding and following periods."

7. *The Baroque Poem*, p. 22.

8. Leo Spitzer, "El barroco español," 21.

9. *La elegía funeral en la poesía española*, p. 172.

10. *Studies in Human Time*, p. 19.

11. Luis Rosales discussed this in greater detail in *El sentimiento del desengaño en la poesía barroca*, pp. 46–47.

12. "A Note on Donne the Preacher," *A Garland for John Donne*, ed. Theodore Spencer (Gloucester, Mass.: P. Smith, 1958), pp. 75–76.

13. "Quevedo, poeta de la muerte," 13.

14. *Studies in Human Time*, pp. 14–15.

15. Emilio Carilla, for instance, has noted the antitheses most favored by Baroque writers in *El barroco literario hispánico*, pp. 73–75: "El escritor barroco vio en el juego de oposiciones y contrastes medios para avanzar en su camino y para procurar encontrar respuestas a sus preguntas . . . Hubo antítesis que gozaron de singu-

lar preferencia: vida y muerte, belleza y fugacidad, tierra y cielo (o humano y divino), sueño y realidad, belleza y fealdad, eternidad y temporalidad, ilusión y desengaño, luz y sombra (o día y noche), verdad y mentira, nieve y fuego, etc., y su variedad de encadenamientos y derivaciones."

16. *The Shakespearian Moment and its Place in the Poetry of the Seventeenth Century*, p. 50.

17. "Quevedo and the Metaphysical Conceit," *Bulletin of Hispanic Studies* 35 (1958), 219.

18. *European Metaphysical Poetry*, pp. 1–2.

19. For further discussion of this, see Stephen Gilman, "An Introduction to the Ideology of the Baroque in Spain," 93.

20. "Quevedo and the Metaphysical Conceit," 217.

21. *European Metaphysical Poetry*, p. 276.

22. Otis Green discusses this in *Spain and the Western Tradition*, 4:22.

CHAPTER 1

1. p. ix. Henceforth, throughout this chapter, documentation for this book occurs in the text. Dronke's work is the most sophisticated study yet on the subject of courtly love and presents a far more comprehensive view of what he convincingly argues is a universal phenomenon, in distinct contrast to earlier authors such as Denis de Rougemont, *Love in the Western World*, tr. Montgomery Belgion, rev. and augm. ed. (New York: Pantheon, 1956); and C. S. Lewis, *The Allegory of Love* (London: Oxford University Press, 1959).

2. Maurice Valency, *In Praise of Love*, p. 259.

3. Dronke attacks the "widespread belief that the poets of *amour courtois*, in particular the troubadours, sang of a quasi-platonic love, which never desired full physical satisfaction at all. . . . It has been a case of reading a notion culled from Andreas Capellanus (*De Amore*, I. 6) back into the lyrics, of attempting to twist his concept *amor purus* into the Provençal *fin' Amors*" (pp. 48–49).

4. Donald Guss, *John Donne, Petrarchist*, pp. 26–27.

5. Ibid., pp. 23–24.

6. For an extensive philological inquiry into the history of *conceptismo* and *culteranismo*, see Andrée Collard, *Nueva poesía: conceptismo, culteranismo en la crítica española*.

7. Citations of Quevedo are from *Francisco de Quevedo, Obras completas*, ed. José Manuel Blecua, I.

8. Citations of Donne are from *John Donne. The Elegies and The Songs and Sonnets*, ed. Helen Gardner.

CHAPTER 2

1. For an extensive discussion of this interrelationship, see Luis Rosales, *El sentimiento del desengaño en la poesía barroca*, p. 47.

2. In each of their poems, Quevedo and Donne, like other Metaphysical poets, created, in Warnke's terms, "a dramatic persona as lyric protagonist" (*Versions of Baroque*, p. 40). With this poetic recourse properly acknowledged, this study will henceforth employ the proper name of each poet in reference to the multiple and quite varied speakers of his poems. Given the nature of this work, this perhaps unorthodox procedure is preferable to the tiring repetition of such phrases as "the speaker of Donne's poem" and "the speaker of Quevedo's sonnet."

3. For further thoughts regarding this, see Stephen Gilman, "An Introduction to the Ideology of the Baroque in Spain," 93.

4. Dronke, *Medieval Latin and the Rise of European Love-Lyric*, p. 189.

5. *Style, Rhetoric, and Rhythm*, p. 208.

6. See Otis Green, *El amor cortés en Quevedo*, for a treatment of the *Poema a Lisi* as poetry in the courtly love tradition.

7. Ibid., p. 111.

8. Alan K. G. Paterson elucidates Quevedo's anti-Petrarchan attitude in an ostensibly Petrarchan sonnet in " 'Sutileza del pensar' in a Quevedo Sonnet," 131–42.

9. *Obras*, p. 440.

10. *The Wit of Love*, pp. 54–55.

11. *La cuna y la sepultura*, ed. Luisa López Grigera, p. 16.

12. *The Sermons of John Donne*, ed. Evelyn M. Simpson and George R. Potter, 10:233.

CHAPTER 3

1. *La poesía metafísica de Quevedo*, p. 132.

2. Ibid., pp. 133–35.

3. Given the currency of the theory of courtly love as an adulterous and, therefore, necessarily secret love, Dronke's clarification in *Medieval Latin and the Rise of European Love-Lyric* of the origin of its secrecy is of great significance: "the secrecy of *amour courtois* springs . . . from the universal notion of love as a mystery not to be profaned by the outside world, not to be shared by any but lover and beloved" (p. 48).

4. *Versions of Baroque*, pp. 100–101.

5. Ibid., p. 62.

6. One of Quevedo's late Baroque contemporaries, Henry Vaughan (1622–1695), was also obsessed with time, its silent inexorability and the relativity of its movement. His "Silence, and stealth of dayes!" reflects his profound kinship with Quevedo and other contemporaries who apprehended the properties of time with greater anguish than perhaps any other representatives of a particular time period in Western Europe.

7. Frank J. Warnke, *Versions of Baroque*, p. 104.

8. For more detailed discussion, see Carlos Blanco Aguinaga's "Dos sonetos del siglo XVII: Amor-Locura en Quevedo y sor Juana."

9. *Versions of Baroque*, p. 70.

10. I am indebted to James C. Smith, "On Metaphysical Poetry," 229, for this idea and to his article as a whole for its particular orientation. It has been reprinted, with careful editing, in the posthumous volume *Shakespearian and Other Essays*, ed. E. M. Wilson (Cambridge: Cambridge Univ. Press, 1974), pp. 262–78.

11. *Medieval Latin and The Rise of European Love-Lyric*, p. 182.

12. Smith, "On Metaphysical Poetry," 230.

13. Much has been written regarding this sonnet, stemming from Amado Alonso's influential study in *Materia y forma en poesía*, pp. 127–32. See also Fernando Lázaro Carreter, "Quevedo, entre el amor y la muerte," *Papeles de Son Armadans* (Palma) 1 (1956), 45–60, and Carlos Blanco Aguinaga, " 'Cerrar podrá mis ojos' . . . Tradición y originalidad."

14. "Quevedo and the Metaphysical Conceit," 218.

15. Ibid., 220.

16. " 'Cerrar podrá mis ojos,' " 76.

17. The concept of love's constancy amid change is clearly within the Petrarchan tradition. Jean de Sponde (1557–1595), France's Metaphysical counterpart of Donne and Quevedo, perhaps exemplifies this constancy with greater insistence than any other Petrarchist of the Baroque period. The first sonnet in his *Sonnets*

d'Amour, for instance, illustrates this central theme of his love lyric, as seen in the tercets:

> Il est ainsi: ce corps se va tout souslevant
> Sans jamais s'esbranler parmi l'onde et le vent.
> Miracle nompareil! si mon amour extresme,
> Voyant ces maux coulans, soufflans de tous costez,
> Ne trouvoit tous les jours par exemple de mesme
> Sa constance au milieu de ces legeretez.

(Jean de Sponde, *Poems of Love and Death*, intro. by Alan J. Steele [Edinburgh: Oliver & Boyd, 1964].) Whereas Donne's emphasis is on temporality, on the mutability that surrounds his immutable love, Sponde stresses the spatial or material aspects of adversity.

18. *Baroque Lyric Poetry*, p. 36.

19. *The Wit of Love*, pp. 57–58.

20. See Emilia N. Kelley, *La poesía metafísica de Quevedo*, pp. 152–54, for her stylistic analysis of this sonnet.

21. Joan Bennett, *Four Metaphysical Poets*, p. 25, for instance, in her brief discussion of "The Anniversarie" affirms its "triumphant close."

22. Ibid., p. 38.

CHAPTER 4

1. The term is Pedro Laín Entralgo's. He discusses the notion of absence in Quevedo's poetry in "La vida del hombre en la poesía de Quevedo," 86–87.

2. For more on the pilgrim image, see Antonio Vilanova, "El peregrino de amor en las *Soledades* de Góngora," and Juergen Hahn, *The Origins of the Baroque Concept of Peregrinatio*.

3. *European Metaphysical Poetry*, p. 275.

4. Peter Dronke, *Medieval Latin and the Rise of European Love-Lyric*, pp. 122–23.

5. See Joseph G. Fucilla, *Estudios sobre el petrarquismo en España*, p. 196.

6. "On Metaphysical Poetry," 234.

CHAPTER 5

1. *The Poetry of Meditation*, pp. 214–15.

2. These are the terms employed in the English translation of Otis Green's *El amor cortés en Quevedo* (*Courtly Love in Quevedo*, University of Colorado Studies, Series in Language and Literature, No. 3 [Boulder, 1952]). Green is referring back to Pedro Laín Entralgo's article "La vida del hombre en la poesía de Quevedo," in which he asserts that Quevedo "es pesimista *quoad vitam*, no *quoad ens*; respecto a la vida terrena, no respecto al verdadero ser del hombre" (p. 79).

CHAPTER 6

1. *Four Metaphysical Poets*, pp. 43–44.

2. Frank J. Warnke, *Versions of Baroque*, p. 70.

3. *Ibid.*, pp. 98–99.

4. *Ibid.*, p. 45.

5. *Poetry and Humanism*, p. 100.

6. *El amor cortés*, pp. 83–84.

7. Francisco de Quevedo, *La cuna y la sepultura*, ed. Luisa López Grigera, pp. 30–31.

8. *The Sermons of John Donne*, ed. Evelyn M. Simpson and George R. Potter, 10:235.

9. See Joseph G. Fucilla, *Estudios sobre el petrarquismo en España*, pp. 200–201: This sonnet echoes two Petrarchan sonnets: *Rime* No. 88 ("Ond'io consiglio voi che siete in via, / Volgete i passi.") and *Rime* No. 272 ("E la morte vien dietro a gran giornate.").

10. Frank J. Warnke, *Versions of Baroque*, p. 52.

CONCLUSION

1. *The Baroque Poem*, p. 22.
2. *Estudios sobre el Barroco*, p. 70.
3. *Practical Criticism: A Study of Literary Judgment*, pp. 290–91.
4. *European Metaphysical Poetry*, p. 4.
5. Ibid., p. 10.

Bibliography

Alberti, Rafael. "Quevedo, poeta de la muerte." *Revista Nacional de Cultura* 22 (1960): 11–23.

Alonso, Amado. "The Stylistic Interpretation of Literary Texts." *Modern Language Notes* 57 (1942): 489–96.

———. *Materia y forma en poesía*. Madrid: Gredos, 1955.

Alonso, Dámaso. *Poesía española: Ensayo de métodos y límites estilísticos*. 5th ed. Madrid: Gredos, 1966.

Andreasen, N. J. C. *John Donne, Conservative Revolutionary*. Princeton: Princeton University Press, 1967.

Astrana Marín, Luis. *Ideario de Don Francisco de Quevedo*. Madrid: Biblioteca Nueva, 1940.

———. *La vida turbulenta de Quevedo*. 2nd ed. Madrid: Editorial "Gran Capitan," 1945.

Ayala, Francisco. "Sueño y realidad en el Barroco. Un soneto de Quevedo." *Ínsula* 184 (marzo 1962): 1.

Baker, Herschel. *The Wars of Truth. Studies in the Decay of Christian Humanism in the Earlier Seventeenth Century*. Cambridge, Mass.: Harvard University Press, 1952.

Bald, Robert Cecil. *John Donne. A Life*. New York: Oxford University Press, 1970.

Bennett, Joan. "The Love Poetry of John Donne: A Reply to Mr. C. S. Lewis." In *Seventeenth Century Studies Presented to Sir Herbert Grierson*. Preface by J. Dover Wilson. Oxford: Oxford University Press, 1938.

———. *Four Metaphysical Poets*. 2nd ed. New York: Vintage-Knopf, 1953.

Bergamín, José. *Fronteras infernales de la poesía*. Madrid: Taurus, 1959.

Blanco Aguinaga, Carlos. " 'Cerrar podrá mis ojos la postrera . . . ': Tradición y originalidad." *Filología* 8 (1962): 57–78.

———. "Dos sonetos del siglo XVII: Amor-Locura en Quevedo y sor Juana." *Modern Language Notes* 77 (1962): 145–62.

Borges, Jorge Luis. "Grandeza y menoscabo de Quevedo." *Revista de Occidente* 6 (1924): 249–55.

Bouvier, René. *Quevedo, "homme du diable, homme de Dieu."* Paris: H. Champion, 1929.

Bradbury, Malcolm, and Palmer, David. eds. *Metaphysical Poetry*. Stratford-upon-Avon Studies, no. 11. London: Edward Arnold, 1970.

Brandenburg, Alice S. "The Dynamic Image in Metaphysical Poetry." *PMLA* 57 (1942): 1039–45.

Brooks, Cleanth. *The Well Wrought Urn*. New York: Harcourt, Brace & Co., 1947.

Bush, Douglas. *English Literature in the Early Seventeenth Century*. 2nd rev. ed. Oxford: Clarendon Press, 1962.

Camacho Guizado, Eduardo. *La elegía funeral en la poesía española*. Madrid: Gredos, 1969.

Campoamor, Clara. *Vida y obra de Quevedo*. Buenos Aires: Ediciones Gay-Saber, 1945.

Carilla, Emilio. *El barroco literario hispánico*. Buenos Aires: Nova, 1969.

———. *Estudios de literatura española*. Rosario, Argentina: Universidad Nacional del Litoral, 1958.

———. *Quevedo entre dos centenarios*. Tucumán: Universidad Nacional de Tucumán, 1949.

Cioranescu, Alejandro. *El barroco o el descubrimiento del drama*. La Laguna de Tenerife, Islas Canarias: Universidad de la Laguna, 1957.

Coffin, C. M. *John Donne and the New Philosophy*. 2nd ed. New York: Humanities Press, 1958.

Cohen, J. M. *The Baroque Lyric*. London: Hutchinson, 1963.

Collard, Andrée. *Nueva poesía: conceptismo, culteranismo en la crítica española*. Madrid: Castalia, 1967.

Consiglio, Carlo. "El poema a Lisi y su petrarquismo." *Mediterráneo* 14 (1956): 76–93.

Coutinho, Afrânio. *A literatura no Brasil*. 4 vols. 2nd ed. Rio de Janeiro: Sul Americana, 1968–71.

Croll, Morris W. *Style, Rhetoric and Rhythm*. Edited by Max Patrick and Robert O. Evans. Princeton: Princeton University Press, 1966.

Crosby, James O. *En torno a la poesía de Quevedo*. Madrid: Castalia, 1967.

———. "Nuevos documentos para la biografía de Quevedo." *Boletín de la Biblioteca Menéndez y Pelayo* 29 (1953): 229–61.

Cruttwell, Patrick. *The Shakespearian Moment and its Place in the Poetry of the Seventeenth Century*. London: Chatto and Windus, 1954.

Daniells, Roy. "English Baroque and Deliberate Obscurity." *Journal of Aesthetics and Art Criticism* 5 (1946): 115–21.

Díaz-Plaja, Guillermo. *El espíritu del barroco: tres interpretaciones*. Barcelona: Apolo, 1940.

Donne, John. *John Donne. The Elegies and The Songs and Sonnets*. Edited by Helen Gardner. Oxford: Oxford University Press, 1965.

———. *The Sermons of John Donne*. Edited by Evelyn M. Simpson and George R. Potter. 10 vols. Berkeley and Los Angeles: University of California Press, 1962.

Dronke, Peter. *Medieval Latin and the Rise of European Love-Lyric*. Oxford: Clarendon Press, 1965.

Durán, Manuel. "El sentido del tiempo en Quevedo." *Cuadernos Americanos* 63 (1954): 273–88.

Fucilla, Joseph G. *Estudios sobre el petrarquismo en España*. Madrid: Ograma, 1960.

Gardner, Helen, ed. *John Donne: A Collection of Critical Essays*. Englewood Cliffs, N.J.: Prentice-Hall, 1962.

Gay-Crosier, Raymond. *Religious Elements in the Secular Lyrics of the Troubadours*. Chapel Hill: The University of North Carolina Press, 1971.

Gilman, Stephen. "An Introduction to the Ideology of the Baroque in Spain." *Symposium* 1 (1946): 82–107.

Gómez de la Serna, Ramón. *Quevedo*. Buenos Aires: Espasa-Calpe, 1953.

Green, Otis H. *El amor cortés en Quevedo*. Zaragoza: Librería General, 1955.

———. *Spain and the Western Tradition*. 4 vols. Madison: University of Wisconsin Press, 1963–66.

Grierson, H. J. C. "John Donne and the Via Media." *Modern Language Review* 43 (1948): 305–14.

———. *Metaphysical Lyrics and Poems of the Seventeenth Century. Donne to Butler*. Oxford: Clarendon Press, 1956.

Guss, Donald L. *John Donne, Petrarchist*. Detroit: Wayne State University Press, 1966.

Hahn, Juergen. *The Origins of the Baroque Concept of Peregrinatio*. Chapel Hill: The University of North Carolina Press, 1973.

Hatzfeld, Helmut. "A Clarification of the Baroque Problem in the Romance Literatures." *Comparative Literature* 1 (1949): 113–39.

———. *Estudios sobre el Barroco*. Madrid: Gredos, 1964.

Hughes, Richard E. *The Progress of the Soul: The Interior Career of John Donne*. New York: W. Morrow, 1968.

Hunt, Clay. *Donne's Poetry, Essays in Literary Analysis*. 3rd ed. New Haven: Yale University Press, 1956.

Keast, W. R. *Seventeenth Century English Poetry*. New York: Oxford University Press, 1962.

Kelley, Emilia N. *La poesía metafísica de Quevedo*. Madrid: Guadarrama, 1973.

Laín Entralgo, Pedro. "La vida del hombre en la poesía de Quevedo." *Cuadernos Hispanoamericanos* 1 (1948): 63–101.

———. *Obras*. 3 vols. Madrid: Editorial Plenitud, 1965.

Lanza Esteban, Juan. "Quevedo y la tradición literaria de la muerte." *Revista de Literatura* 4 (1953): 367–80.

Láscaris, Constantino. "Senequismo y agustinismo en Quevedo." *Revista de Filosofía* 2 (1950): 461–85.

Lázaro Carreter, Fernando. *Estilo barroco y personalidad creadora*. Salamanca: Anaya, 1966.

Leishman, J. B. *The Monarch of Wit*. 5th ed. London: Hutchinson, 1962.

Lewis, C. S. "Donne and Love Poetry in the Seventeenth Century." In *Seventeenth Century Studies presented to Sir Herbert Grierson*. Oxford: Oxford University Press, 1938.

Lida, Raimundo. "Estilística, un estudio sobre Quevedo." *Sur* 4 (1931): 163–72.

Lira Urquieta, Pedro. *Sobre Quevedo y otros clásicos*. Madrid: Ediciones Cultura Hispánica, 1958.

Mahood, M. M. *Poetry and Humanism*. 2nd ed. London: Cape, 1970.

Martz, Louis L. *The Poetry of Meditation*. 2nd ed. New Haven: Yale University Press, 1962.

———. *The Wit of Love*. Notre Dame: University of Notre Dame Press, 1969.

Mas, Amédée. *La caricature de la femme, du mariage et de l'amour dans l'oeuvre de Quevedo*. Paris: Ediciones Hispano-Americanas, 1957.

May, T. E. "An Interpretation of Gracián's *Agudeza y arte de ingenio*." *Hispanic Review* 16 (1948): 275–300.

Mazzeo, J. A. "A Critique of Some Modern Theories of Metaphysical Poetry." *Modern Philology* 50 (1952): 88–96. Reprinted in W. R. Keast. *Seventeenth Century English Poetry*. New York: Oxford University Press, 1962.

———. "A Seventeenth-Century Theory of Metaphysical Poetry." *Romanic Review* 42 (1951): 245–55.

Menéndez Pidal, Ramón. "Oscuridad, dificultad entre culteranos y conceptistas." *Romanische Forschungen* 56 (1942): 211–18.

Mérimée, Ernest. *Essai sur la vie et les oeuvres de Francisco de Quevedo*. Paris: Alphonse Picard, 1886.

Miner, Earl. *Seventeenth-Century Imagery*. Berkeley and Los Angeles: University of California Press, 1971.

Moloney, Michael Frances. *John Donne, His Flight from Mediaevalism*. 2nd ed. New York: Russell and Russell, 1965.

Mourges, Odette de. *Metaphysical, Baroque and Précieux Poetry*. Oxford: Clarendon Press, 1953.

Nelly, Una. *The Poet Donne: A Study in his Dialectic Method*. Cork: Cork University Press, 1969.

Nelson, Lowry, Jr. *Baroque Lyric Poetry*. New Haven: Yale University Press, 1961.

Neruda, Pablo. *Viajes al corazón de Quevedo*. Santiago: Sociedad de escritores de Chile, 1947.

Newman, F. X. *The Meaning of Courtly Love*. Albany: State University of New York Press, 1968.

Papell, Antonio. *Quevedo: su tiempo, su vida, su obra*. Barcelona: Editorial Barna, 1947.

Parker, A. A. "La 'agudeza' en algunos sonetos de Quevedo." In *Estudios dedicados a Menéndez Pidal*, vol. 3. Madrid: CSIC, 1952.

Paterson, Alan K. G. "'Sutileza del pensar' in a Quevedo Sonnet." *Modern Language Notes* 81 (1966): 131–42.

Petrarca, Francesco. *Rime*. Edited by Siro Attilo Nulli. Milano: U. Hoepli, 1956.

Poulet, Georges. *Studies in Human Time*. Translated by Elliott Coleman. Baltimore: Johns Hopkins Press, 1956–59.

Quevedo, Francisco de. *La cuna y la sepultura*. Edited by Luisa López Grigera. Madrid: Anejos del Boletín de la Real Academia Española, 1969.

———. *Obras completas. Poesía original*. Edited by José Manuel Blecua. 2nd ed. Vol. 1. Barcelona: Planeta, 1968.

———. *Obra poética*. Edited by José Manuel Blecua. 3 vols. Madrid: Castalia, 1969–71.

Richards, I. A. "The Interactions of Words." In *The Language of Poetry*. Edited by Allen Tate. Princeton: Princeton University Press, 1942.

———. *Practical Criticism: A Study of Literary Judgment*. 2nd ed. New York: Harcourt, Brace & Co., 1956.

Rivers, Elias, ed. *Renaissance and Baroque Poetry of Spain*. New York: Dell Publishing Co., 1966.

Rosales, Luis. *El sentimiento del desengaño en la poesía barroca*. Madrid: Ediciones Cultura Hispánica, 1966.

Segel, Harold B. *The Baroque Poem*. New York: E. P. Dutton & Co., 1974.

Simpson, Evelyn M. "Donne's Spanish Authors." *Modern Language Review* 43 (1948): 182–85.

Smith, A. J. "The Metaphysic of Love." *The Review of English Studies* 9 (1958): 362–75.

Smith, James C. "On Metaphysical Poetry." *Scrutiny* 2 (1933): 222–39. Reprinted in *Shakespearian and Other Essays*. Edited by E. M. Wilson. Cambridge: Cambridge University Press, 1974.

Spencer, Theodore, ed. *A Garland for John Donne*. 2nd ed. Gloucester, Mass.: P. Smith, 1958.

Spitzer, Leo. "El barroco español." *Boletín del Instituto de Investigaciones Históricas* 28 (1943–44): 17–30.

———. *Linguistics and Literary History*. Princeton: Princeton University Press, 1948.

Stampfer, Judah. *John Donne and the Metaphysical Gesture*. New York: Funk and Wagnalls, 1970.

Stauffer, Donald. *The Nature of Poetry*. New York: W. W. Norton, 1946.

Sypher, Wylie. *Four Stages of Renaissance Style: Transformations in Art and Literature, 1400–1700*. Garden City, N.Y.: Doubleday, 1955.

Tate, Allen. *On the Limits of Poetry*. New York: Swallow Press, 1948.

Terry, Arthur. "A Note on Metaphor and Conceit in the Siglo de Oro." *Bulletin of Hispanic Studies* 31 (1954): 91–97.

Valency, Maurice. *In Praise of Love*. New York: Macmillan, 1958.

Vilanova, Antonio. "El peregrino de amor en las *Soledades* de Góngora." In *Estudios dedicados a Menéndez Pidal*, vol. 3. Madrid: CSIC, 1952.

_____. "El peregrino andante en el *Persiles* de Cervantes," *Boletín de la Real Academia de buenas letras de Barcelona* 22 (1949): 97–159.

Vossler, Karl. *La poesía de la soledad en España*. Translated by Ramón de la Serna y Espina. Buenos Aires: Losada, 1946.

Wagner de Reyna, Alberto. "Quevedo ante la vida y la muerte." *Realidad* 6 (1949): 154–76.

Warnke, Frank J. *European Metaphysical Poetry*. Elizabethan Club, Series 2. New Haven: Yale University Press, 1961.

_____. *Versions of Baroque: European Literature in the Seventeenth Century*. New Haven: Yale University Press, 1972.

Wellek, René. "The Concept of Baroque in Literary Scholarship." *Journal of Aesthetics and Art Criticism* 5 (1946): 77–109.

Wiley, Margaret L. *The Subtle Knot*. Cambridge, Mass.: Harvard University Press, 1952.

Williamson, George. "The Libertine Donne." *Philological Quarterly* 13 (1934): 276–91.

_____. "Mutability, Decay and Seventeenth-Century Melancholy." *A Journal of English Literary History* 2 (1935): 121–50.

Wilson, F. P. *Elizabethan and Jacobean*. Oxford: Clarendon Press, 1945.

Xirau, Ramón. *Sentido de la presencia*. Mexico City: Tezontle, 1953.

Index

V

Valency, Maurice, 8
Vega, Garcilaso de la: 10, 27, 52–53, 87, 120, 152, 159; "Égloga III," 52, 120, 159
Vega, Lope de: 32, 55; *La Dorotea*, 32; *Rimas Sacras*, 55
Violence, Baroque, 152–55
Virgin, worship of, 11

W

Warnke, Frank J.: xv, xvi, xxii, xxiv, 61, 63, 70, 91, 172, 182, 209; *European Metaphysical Poetry*, xv; *Versions of Baroque*, xv
Wit, 11, 93–94, 147
Wyatt, Sir Thomas, 10